DO776777

STUDIES OF THE AMERICAS
edited by
James Dunkerley
Institute for the Study of the Americas
University of London
School of Advanced Study

Titles in this series are multi-disciplinary studies of aspects of the societies of the hemisphere, particularly in the areas of politics, economics, history, anthropology, sociology and the environment. The series covers a comparative perspective across the Americas, including Canada and the Caribbean as well as the USA and Latin America.

Titles in this series published by Palgrave Macmillan:

Cuba's Military 1990–2005: Revolutionary Soldiers during Counter-Revolutionary Times
By Hal Klepak

The Judicialization of Politics in Latin America
Edited by Rachel Sieder, Line Schjolden, and Alan Angell

Latin America: A New Interpretation
By Laurence Whitehead

Appropriation as Practice: Art and Identity in Argentina
By Arnd Schneider

America and Enlightenment Constitutionalism
Edited by Gary L. McDowell and Johnathan O'Neill

Vargas and Brazil: New Perspectives
Edited by Jens R. Hentschke

When Was Latin America Modern?
Edited by Nicola Miller and Stephen Hart

Debating Cuban Exceptionalism
Edited by Bert Hoffmann and Laurence Whitehead

Caribbean Land and Development Revisited
Edited by Jean Besson and Janet Momsen

The Hispanic World and American Intellectual Life
By Iván Jaksic

Bolivia: Revolution and the Power of History in the Present
By James Dunkerley

Brazil, Portugal, and the Black Atlantic
Edited by Nancy Naro, Roger Sansi-Roca, and David Treece

The Role of Mexico's Plural in Latin American Literary and Political Culture
By John King

Democratization, Development, and Legality: Chile 1831–1973
By Julio Faundez

The Republican Party and Immigration Politics in the 1990s: Take Back Your Tired, Your Poor
By Andrew Wroe

Faith and Impiety in Revolutionary Mexico
By Matthew Butler

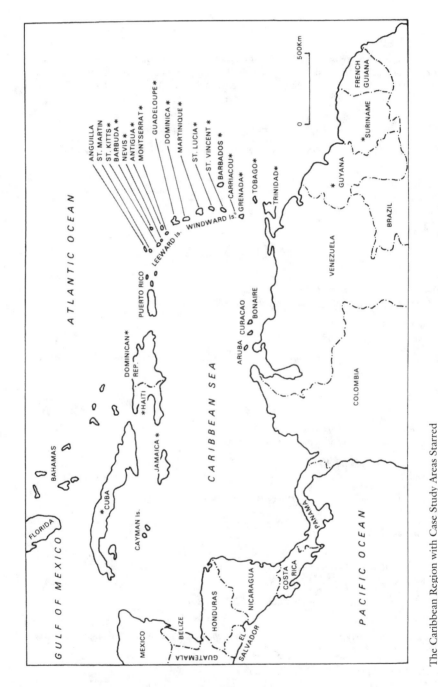

The Caribbean Region with Case Study Areas Starred

Source: Revised and redrawn from J. Besson and J. Momsen (eds.), *Land and Development in the Caribbean* (London and Basingstoke: Macmillan Caribbean, 1987), Map 1, p.xii.

Caribbean Land and Development Revisited

Edited by

Jean Besson
and
Janet Momsen

palgrave
macmillan

CARIBBEAN LAND AND DEVELOPMENT REVISITED

First published in 2007 by
PALGRAVE MACMILLAN™
175 Fifth Avenue, New York, N.Y. 10010 and
Houndmills, Basingstoke, Hampshire, England RG21 6XS
Companies and representatives throughout the world.

PALGRAVE MACMILLAN is the global academic imprint of the Palgrave Macmillan division of St. Martin's Press, LLC and of Palgrave Macmillan Ltd. Macmillan® is a registered trademark in the United States, United Kingdom and other countries. Palgrave is a registered trademark in the European Union and other countries.

ISBN-13: 978–1–4039–7392–4
ISBN-10: 1–4039–7392–X

Library of Congress Cataloging-in-Publication Data

Caribbean land and development revisited / edited by Jean Besson and Janet Momsen.
p. cm. ("Studies of the America" series)
ISBN: 1–4039–7392–X (alk. paper)
1. Land use—Caribbean Area. 2. Real estate development—Caribbean Area.
3. Agriculture—Caribbean Area. I. Besson, Jean, 1944– II. Momsen, Janet Henshall.

HD403.2.C374 2007
333.7309729—dc22   2006033724

A catalogue record for this book is available from the British Library.

Design by Newgen Imaging Systems (P) Ltd., Chennai, India.

First edition: July 2007

10   9   8   7   6   5   4   3   2   1

Printed in the United States of America.

To John (JB)
Rick and Magnus (JM)

Contents

Part I   Historical Perspectives on Land and Crop Production

Part II   Policy, Planning, and Management

List of Figures

List of Maps

List of Tables

Preface

In the 20 years since our first collaboration Jean Besson has moved from Aberdeen to London and Janet Momsen from Newcastle upon Tyne to California. However, new electronic communication has bridged the spatial distance. Face to face work was made possible by Jean's leave from Goldsmiths College and Janet's sabbatical leave in the United Kingdom in spring 2006. This meant that we could spend long hours working in Jean's conservatory jointly editing and making decisions about the shape of the book. We thank John Besson for his patience and practical help while we worked on the book. Janet's children, Rick and Magnus, are now grown-up, but they continue to be supportive of her work for which she is very grateful.

We also thank John's sister Daphne Besson for so willingly taking on the translation of the paper submitted by a French author. This was an enormous help to progress on the book. We are also grateful to Peggy Hauselt of the University of California, Davis for drawing the Frontispiece and Maps 13.1 and 13.2.

Our Editor at Palgrave Gabriella (Ella) Georgiades has been consistently responsive to our queries while preparing the manuscript. We appreciate her help. We also thank James Dunkerley, Director of the Institute for the Study of the Americas (ISA), University of London School of Advanced Study, and General Editor of ISA's Studies of the Americas Series for his enthusiastic support of our book.

This sequel to our 1987 *Land and Development in the Caribbean* (Macmillan) has only David Lowenthal and the editors who also contributed to the earlier book. We now have a much wider coverage of the region and of issues related to land and development. This completely new volume includes both well-established scholars as well as those who have only recently finished their PhDs. We thank them all for their contributions.

Introduction

Jean Besson and Janet Momsen

Land has been central to the development of the Caribbean region for more than 500 years, from Columbus's landfall in 1492 to the twenty-first century. These issues were foregrounded in our edited collection of essays by anthropologists, geographers, and historians in 1987, entitled *Land and Development in the Caribbean*,[1] which was described as a milestone "on the road to a deeper understanding of contemporary Caribbean rural economy"[2] and opened up these issues to extensive and continuing discussion and debate.[3]

The present book revisits these themes in a new millennium, with fresh perspectives and a new cast of authors brought together by the editors some 20 years on. The new authors include anthropologists, geographers, historians, a sociologist, practitioners in land policy, planning, and management, and a consultant in human rights law. These contributors are based at universities and other institutions in the Caribbean, the United Kingdom, France, The Netherlands, Canada, and the United States. This sequel, an interdisciplinary collection of 18 new chapters plus our editorial introduction, on a range of territories in the Anglophone, Francophone, Hispanic, and Dutch Caribbean, expands the perspectives of our earlier book—providing new directions in the exploration of Caribbean land and development based on both historical and contemporary research.

The Scope and Focus of the Book

These essays draw on a sociocultural definition of the Caribbean region as the world's oldest colonial/postcolonial sphere (originally conquered by the Spanish and then fractured by British, Dutch, French, Scandinavian, and U.S. control), which includes the Antilles or islands of the Caribbean Sea and certain neighboring mainland territories of the Americas that share a common colonial history, especially the Guianas and Belize.[4] Against this regional background, the book includes essays on Cuba and the Dominican Republic in the Hispanic Caribbean; Francophone Haiti, Guadeloupe, and Martinique; Suriname (formerly Dutch Guiana); and much of the English speaking Caribbean including Barbados, Barbuda, Carriacou, Jamaica, Montserrat, Nevis, St. Vincent, Trinidad and Tobago, and St. Lucia in the Commonwealth

Caribbean. However, St. Lucia is also Francophone due to its colonial history, in which it changed hands 14 times between the French and the British, and Trinidad was impacted by Spanish, French, and British colonial influences.

In the twenty-first century, in addition to postcolonial territories (e.g., Haiti, Cuba, the Dominican Republic, Jamaica, Trinidad and Tobago, St. Lucia, Barbados, and Suriname), external and internal colonial relationships persist: Guadeloupe and Martinique are Overseas Departments of France; Montserrat is a British Dependent Territory; Barbuda is a dependency of Antigua; and Carriacou is part of Grenada's tri-island state (which also includes Petite Martinique). In addition, Cuba (with some help from Venezuela) is trying to make its way in the world economy after a complex history of Hispanic, American, and Soviet control.

With populations descended in varying degrees from European colonizers, African slaves, and indentured laborers from Africa, India, China, Java, and Europe, all of these societies are variations on pan-Caribbean themes.[5] Such themes include a long history of population movements into, out of, and within the region, beginning with Native American migrations and followed by the demographic movements of colonization, indenture, and slavery. Since emancipation, emigration to Central America, North America, Europe, and within the Caribbean has become a marked characteristic of the region, as has return migration and circulatory migration. Other pan-Caribbean contours include race-class stratification and various Creole ethnicities.

Within these global and regional contexts, the book explores colonial and postcolonial issues such as access to land, environmental and planning policies, food production and trade, perceptions of land and landscape, tourism and other development concerns, and transnational migration. These themes overlap between the various parts and chapters of the book.

The issue of access to land runs through many of the chapters. Variations on this central theme include plantations, and peasantries (Richardson, Grossman, Taitt, Besson, Lowenthal and Clarke, Chivallon, Momsen, and Mills); land tenures, including informal occupation or "squatting" and the issue of indigenous and tribal land rights (Kambel, Stanfield and Wijetunga, Macleod, Miller and Barker, Besson, Lowenthal and Clarke, Sheller, and Mills); land loss, due to legal centralism (Kambel), tourism (Macleod, Momsen), suburbanization (Momsen), soil erosion (Grossman), and environmental disasters—as in Montserrat, despite the increased acreage of the island after the volcanic eruption (Skinner). Access to marine resources is another variation on this theme, as in the competition between fishing and tourism (Pugh, Macleod).

Closely related to the issue of land access is the theme of environmental and planning policies. This includes a historical perspective in relation to soil erosion (Grossman) and contemporary analyses of fishing and tourism (Macleod, Pugh), control of state land (Kambel, Stanfield and Wijetunga), agrobiodiversity (Spence and Thomas-Hope), and land and development for the twenty-first century (Miller and Barker). Food production and trade are especially addressed by Taitt, Torres, Momsen and Niemeier, Momsen, Spence and Thomas-Hope.

Paradoxical attitudes to land, as economic and symbolic, and as limited and unlimited, formed a central theme in our earlier collection of essays.[6] This theme is picked up and expanded in the present book through explorations of perceptions of land and landscape. Variations on these themes include imposed colonial landscapes (Richardson, Grossman, Chivallon); landscapes of power and resistance (Macleod, Besson, Chivallon, Sheller); fishing spaces as places of the past (Pugh); and imagined landscapes that anchor dispersed transnational communities, such as the virtual landscape of Montserrat (Skinner) and migrants' perceptions of land on Carriacou (Mills).

Imposed and participatory development (including Creole wisdom) was another central issue in our earlier volume,[7] which is expanded and explored in several chapters of this book. Discussion focuses around plantation and peasant production (Richardson, Grossman, Taitt); state-owned versus private land (Torres et al., Stanfield and Wijetunga); legal versus customary tenures, including the issues of indigenous and tribal (maroon) land rights, land titling, and "squatting" (Kambel, Besson, Lowenthal and Clarke, Sheller, Mills); environmental conservation in fishing, bauxite mining, and tourism (Pugh, Kambel, Macleod); biodiversity in agriculture (Spence and Thomas-Hope); changing settlement patterns, including house construction and suburbanization (Macleod, Besson, Momsen, Skinner, Mills, and Byron); and regulated foreign access to land (Mills).

The Caribbean region has long been characterized by population mobility, but increased air travel and electronic communications have intensified and reinforced transnational networks and communities. The impact of migration has been particularly pronounced in the smaller islands, such as Montserrat (where migration has been recently exacerbated by a volcanic eruption), Nevis, Carriacou, and Barbuda. Several chapters reflect such issues, but those by Lowenthal and Clarke, Skinner, Mills and Byron especially discuss these themes.

The Structure and Arguments of the Book

While these overlapping issues link the various parts and chapters of the book, parts 1–4 structure the 18 chapters more tightly around specific approaches to Caribbean land and development. Part 1 explores "Historical Perspectives on Land and Crop Production." Part 2 examines "Policy, Planning, and Management." Part 3 interrogates the question of "Land for the Peasantry?" Part 4 looks at "Landscape, Migration, and Development."

Historical Perspectives on Land and Crop Production

Part 1, "Historical Perspectives on Land and Crop Production," highlights and assesses, through four historical essays (Richardson, Grossman, Taitt, and Torres et al.), the important role of colonialism and postcolonialism in shaping and controlling Caribbean land and crop production, particularly in relation to the tension between plantation export crops and small-scale domestic food cultivation. The essays focus on the former British West Indies, on French Guadeloupe and on Spanish-speaking Cuba.

In chapter 1, "The Importance of the 1897 British Royal Commission," Bonham C. Richardson focuses on the West India Royal Commission of 1897, which identified different agricultural paths for different British West Indian islands that have led to intraisland land-use variations. The Commission also initiated the development of the sparsely settled interiors of the Windward Islands and Trinidad. However, Richardson shows that the Commission was not a purely imperial event but was also a grassroots phenomenon, as it was precipitated by Caribbean labor disturbances in the 1890s. It established a mechanism for the devolution of large-scale plantations into land settlements of small-scale peasant plots, notably on St. Vincent and Carriacou, which led to later development of land settlements in these islands and elsewhere in the region.[8] The case of Carriacou is explored more fully in chapter 17 by Mills, who brings the analysis up to the present.

In chapter 2, "The Colonial Office and Soil Conservation in the British Caribbean, 1938–1950," Lawrence S. Grossman continues the historical focus on external initiatives by exploring the role of the British Colonial Office in controlling soil erosion and environmental degradation in the mid-twentieth century. The Colonial Office was not motivated by concerns related particularly to problems in the Caribbean. It stressed the need to implement soil conservation in the context of its concerns that the future of the entire British Empire was being threatened by environmental degradation and population growth. "Efforts to introduce soil conservation policies were not simply environmental initiatives alone. They reflected broader attempts by the Colonial Office to transform land tenure relationships, introduce more permanent forms of agriculture, and increase direct state intervention in and control over the peasant production process."

Sir Frank Stockdale, as Comptroller for Development and Welfare in the West Indies from 1940 to 1945, persuaded many parts of the region to abandon freehold tenure on land settlements and replace it with leasehold arrangements. This reassessment of Eurocentric perspectives imposed on the British West Indies, as identified by Richardson and Grossman, is echoed in later chapters on the Hispanic and Francophone Caribbean (chapters 8, 12, and 15, by Macleod, Chivallon, and Sheller).

In chapter 3, "Domestic Food Production in Guadeloupe in World War II," Glenroy Taitt focuses on French Guadeloupe in World War II. On the eve of World War II, agriculture in Guadeloupe was largely based on the export of the plantation crops of sugar and bananas. When France capitulated to Germany in 1940 the Governor of Guadeloupe pledged allegiance to Vichy against the will of the majority of the people of Guadeloupe. Vichy control of Guadeloupe lasted from 1940 to 1943. This led to a blockade being imposed by the Allies against the French West Indies. The blockade was not meant to starve the colonies but to nudge them into the allied camp. The United States of America made money available from blocked French accounts to purchase essential commodities. Thus trade with France was cut off and replaced by U.S. imports much to the annoyance of the government of Guadeloupe. However, the United States was unable to supply Guadeloupe with its usual quantities of food. All cultivators were ordered to plant idle lands in food crops. The sugar industry was largely uncooperative, but much of the banana land went into food crops. Overall it was the peasant zones of Grands-Fonds in Grande-Terre and the leeward coast of Basse-Terre that fed Guadeloupe throughout the war. This was a very prosperous period for the peasant farmers of Grands-Fonds with buyers coming to the farm gate to purchase produce. For the farmers there was competition between domestic food production and export agriculture as well as with imports.

In chapter 4, "Cuba's Farmers' Markets in the 'Special Period,' 1990–1995," Rebecca Torres, Janet Momsen, and Debbie A. Niemeier explore a parallel theme to that of chapter 3 looking at the impact of the ending of the Cold War and the collapse of the USSR on food production in postrevolutionary Cuba. The loss of a subsidized sugar market in the Soviet Union and the related reduction in the import of food and agricultural inputs resulted in a crisis in Cuba's food supply. This crisis was exacerbated by the continuing U.S. blockade. However, Cuba is fortunate in having the best people to land ratio in the Antilles. Within this context and that of the "Special Period" in the mid-1990s, the Cuban state partially reversed the emphasis on state ownership of land thereby allowing an increase in private food production, including urban gardening in order to improve nutrition levels. The lifting of constraints on private crop sales led to the setting up of farmers' markets, which parallel the peasant markets that have long been a feature of many other Caribbean societies such as Francophone Haiti and Anglophone Jamaica (see, e.g., Besson and Sheller, chapters 10 and 15, respectively, in later parts of the book).[9] Today, farmers selling in these markets make the highest incomes among all Cuban agriculturists.

Policy, Planning, and Management

Part 2, "Policy, Planning, and Management," critically explores through five essays (Kambel, Stanfield and Wijetunga, Pugh, Macleod, Miller and Barker) the dialectical themes of state policy and participatory planning. In chapter 5, "Land, Development, and Indigenous Rights in Suriname: The Role of International Human Rights Law," Ellen-Rose Kambel explores the current debate in Suriname on the land rights of indigenous and tribal peoples (maroons). Dutch colonial land policy from 1650 to 1945 first favored plantation agriculture on the coastal strip (occupied by the majority of the population who are descendants of Dutch planters, African slaves, and indentured laborers from India and Java). Then, after the decline of the plantation system following emancipation in 1863, colonial policy encouraged the exploitation of gold, bauxite, and natural rubber in the hilly and forested interior that is home to four Native American groups and six maroon tribes of African descent who comprise approximately 20 percent of the population. The introduction of imposed resource exploitation, including bauxite mining, from 1945 to independence in 1975 damaged much of the land occupied by the indigenous and tribal peoples (compare Miller and Barker, and Besson, chapters 9 and 10) who were regarded as having no title to their lands. These lands were portrayed in the colonial legal system as being state-owned, a false notion reinforced by the ideology of legal centralism, the economic interests of a light-colored Creole elite aspiring to Dutch culture, and national development ideology that portrayed the indigenous and tribal peoples as needing to be "developed." Kambel shows how, since the 1990s, indigenous peoples and maroons have used international human rights law to challenge this situation, by arguing for land rights (including the right to participate in the management and development of their resources) based on land titles. This approach is having partial success. This Suriname case study of the use of international human rights law to reinforce Native American land titles and maroon territorial treaties provides an important variation on the current global issue of land titling and legal property rights, which are generally designed to expand land markets (see Stanfield and Wijetunga, chapter 6 and, Besson, chapter 10).

In chapter 6, "The Management of State Lands in Trinidad and Tobago," J. David Stanfield and A. A. Wijetunga assess public land management in Trinidad and Tobago, where the state owns approximately 52 percent of the total land area, which is generally managed through private leases. In 1994, a Land Management Authority (LMA) was proposed by government to acquire and manage state lands, including the containment of squatting. By the late 1990s, after further proposals for the LMA such as regularization of tenure and land registration, duplications and contradictory policies emerged. The chapter explores studies undertaken by the authors in 2000, as part of the Land Use Policy and Administration Project (LUPAP), which examined 11 core state land management institutions that use leases to manage state lands. The analysis concludes that the Commissioner of State Lands, who manages the largest amount of public land, is a relatively costly and ineffective manager. The chapter also reveals the institutional root causes of this ineffectiveness and proposes a new Land Management Authority. The cases of Trinidad and Tobago, and Cuba (Torres et al., chapter 4) present an interesting paradox and contrast. While postrevolutionary Cuba shifted emphasis from state farming to private production in the Special Period due to pressure on food production, in capitalist Trinidad and Tobago over half the land is still owned by the state.

Chapter 7, "The Participation Paradox: Stories from St. Lucia," by Jonathan Pugh focuses on the Soufrière Marine Management Area (SMMA), one of the most prestigious and rare examples of communicative planning in the Caribbean and the global South. The SSMA won the first British Airways Tourism for Tomorrow/World Conservation Union Special Award for National Parks and Protected Areas in 1997 "for its ability to shape a local consensus between the different conflicting interest groups, empowering these groups in the process" especially with regard to fishing and tourism. Pugh critically assesses the model of communicative planning, pointing out that actors have multiple identities rather than being part of a homogeneous "interest group," and arguing that this approach can only result in exclusions. In this way, stereotyping excludes fisherpeople and privileges tourism.

Donald Macleod deals with similar themes in the Hispanic Caribbean in chapter 8, "Land Disputes and Development Activity in the Dominican Republic," from both historical and contemporary perspectives. Focusing on the coastal village of Bayahibe in the southeast of the Dominican Republic, "a fishing community increasingly influenced by tourism, situated next to what is now the Del Este National Park," Macleod explores both the land disputes and the development initiatives in the context of the community's history and the country's distribution of power. Like Pugh's chapter on Anglophone/Francophone St. Lucia, the case study has wide relevance to the Caribbean region, with its escalating tourist industry built on the foundations of colonialism and postcolonial independence (see, e.g., chapters 10, 11, and 13 by Besson, Lowenthal and Clarke, and Momsen), and a related increase in the introduction of national parks that reinforce the land scarcity of the peasantries (discussed in parts 1 and 3).

In chapter 9, "Land Policy in Jamaica in the Decade after Agenda 21," Learie A. Miller and David Barker highlight a number of initiatives relating to land policy and development that were undertaken in Jamaica in the 1990s, in response to the United Nations Conference on Environment and Development, and Agenda 21. These include the development of major policy documents on land, protected areas, biodiversity strategy, forestry, sustainable watershed management, settlements, and tourism. Other issues of land and development, such as bauxite mining, squatter settlements, and the withdrawal of agricultural lands from primary production also continue to be concerns of national policy makers. Setting this range of issues in both historical and global contexts, Miller and Barker reveal however that the results for the country have been rather mixed.

Land for the Peasantry?

The five essays in part 3, "Land for the Peasantry?" (Besson, Lowenthal and Clarke, Chivallon, Momsen, and Spence and Thomas-Hope) pick up and expand with fresh perspectives the focus in our earlier book on land and development among Caribbean peasantries[10] from both historical and contemporary points of view (see also parts 1 and 2).

In chapter 10, " 'Squatting' as a Strategy for Land Settlement and Sustainable Development," Jean Besson, who in our earlier book focused on Caribbean "family land," turns here to explore the significance of informal occupation or "squatting" among Caribbean peasantries. This customary tenure has, both historically and recently, been criticized as an obstacle to development on a global as well as a national and regional scale, with recommendations for either eviction or land sales, registration, titling, and taxation (see also chapters 1, 6, 8, 9, 11, 12, and 17 by Richardson, Stanfield and Wijetunga, Macleod, Miller and Barker, Lowenthal and Clarke, Chivallon, and Mills). Against these global, regional, and national backgrounds, Besson focuses on maroons (compare Kambel, chapter 5), free villages, and a Revivalist-Rastafarian squatter settlement in western Jamaica, an area of intense Euro-American land monopoly through plantations, bauxite mines, and tourism. Besson's ethnographic perspective highlights the creativity of "squatting" as a strategy for peasantization, from the slavery era to the twenty-first century. This includes the role of squatting in laying the foundation for legal tenures, like purchased land and maroon treaty land, which may then evolve into Creole tenures such as family land and sacred landscapes that provide a basis for both productivity and identity. Squatting may therefore be as effective a strategy of land settlement as colonially imposed land settlements, such as those described by Janet Momsen for the British West Indies in our earlier book.[11]

This theme of squatting as a creative strategy for land settlement and peasantization is reinforced and elaborated in chapter 11, "The Triumph of the Commons: Barbuda Belongs to All Barbudans Together," by David Lowenthal and Colin Clarke, who take a long-term view on land and development on Barbuda from the seventeenth to the twenty-first century. On Barbuda, enslaved Africans and their descendants were never subjected to sugar plantation labor and, during the eighteenth century, planted ground provisions and reared stock for their owners, the Codringtons, who leased the island from the Crown, though some slaves were removed to Codrington sugar estates in Antigua. On this dry limestone colony, the slaves filched as much time as possible from their owners to engage in their own agricultural and fishing enterprises, also salvaging from ships wrecked on the reefs. After emancipation in 1834 (there was no Apprenticeship in either Antigua or Barbuda, due to the plantation stranglehold on Antigua and benign neglect on Barbuda), the freed slaves had no legal access to land. However, by the end of the nineteenth century, the Codringtons had withdrawn, subsequent lessees had failed economically, and the Crown had stepped in to establish cattle and cotton estates. This imposed development likewise failed and by 1983, when the colony reluctantly became part of the independent nation-state of Antigua-Barbuda, Barbudans de facto controlled all of their island's resources including the common land appropriated from the time of slavery. In the new millennium the expanding Barbudan population is made up of peasant farmers and migrants who continue to perceive the island as a basis of both livelihood and identity (compare Mills, chapter 17), and to contest external attempts to develop the island—now through sand excavation and tourism. The triumph of the Barbudan commons, like the sustainability of the common land of the Jamaican Accompong Maroons (Besson, chapter 10) challenges Hardin's classic thesis of the "tragedy of the commons."[12] This chapter by geographers complements and updates the anthropological perspectives on Barbuda in our earlier book.[13]

Christine Chivallon picks up the historical and contemporary theme of Caribbean peasantization in chapter 12, "The Contested Existence of a

Peasantry in Martinique: Scientific Discourses, Controversies, and Evidence," in the context of the French West Indies. Chivallon identifies and reassesses a widely held interpretation that a peasantry did not emerge in Martinique after emancipation in 1848. She shows that this "classical" interpretation denying the existence of a Martinican postslavery peasantry is based on three main arguments: that the occupation of the highland *mornes* by freed slaves was mainly by squatting, that the scale of such land acquisition was very limited, and that fragmentation through inheritance resulted in inefficient land management. Drawing on her research on land and kinship in seven rural districts of highland Martinique, combined with historical documentary sources, Chivallon reappraises these arguments for the period 1840–1988. She reveals the significant development of peasant property through legal land sales, the extensive scale of such land purchases, and the preservation of the patrimony through rational strategies of land management including joint ownership in undivided land. This form of tenure has parallels to "family land" elsewhere in the Caribbean region, as explored in our earlier book and advanced by Sheller, Mills, and Byron in this present volume (chapters 15, 17, and 18). Like Kambel's essay on the use of international human rights law by indigenous and tribal peoples in Suriname (chapter 5), Chivallon's analysis also highlights how Caribbean subaltern groups may draw on legal systems to reinforce or acquire land rights.

In chapter 13, "The Waxing and Waning of Land for the Peasantry in Barbados," Janet Momsen continues the peasantization theme in the Eastern Caribbean, exploring this through new research within the context of intense land scarcity for the Barbadian peasantry. As Momsen shows, "Barbados was the only older sugar colony in the Caribbean able to increase sugar production after slavery ended, as a result of the planters' monopoly of agricultural land." However, even during slavery, slaves cultivated food on small plots of plantation land for subsistence and sale, and when plantation agriculture became less profitable the postslavery peasantry was able to increase their access to land. However, new forms of development including suburbanization and tourism have reinforced land scarcity for the peasantry. Focusing on the last half century, Momsen's chapter "examines the adaptability of the small farm sector in the face of the changing competition between land and development" in the island, exploring the changing use of farmland "based on the interpretation of aerial photographs from 1951, 1964, and 1989 and surveys of small-scale agriculture undertaken in 1963, 1987, and 2003." While Besson highlights the creativity of the Jamaican peasantry, Lowenthal and Clarke reveal the tenacity of the Barbudan peasantry, and Chivallon identifies the "invisibility" of the peasantry in Martinique, Momsen focuses on the dynamism of the Barbadian peasants. She shows that, with a shift to crop production for tourism and export supported by the government, they are now more like small farmers in the global North than like the traditional Barbadian peasantry.

While there has been more land available to the peasantry in the larger island of Jamaica with its mountainous interior than in the small lowland island of Barbados, Balfour Spence and Elizabeth Thomas-Hope return to the issue of persisting land scarcity for the Jamaican peasantry (compare Besson's chapter 10 on western Jamaica) in chapter 14, "Agrobiodiversity as an Environmental Management Tool in Small-Scale Farming Landscapes: Implications for Agrochemical Use." Like Momsen on Barbados (chapter 13), Spence and Thomas-Hope focus on the marginalized small-scale agricultural landscape that, in Jamaica, is manifested in small, fragmented land parcels situated on steep, unstable slopes or on bottom lands that are vulnerable to flooding, exacerbated by the absence of infrastructural support in terms of marketing, credit, and extension, noting that there has been little research on this issue. The authors' own research rectifies this neglect as part of the People, Land Management and Environmental Change (PLEC) project that looked at biodiversity in small farming landscapes globally as a means of environmental and economic sustainability. Based on a sample of 52 field types managed by 53 farmers, Spence and Thomas-Hope reveal an inverse relationship between plant species diversity and the use of agrochemicals, indicating that land-use stages that are characterized by high levels of plant species diversity have the potential to be more sustainable than those that promote monoculture. This conclusion has important implications for land and development in the Rio Grande Valley in eastern Jamaica, where banana monoculture has until recently predominated, showing that agricultural sustainability depends on the introduction of plant species diversity and the acceptance by farmers of such biodiversity initiatives.

Landscape, Migration, and Development

The four essays in part 4, "Landscape, Migration, and Development" (Sheller, Skinner, Mills, and Byron) reinforce and expand issues on landscape and development from the preceding sections and also relate these themes to transnational networks and migration (see also chapters 10 and 11 by Besson, and Lowenthal and Clarke), which are crucial dimensions for understanding Caribbean societies, economies, and cultures.

In chapter 15, Mimi Sheller expands the regional and landscape perspectives of the book in her essay on "Arboreal Landscapes of Power and Resistance." She sees land and its uses as "one of the key sites of social struggle in postslavery societies." Sheller argues that "social relations of power, resistance, and oppositional culture-building are inscribed into living landscapes of farming, dwelling, and cultivation," and that "claims to power (both elite and subaltern) are marked out by landscape features such as plazas, roads, pathways, vantage points, and significant trees, all of which proclaim use-rights, ownership, or the sacrality of particular places." She draws on "literary sources and visual imagery from the Anglophone and Francophone Caribbean" (especially Jamaica and Haiti), to build on emerging cultural approaches in the geography, sociology, and political economy of land in the Caribbean. Her chapter contributes to this book by focusing on trees especially, which "have been used to identify, symbolize, demarcate, and sustain various Caribbean places, meanings, and lives." Sheller first traces "the importance of trees in the development of plantation economies and discourses of empire" and then explores "the contestation of these colonial arboreal landscapes by Afro-Caribbean agents who claimed particular trees for their own projects of survival and meaning-making—sacred ancestral trees, liberty trees, family land trees, gathering-place trees." Her chapter concludes with "some reflections on the 'cultural turn' in development studies" to highlight "a multimethod approach to tracing social struggles over land, landscape, place, and space."

Jonathan Skinner in chapter 16, "From the Pre-Colonial to the Virtual: The Scope and Scape of Land, Landuse, and Landloss on Montserrat," turns attention to one of the enduring Caribbean colonies (compare Taitt and Chivallon, chapters 3 and 12, on French Guadeloupe and Martinique). However, while colonialism has endured on Montserrat, now a British Dependent Territory, land has not, for the volcanic eruptions of Chances Peak since 1995 have destroyed or endangered this Caribbean landscape and generated explosive land development issues. These issues, which include rapid—and in many cases irrational—development by British development workers, are set in historical and transnational contexts, as Skinner explores practices of landuse and changing conceptualizations of land on the island from pre-colonial settlement and Amerindian activity through to contemporary post-disaster diasporic imaginations. These historical and global perspectives also reveal the significant plantation and peasant agricultural competition in Monserratian history, Caribbean themes of land and development that weave through all of the chapters in this book.

In chapter 17, " 'Leave to Come Back': The Importance of Family Land in a Transnational Caribbean Community," Beth Mills picks up the themes of land as a basis for both development and identity in Caribbean culture and the significance of land in the region's transnational networks (see, e.g.,chapters 10, 11, and 16 by Besson, Lowenthal and Clarke, and Skinner) by focusing on family land in Carriacou, Grenada. As Mills highlights, building on the insights of our earlier book, family land in the Caribbean is a type of customary tenure whereby members of a kinship group descended from a common ancestor share the ownership of a piece of land equally over generations.[14] These land rights are retained by migrant kin dispersed in various parts of the globe, underlining the basis of Caribbean land as a source of diasporic imaginings (compare Skinner, chapter 16). Mills explores variations on these themes, foregrounding the case of Carriacou (where plantations devolved into peasant plots and land settlements see Richardson's chapter 1). Her analysis reveals the significance of family land to members of the transnational community living in the United States of America in New York and in Toronto, Canada, showing that "the concept of family land created by the transnational imagination is arguably the most important role of family land in contemporary Carriacou society." However, this transnational imagination of family land has important development implications for the island, reinforcing the homeward flow of overseas migrant remittances.

Chapter 18, "Collateral and Achievement: Land and Caribbean Migration" by Margaret Byron, complements the analyses of Skinner and Mills (chapters 16 and 17) and concludes the book by exploring further the relationship between migration and Caribbean land and development issues throughout the region. Byron discusses the role of land in "the increasingly transnational condition of Caribbean communities." Against the historical background of the postemancipation struggle for land and variations on this plantation-peasant dialectic across the region (see parts 1–3), Byron argues that Caribbean laboring classes incorporated migration as an income improvement strategy early in the postemancipation era, highlighting that remittances were partly directed into investment in house lots and later in land for cultivation. Elaborating this theme of land and development, she shows that "the wealthiest returnees, often those artisans who had the opportunity to take skilled jobs in the destination countries," used their savings to invest in estate land (sugar plantations that were no longer profitable) and that "the subdivision and resale of this land created a small, relatively wealthy middle class in many territories." Focusing on the postwar migration to Britain, in comparison to Mills's focus on Canada and the United States of America, Byron argues that for many would-be migrants, family land provided essential collateral. She also shows that migration enabled many others to purchase their own land thus increasing their security in the home island. Her analysis is mainly based on Nevis, a small dry island similar in resource levels to Carriacou. She reveals that "this land ownership paralleled social ties in maintaining firm links between migrants and their countries of origin," as "it underpins the 'transnational existence' for many migrants and is usually the first stage of realizing the return goal."

Conclusion

Together, then, these 18 chapters pursue both enduring and new directions on Caribbean land and development, based on recent research enriched by the groundbreaking perspectives of the pioneering essays in the editors' earlier book.[15] This new cast of authors takes these approaches further in the new millennium, expanding our knowledge geographically across the region. They highlight the persisting and changing themes of land and its links to development in the Caribbean region that, as the oldest area of European expansion, continues to mirror in microcosm important global issues into the twenty-first century.

Notes

1. Jean Besson and Janet Momsen (eds.), *Land and Development in the Caribbean* (London: Macmillan, 1987).
2. David Barker, Review of *Land and Development in the Caribbean*, Jean Besson and Janet Momsen (eds.), and *Small Farming and Peasant Resources in the*

Caribbean, John S. Brierley and Hymie Rubenstein (eds.), *Social and Economic Studies* 38, no. 4 (1989): 265–274, at 272.

3. See, e.g., David T. Edwards, Review of *Land and Development in the Caribbean*, Jean Besson and Janet Momsen (eds.), and *Small Farming and Peasant Resources in the Caribbean*, John S. Brierley and Hymie Rubenstein (eds.), *Nieuwe West Indische Gids* 64 (1990): 57–60; Elizabeth M. Thomas-Hope, Review of *Land and Development in the Caribbean*, Jean Besson and Janet Momsen (eds.), *Slavery and Abolition* 11, no. 3 (1990): 420–422; Tracey Skelton, " 'Cultures of Land' in the Caribbean: A Contribution to the Debate on Development and Culture," *Journal of Development Research* 8, no. 2 (1996): 71–92; Allan N. Williams (ed.), *Land in the Caribbean: Proceedings of a Workshop on Land Policy, Administration and Management in the English-Speaking Caribbean* (Mt. Horeb, Wisconsin: Land Tenure Center, University of Wisconsin-Madison, 2003); Robert Home and Hilary Lim (eds.), *Demystifying the Mystery of Capital: Land Tenure and Poverty in Africa and the Caribbean* (London: Cavendish, 2004).

4. Sidney W. Mintz, *Caribbean Transformations* (New York: Columbia University Press, 1989); Sidney W. Mintz, "Enduring Substances, Trying Theories: The Caribbean Region as *Oikoumené*," *Journal of the Royal Anthropological Institute* 2, no. 2 (1996): 289–311.

5. See, e.g., David Lowenthal, *West Indian Societies* (London: Oxford University Press, 1972); H. Hoetink, " 'Race' and Color in the Caribbean," in Sidney W. Mintz and Sally Price (eds.), *Caribbean Contours* (Baltimore: Johns Hopkins University Press, 1985), 55–84.

6. Besson and Momsen (eds.), *Land and Development in the Caribbean.*

7. Besson and Momsen (eds.), *Land and Development in the Caribbean.*

8. Janet Momsen, "Land Settlement as an Imposed Solution," in Besson and Momsen (eds.), *Land and Development in the Caribbean*, 46–69.

9. See also, e.g., Sidney W. Mintz, "Peasant Markets," *Scientific American* 203, no. 2 (1960): 112–122; Mintz, *Caribbean Transformations*, 180–224; Sidney W. Mintz and Richard Price, *The Birth of African-American Culture* (Boston: Beacon Press, 1992), 77–80; Sidney W. Mintz, *Tasting Food, Tasting Freedom* (Boston: Beacon Press, 1996), 33–49; Jean Besson, "Gender and Development in the Jamaican Small-Scale Marketing System: From the 1660s to the Millennium and Beyond," in David Barker and Duncan McGregor (eds.), *Resources, Planning and Environmental Management in a Changing Caribbean* (Kingston, Jamaica: University of the West Indies Press, 2003), 11–35.

10. There has been much controversy on the definition of the concept of peasantry in general and in relation to the Caribbean region (e.g., Jerome S. Handler, "Small-Scale Sugar Cane Farming in Barbados," *Ethnology* 5 (1966): 64–83; Lambros Comitas, "Occupational Multiplicity in Rural Jamaica," in Lambros Comitas and David Lowenthal (eds.), *Work and Family Life: West Indian Perspectives* [Garden City: Anchor Press/Doubleday, 1973], 157–173). We find especially useful the characterizations by George Dalton of peasantries in anthropology and history and Sidney Mintz's delineations of Caribbean peasantries (see, e.g., Jean Besson, *Martha Brae's Two Histories: European Expansion and Caribbean Culture-Building in Jamaica* [Chapel Hill and London: University of North Carolina Press, 2002], 6–7, 215.)

    Dalton defined "peasant" as a broad middle category between the two extremes of "tribal" (subsistence economy) and "post-peasant modern farmer," with socioeconomic organization typified by subsistence production combined with production for sale, the virtual absence of machine technology, a significant retention of traditional social organization and culture, and "incomplete" land and labor markets—i.e., land and work are partly embedded in social relations (George Dalton, "Primitive Money," in George Dalton (ed.), *Tribal and Peasant Economies* [Garden City: Natural History Press, 1967], 254–281, at 265–267; George Dalton, "Peasantries in Anthropology and History," in George Dalton (ed.), *Economic Anthropology and Development* [New York: Basic Books, 1971], 217–266). Dalton's definition of peasantry encompassed various subtypes, including the "hybrid/composite peasantries" of Latin America and the Caribbean and within this subtype Caribbean "reconstituted peasantries" as defined by Sidney Mintz may be identified.

Mintz defined "peasantry" in general as "a class (or classes) of rural landowners producing a large part of the products they consume, but also selling to (and buying from) wider markets, and dependent in various ways upon wider political and economic spheres of control" (Mintz, *Caribbean Transformations*, 132). He later qualified the criterion of land ownership by noting that peasants are "small-scale cultivators who own or *have access to* land" (Mintz, *Caribbean Transformations*, 141, our emphasis). He further argued that "Caribbean peasantries are, in this view, *reconstituted peasantries*, having begun other than as peasants—in slavery, as deserters or runaways, as plantation laborers, or whatever—and becoming peasants in some kind of resistant response to an externally imposed regimen" (Mintz, *Caribbean Transformations*, 132).

These definitions enable analysis of variations of peasantization, the internal differentiation of peasantries, the combination of cultivation and the sale of labor in "occupational multiplicity," and the coexistence of small-scale legal and customary land tenures (see, e.g., Besson, *Martha Brae's Two Histories*, especially 215).

11. Momsen, "Land Settlement as an Imposed Solution."
12. Garett Hardin, "The Tragedy of the Commons," *Science* 162 (1968): 1243–1248.
13. Riva Berleant-Schiller, "Ecology and Politics in Barbudan Land Tenures," in Besson and Momsen (eds.), *Land and Development in the Caribbean*, 116–131; Jean Besson, "A Paradox in Caribbean Attitudes to Land," in Besson and Momsen (eds.), *Land and Development in the Caribbean*, 38–40, n. 5.
14. See especially Jean Besson, "A Paradox in Caribbean Attitudes to Land," in Besson and Momsen (eds.), *Land and Development in the Caribbean*, 13–45.
15. Besson and Momsen (eds.), *Land and Development in the Caribbean*.

Part I

Historical Perspectives on Land and Crop Production

Chapter 1

The Importance of the 1897 British Royal Commission

Bonham C. Richardson

The report of the 1897 Commission may be regarded as the Magna Charta of the West Indian peasant.

> C. Y. Shepherd, "Peasant Agriculture in the
> Leeward and Windward Islands,"
> *Tropical Agriculture*, 1947: 63

In December 1896, a full-scale Royal Commission was convened to assess a widespread economic malaise in the British Caribbean. It was the first comprehensive investigative commission to deal with the British Caribbean in its entirety since 1842. Late in the 1800s a severe economic depression, owing to the decline of the local sugarcane industries, had created misery throughout the British Caribbean colonies. Especially in the smaller places, antiquated infrastructures and worn-out soils could not compete with the new economies of scale that were by now producing enormous quantities of cane sugar with modern equipment in such rival tropical areas as Fiji, Natal, Brazil, and Java, as well as Cuba and the Dominican Republic in the greater Caribbean region itself. Even worse, European beet sugar, supported by government subsidies that came to be known as "bounties," had undercut British Caribbean sugar on the London market; a precipitous drop in the price of sugar in 1884 was attributed to the dumping of beet sugar in London, mainly by German producers. The resulting low wages and unemployment in the British Caribbean led to terrible local conditions. This chapter briefly outlines these conditions, yet its main focus is on the formation of the 1897 commission, its activities and conclusions, and the early implementations of some of the commission's suggestions.[1]

The British government commission was appointed in December 1896. It held hearings in London before traveling to the Caribbean where, in the first months of 1897, it heard from planters, government officials, and even laborers throughout the region. The testimony, economic data, and allied information generated by the commission's activities filled thousands of pages and remain an extremely valuable resource for researchers.[2] The commission's principal recommendation was for the widespread establishment of smallholders but not if such a development were to lead to squatting or to the abandonment of ongoing sugar estates by their workers. The commission's findings and recommendations represented an important geographical watershed for the British Caribbean because it justified the emergence of smallholders on several islands heretofore monopolized by planters. But large numbers of smallholders did not appear on all of the islands; some colonies continued and even intensified plantation-based sugarcane production, so that the exuberant "Magna Charta" pronouncement by economist C. Y. Shepherd published 50 years after the commission report did not necessarily apply everywhere in the British Caribbean.[3]

The Commission's Origins

Few documents are as useful to historically oriented scholars of the British Caribbean as those associated with Royal Commissions of Enquiry. These commissions themselves were occasional, problem-oriented surveys or investigations, and they provided particularly important documentary evidence of conditions immediately prior to and following emancipation. Especially in the mid- to late nineteenth century, when planters and former slaves were coming to grips with new social and economic arrangements in an environment clouded with old animosities, a number of commissions dealt with local issues such as sugarcane production, migration, finances, and social disturbances.[4] The commissioners usually were sent from London to assess local problems. These problems were normally confined to a particular theme, island, or event, although on rare occasions (such as in 1897) the assessment was of the whole British Caribbean. Since these commissions addressed local issues in which points of view usually conflicted, the records of these commissions were often spiced with candid testimony that provide windows into the region's past.

The nineteenth-century heyday of the royal commissions dealing with the British Caribbean coincided with what has been called The Great Era of the royal commissions in general, most of which dealt with nineteenth-century social and industrial problems in the British Isles.[5] Deriving their formal authority directly from the Crown, the commissions actually were appointed by ministers whose political parties held a majority in the House of Commons. Although the commissions were thereby part of the formal British political structure, they were often given the latitude to seek answers outside normal political channels. Commissions dealt with issues that often were too immediate, complex, delicate, or technical to be trusted to normal government routine. Their recommendations, though lacking legal authority, usually carried extraordinary weight, and many policy changes in British social history may be traced to the findings and recommendations of Royal Commissions of Enquiry.

Since commissioners usually were sent from Britain and were men with wide colonial experience, it was inevitable that commissioners compared social and economic issues across different regions and different cultures. It is therefore common to see commentary in commission proceedings in which colonial officials compared conditions in, for example, British Guiana with those in Ceylon or the Transvaal. Commissioners were also well read, and many were familiar with the writings of such authors as James Anthony Froude, the Regius Professor of Modern History at Oxford University. Froude toured the British Caribbean during 1886–1887 with an eye to assessing the possibility of some form of parliamentary self-rule for the islands. His resulting book was a chronicle of remarkably naïve travel vignettes that depicted the black West Indians as childish, backward, and primitive people who had never really lost their "African" savagery.[6] Although Froude's work had a number of contemporary detractors, mainly because it was thoroughly racist, even in the context of the late 1800s, he was sufficiently influential that Colonial Office bureaucrats occasionally cited him to justify particular policies.

Yet there were enlightened attitudes at the time with which British decision makers were also familiar. In the latter decades of the nineteenth century the writing and thinking of John Stuart Mill and others began to champion the practicality of peasant proprietorship of land in certain parts of the British Empire.[7] Mill drew examples from Ireland and India to champion the formation of a smallholder populace as a fair, prudent, and forward-looking strategy for matching people with land. His views inspired opposition among some in Britain, and his views were considered near unthinkable among many West Indian planters. Despite this opposition Mill's ideas were sufficiently attractive to some of the younger members of the Colonial Office that commentary about the feasibility, even the desirability, of "peasant proprietary schemes" for some of the British Caribbean colonies began to appear in official correspondence as early as the 1870s.

The fall in British West Indian sugar prices in the early 1880s resulted directly from competition with European sugar beets. In order to stimulate local sugar beet production, European governments had introduced a complex system of refunds of local excise taxes for producers and refiners who realized high sugar content for given weights of beets. These rebates or bounties encouraged ever-greater production that found its natural market in Britain which had adopted its laissez-faire market policies in light of its own industrial surpluses. Cheap European beet sugar, further, was a boon to British workers who were consuming sugar as food additives as never before.[8] As a result, British Caribbean sugarcane producers were realizing greatly reduced profits at a time when the London sugar market actually was expanding, an issue that cane planters and some colonial officials complained about incessantly. Reading the reports and memoranda from the British Caribbean colonies in the late 1880s suggests that the last two decades of the century consisted of one long planter meeting after another, all condemning London's free trade policies. During this same period a number of the oldest merchant houses in the region—traditional sources of credit for local planters—failed.

Yet the real impact of the sugar bounty depression fell directly on Caribbean laborers.[9] The descendants of black slaves in the region never had prospered in the half century since emancipation, but in most places they had established village-based societies that were partly independent from ongoing estates, and a growing number of black and brown peoples of the British Caribbean had become artisans and shopkeepers and had profited from a modicum of education. Then in the 1880s depression-lowered wages quickly absorbed household savings, reduced the quantity and variety of food imported to augment village subsistence crops, and sent laborers in droves to distant estates and other islands to seek work, only to find that these places also were affected by depression conditions.

Scarcely a week passed at the British Colonial Office in London in the last two decades of the nineteenth century without officials there receiving a report from the Caribbean colonies outlining in poignant detail estates closing or reducing their labor needs, thereby leading to the impoverishment of working peoples, or widespread malnourishment accented by disease, all of these conditions exacerbated by the depression. The depression's effects were most severe in the smaller places that were, for all practical purposes, totally dependent on sugar production, mainly Barbados, St. Kitts, and Antigua. Islands with highland subsistence refuges such as Grenada, Dominica, Nevis, St. Lucia, and St. Vincent were only slightly better off. The larger colonies, British Guiana with rice, Trinidad with cacao and asphalt, and Jamaica with bananas had economic alternatives to sugarcane, but they also had larger populations to sustain.

Like every major Royal Commission of Enquiry, the 1897 commission was called for a number of interrelated reasons, and it would be pointless to seek a single cause for it. The formal charge given the commission, "to inquire into the present condition and future prospects of the sugar-growing Colonies of the West Indies" was stated in bland Victorian prose as a preamble to the final written report. But terrible, economically depressed conditions had existed in the region for well over a decade.[10] Why, then, did it take so long for an official commission to be formed and thereby acknowledge fully the serious distress in the British Caribbean in the late 1800s, when officials in the London Colonial Office had for years perused and answered reports that detailed case after case of depression-induced misery sent from the islands?

I have suggested elsewhere that it seems more than coincidental that a number of depression-influenced civil disturbances were growing during the same years, riots and protests that caught and held London's official attention far more readily than did the many sorrowful accounts of local West Indian malnutrition sent by parish medical inspectors.[11] Along with the documentation of human misery, reports of grumbling and threats by black workers in various islands were causes for official speculation and even alarm. Minor protests on individual plantations could be handled by a detachment of police, but major conflagrations that threatened to engulf entire islands were of an entirely different magnitude. Something approximating an islandwide riot occurred in Kingstown, St. Vincent, in November 1891 when an estimated 2,000 men marched into the capital town and were dispersed by British bluejackets. In April 1893, the police shot and killed four men protesting police interference on Dominica's windward coast. Far more serious disturbances, significantly involving sugar estate workers, took place in the region in 1896. In January and February in St. Kitts, hundreds of estate workers marched into Basseterre, burned buildings, and came under control only through the joint efforts of local police and British marines who shot two rioters dead. In October of the same year, indentured Indians rioted on a plantation in British Guiana, provoking a local police detachment to open fire on the crowd, killing five.

Within the context of London's overall colonial strategy—by this time being played out on a truly global scale—the West Indian depression riots were probably only minor nuisances. But if these disturbances continued and escalated, they could have distracted the Colonial Office from its preoccupation with the newer, larger, and richer parts of the empire. It therefore seems more than likely that the riots—especially those in 1896—helped greatly in precipitating the decision to call the commission. And since the commission itself led to important changes in the British Caribbean, it seems reasonable to suggest that local working-class disturbances helped create major material changes in the region. This suggestion, furthermore, is consistent with the general acknowledgment that Caribbean resistance is not simply an academic slogan that does little other than romanticize the plight of the region's oppressed people, but that it has represented, among many other things, a means by which Caribbean peoples have bettered themselves.

The Commission's Composition, Deliberations, and Conclusions

The five men who composed the Royal Commission of Enquiry already had vast experience in the British Caribbean, and they likely brought with them preconceptions as to what solutions might be best for the region. Yet most of their individual experiences were with particular island colonies. The four months they spent in the region, on the other hand, provided close looks at a regional differentiation and variety from one island to the next that they emphasized over and over in their final written findings. The commission's chairman was Henry Wylie Norman who, at age 70, had been a military official in India and later the Governor of Jamaica and also of Queensland. His two fellow commissioners were David Barbour, author of a number of economic treatises, and Edward Grey, who had served the Crown in a number of official capacities, including as the Colonial Office's desk officer for the Caribbean region. The commission's Secretary Sydney Olivier had been a Colonial Office official since 1882 and had acted as Secretary of the Fabian socialist society from 1886 to 1890; Olivier would later become the Governor of Jamaica. Daniel Morris, the Assistant Director of Kew Gardens, accompanied the commission to provide agricultural and botanical expertise;

Morris had been the Chief Agricultural Officer of Jamaica for years, and during that time he had traveled extensively in the British Caribbean, making recommendations, publishing pamphlets, and lecturing officials and planters alike about the latest techniques in tropical agriculture. The five men interviewed witnesses in London in the first week of 1897, sailed from Southampton on January 13, and, after two weeks at sea, arrived in Georgetown, British Guiana, on January 27, 1897.

As the commissioners made their way north through the region, their schedules and activities were publicized in local newspapers. On their arrival at a particular place, insular officials provided lists of economic data later published in the final written report, and occasional on-site visits to sugarcane estates took place, yet the bulk of the information gathered was through hearings held at the public buildings in the capital cities and towns. Usually the hearings were dialogues among the commissioners and a given island's public officials—police commissioners, public health officials, and of course governors and their staff members—providing opportunities for local officials to ingratiate themselves to the visitors from London. In general, more candid and sometimes contested testimony came from colonial sugarcane planters, many of whom considered the ineffectual diplomacy on the part of the British government as the primary cause of their problems because London had allowed the European sugar bounties to ruin their crops' prices.

Even more contentious were the occasional testimonies of working-class representatives who at times condemned local planters and officials alike and who saw the commission hearings as their only chance to appeal directly to representatives of the Crown, thereby going over the heads of local governments, men for whom they often harbored intense dislike and even disdain. When the commissioners reached St. Vincent early in February, they received, among other memoranda, a handwritten statement signed by 21 men and women from Barrouallie, on the island's leeward coast, likening the commissioners' arrival to the coming "of Moses of yore into Egypt, delivering the children of Israel from Pharoah's bondage."[12] The commission's findings indeed eventually influenced important land changes on St. Vincent, though perhaps not to the extent that those composing this baroque proclamation might have expected.

Although the most important of the commission's final recommendations was that of establishing settlements of British West Indian laborers "on small plots of land as peasant proprietors," there were also four other unanimous recommendations: the improvement of minor agricultural industries and cultivation systems in general for small proprietors, better interisland communications, the establishment of a trade in fresh tropical fruit with New York and eventually London, and the "grant of a loan from the Imperial Exchequer for the establishment of Central Factories in Barbados." The region's far-flung insularity and geographical variation precluded the commission recommending some sort of interisland political federation as some writers and observers had suggested.[13]

Nor did the three-man commission achieve unanimity on perhaps the single most important issue facing them: whether to propose countervailing tariffs to protect the British Caribbean sugar industry from bounty-supported beet sugar from the Continent. Although Barbour and Grey declined to recommend such tariffs, the Chairman Henry Norman, urged that for sugar imported by the United Kingdom "duties . . . be levied . . . to an amount equal to the bounty that has been paid on it by any foreign Government." Failure to adopt these measures, according to Norman, would ruin West Indian planters, distress the British Caribbean workers and artisans, perhaps lead to strife that would render the islands ungovernable, and lead the region to "serious disaster."[14] So after three months' travel in the Caribbean combined with preliminary and concluding hearings in London, all of which resulted in volumes of written testimony, the commission fell short of making a single unanimous decision about the underlying macro-economic cause of the depression.

The commissioners' report disappointed the British Secretary of State for the Colonies Joseph Chamberlain. Certainly the commissioners had empha-sized the terrible plight of the Caribbean colonies—something everyone had known for a decade—but their equivocal position as to a real remedy left the overall responsibility for a decision with the London Colonial Office. In early November 1897, Chamberlain circulated a memorandum to fellow Cabinet members that advocated placing "considerable duties" on bounty-supported beet sugar produced in Europe. He added that the decision had been left to him because "the Royal Commission has not given much assistance to the solution of the problem."[15]

Chamberlain's suggested tariff reform was not approved by the British Cabinet. His opponents suggested that the placing of duties on bounty-fed sugar imports would be too costly to British consumers and therefore dangerous polit-ically. Chamberlain then countered that the only other way to save the West Indian colonies from complete ruin was by government intervention of a dif-ferent kind: a series of financial grants for local economic transformations—a solution the commissioners had originally recommended in concluding their report. Chamberlain then added that the commissioners' original esti-mate of £580,000 to implement the proposed changes throughout the islands was "totally inadequate." Neither Chamberlain nor the Chancellor of the Exchequer Michael Hicks Beach was completely pleased with any direct imperial financial intervention because it ran counter to Britain's prevailing laissez-faire policies and lacked precedent.[16]

Implementation and Results

The commission's overall importance had not been in providing the imperial government with a clear and unanimous solution to the region's problems. Yet it had emphasized the severity of these problems and made several useful suggestions leading to important changes in the Eastern Caribbean. The most immediate and some of the most profound changes came in St. Vincent.

As early as October 1897, groups of laborers around the island—following the newspaper accounts of the report's recommendations—endorsed the breaking up of local estates. Despite resistance to these ideas by leading planters on St. Vincent, conditions there had become so severe that there was little turning back from the several years of planning, land surveys, and other discussions that had preceded the commissioners' visit. In mid-March 1898, the British Parliament approved a sum of £15,000 to settle landowners on the island. When notified of the grant for land acquisition, the island's Governor then drafted a local land acquisition bill, and the administrator identified 29 "abandoned" estates suitable for acquisition. Not all of the precedent for these ideas and developments had come from the commission's work in the Caribbean; earlier, in introducing the bill to the Imperial Parliament in London, Colonial Secretary Chamberlain had explained that the presence on St. Vincent of abandoned lands and underemployed working peoples was analogous to the situation in Ireland where lands and people recently had been brought together only after land expropriation schemes were accomplished with government funds.[17]

The breakup of large landholdings on St. Vincent was reinforced, indeed accelerated, when a massive hurricane hit the island early in September 1898. After passing over the southern half of Barbados and creating widespread damage to crops and settlements there, the storm's eye apparently passed directly over St. Vincent before it swerved north and grazed St. Lucia, bringing torrential rains and creating mudslides. After the immediate storm damage was absorbed and while relief ships were still dispensing food and blankets to dazed Vincentians, the Governor contacted Daniel Morris, the erstwhile technical expert of the 1897 commission, to visit St. Vincent and to help draw up plans for further small-scale land schemes. The eventual implementation of these schemes was made all the easier by the 1902 eruption of St. Vincent's volcanic Mt. Soufrière; the combination of hurricane and eruption within the space of four years on an island already identified as ideal for land devolution reduced planter enthusiasm for continuing large-scale agriculture and drove many of them away.[18]

In late July 1898, one-and-a-half months prior to the hurricane, Joseph Chamberlain, emboldened by the British Parliament's approval of the St. Vincent grant, issued a circular letter to West Indian governors, advocating the formation of small-scale settlements as had been suggested in the commission report. In the letter Chamberlain stipulated ideal characteristics of these settlements, remarks that eventually became incorporated into subsequent planning suggestions. These new settlements, according to Chamberlain, should be "carefully chosen" as well as within "comparatively easy reach of a market" and of a "permanent character" rather than temporary squatter settlements which were considered detrimental to timber supplies, soil fertility, and water availability. These new settlements, Chamberlain cautioned further, should not be sited so that there was competition with sugarcane plantations for labor.[19]

The incipient planning guidelines implied in Chamberlain's letter was only a small sample of the overall control and direction that the British intended to impose on new British West Indian settlements. Although advocating small-scale peasant communities, British government officials apparently were unable to imagine these settlements thriving without their expert, civilizing guidance. In early 1899 St. Vincent's Governor Alfred Moloney specified, besides settlement accessibility via improved road quality, ideal plot size. Moloney thought that land parcels should be from 5 to 15 acres, anything smaller being a subsistence "yam-piece." Also, he considered proximity to alternative wage sources important. Moloney also thought that a spirit of community would be necessary for success; he noted favorably such camaraderie that he had witnessed in Grenada, the smallholder island that the commissioners tirelessly had held up as a worthy model to emulate. Moloney's further notion that individual cottages should be centered on land plots was disputed by London officials who thought that such a scattering of farmsteads would inhibit the provision of services.

While British officials were divided as to specific planning techniques or strategies, they were unanimous in their opposition to informal settlements scattered throughout the hills and mountains; widespread forest hamlets were inconsistent with central colonial control and represented locales that could encourage relapse into "African" livelihood patterns. Discussions of these points, further, reawakened fears in the region that were decades old. Releasing the black labor force from a subservient, supervised existence might easily lead to trouble; these possibilities had been articulated by, among others, Professor Froude, who had ranted about the supposedly infectious savagery in "Hayti" during his travels in the 1880s. The problems associated with retrogressive "African" customs and behavior, moreover, had been a staple of the testimony gathered by the royal commissioners, particularly in relation to villages in remote highland island interiors.[20]

As mentioned, the island most quickly influenced by the 1897 commission's principal recommendation, the one for peasant proprietor holdings, was St. Vincent. The financial grant of 1898 was followed by other financial grants after the twin disasters of the 1898 hurricane and 1902 eruption, and by March 1904, almost £14,000 had been disbursed to purchase land on abandoned estates with an additional £10,000 approved in June of that year for land for small-scale settlers. Next to St. Vincent, Carriacou, the largest of the Grenadines, was influenced most by the commission's peasant proprietor recommendation. The colonial government began discussions in 1901 with absentee owners of three local estates there, and by 1903 lots on Carriacou were being parceled out and sold. Grenada already was an island of smallholders, and a principal caution for Grenada by the commissioners had been to curtail forest clearance to the higher mountain slopes. St. Lucia continued a trend toward small landholding, often through squatting and joint ownership of individual land plots.[21] Jamaica, larger than any other British West Indian island, far to the west, and not considered as severely affected by the depression as were the smaller places, already had seen the development of smallholder settlements as early as 1838.[22]

The commission's recommendation for a financial grant for the establishment of central sugarcane milling in Barbados resulted in a £80,000 "free grant" to the island in 1902, the same year Joseph Chamberlain helped negotiate a rescinding of European sugar bounties.[23] Although the parliamentary grant was not used for Barbados factory construction, the island's planters borrowed from the fund to finance annual crops and to modernize their equipment. Such modernization was necessary in light of the exodus of many among the Barbadian labor force to the Panama Canal starting in 1904, and it was advantageous when sugar prices rose during World War I. In the second decade of the twentieth century, the number of grinding mills in Barbados fell from 329 to 263 at the same time the island's sugarcane acreage was expanding, reflecting the closing of older, inefficient, wind-powered grinding mills. By 1921 there were 19 sugarcane factories whose capacities were sufficiently large to process cane from more than one estate.[24] Rising sugar prices also helped to inspire the construction of a small-gauge railway around St. Kitts, thereby consolidating the island's sugarcane plantations that became tributary to a single large factory.

In 1899 a regional agricultural department was established in Barbados. It was a result of the commission's principal recommendation concerning smallholders combined with the European penchant for supervision and control of small settlers. Daniel Morris became director in 1900 and held several conferences in order to coordinate the activities and incipient extension work by local agricultural officers and officials of botanic gardens in the region. The spirit of these botanic gardens was extended further into the twentieth century with the establishment of the Imperial College of Tropical Agriculture east of Port of Spain, Trinidad, in 1922. The college's buildings were constructed on the grounds of St. Augustine estate, originally purchased by the local government in 1900 for experimental agricultural research.[25]

Discussion

Although the 1897 royal commission was the first comprehensive assessment of local conditions in the British Caribbean for over 50 years, the region had always been a locus for observation, experimentation, planning, and projects sponsored by Europeans. The historian Jack Greene asserts that during the first three centuries of colonization, "America . . . came to be known primarily as a place to be acted upon by Europeans."[26] Later, by the eighteenth century, most of the Caribbean region had been irrevocably transformed by plantation clearing; yet it was still an important "biocontact zone," studied and scoured by European "bioprospectors" who sought new plants and animals of scientific, commercial, and medical value.[27] Then in the nineteenth century, the British Caribbean, along with other tropical areas of the world, provided the biological bases for scientific development through which Britain hoped to "improve" the British Empire.[28]

The 1897 commission's effects were to point in promising directions after an exhaustive and clear-eyed assessment of the region's problems and constraints, island by island. Throughout their travels and in their written reports and summaries, the commissioners were almost apologetic when, time after time, they emphasized the region's maddening interisland variety. So it is not entirely surprising that their recommendations were different for some islands than it was for others. Some of the places (notably St. Vincent and Carriacou) were considered suitable for smallholder settlements. In contrast, Barbados's sugarcane identity was to be reinforced. The region's colonial preoccupation with sugarcane cultivation, which had begun to fade in the smaller places by the late nineteenth century, was beginning to be confined to a few select places. The other islands were to go their own ways. As colonialism's domination eased and as sugarcane's superficial veneer over a region of great physical and cultural variety disappeared, the different islands of the British Caribbean began to emerge as distinct and different societies. They were all parts of a "region" whose coherence and togetherness had possibly never really existed except in the minds of the men consulting the wall map hanging at the London Colonial Office.

Notes

1. Generous support from several agencies, mainly the National Geographic Society, the National Science Foundation of the United States, and Virginia Polytechnic Institute and State University, made the research possible for this chapter.

2. *Report of the West India Royal Commission* (London: HMSO, 1897). This massive document is available in its microcard version of the British Sessional Papers in many university libraries. The report is referred to as RC (1897) in subsequent references in this chapter.

3. C. Y. Shepherd, "Peasant Agriculture in the Leeward and Windward Islands," *Tropical Agriculture* 24 (1947): 61–71.

4. Eric Williams, *From Columbus to Castro: The History of the Caribbean, 1492–1969* (London: André Deutsch, 1970), 535–537.

5. Hugh M. Clokie and J. William Robinson, *Royal Commissions of Enquiry: The Significance of Investigations in British Politics* (New York: Octagon Books, 1969; original edition 1937), 54–79.

6. James Anthony Froude, *The English in the West Indies, or the Bow of Ulysses* (London: Longmans, 1888).

7. Thomas C. Holt, *The Problem of Freedom: Race, Labor, and Politics in Jamaica and Britain, 1832–1938* (Baltimore: Johns Hopkins University Press, 1992), 322–332.

8. Sidney W. Mintz, *Sweetness and Power: The Place of Sugar in Modern History* (New York: Viking, 1985), 143.

9. Bonham C. Richardson, *Economy and Environment in the Caribbean: Barbados and the Windwards in the Late 1800s* (Barbados, Jamaica, Trinidad and Tobago: University of the West Indies Press, 1997), 18–66.

10. RC (1897), v.

11. Bonham C. Richardson, "Depression Riots and the Calling of the 1897 West India Royal Commission," *Nieuwe West-Indische Gids* 66 (1992): 169–191. For further information about the British West Indian labor disturbances see C.O. 884/9/no. 147, "Notes on West Indian Riots, 1881–1903," PRO (Public Record Office).

12. RC (1897), Appendix C, Part VIII, "St. Vincent," 119–120.

13. RC (1897), 23, 70.

14. RC (1897), 72, 74.

15. I. M. Cumpston, ed., *The Growth of the British Commonwealth, 1880–1932* (London: Edward Arnold, 1973), 103–106.

16. R. V. Kubicek, *The Administration of Imperialism: Joseph Chamberlain at the Colonial Office* (Durham: Duke University Press, 1969), 76–78.

17. Richardson, *Economy and Environment in the Caribbean*, 214.

18. Bonham C. Richardson, "Catastrophes and Change on St. Vincent," *National Geographic Research* 5, no. 1 (1989): 111–125.

19. Holt, *The Problem of Freedom*, 335.

20. Froude, *The English in the West Indies*; and C.O. 321/125 (Confidential), "Peasant Proprietary," May 10, 1890, PRO.

21. Richardson, *Economy and Environment in the Caribbean*, 221–226.

22. Hugh Paget, "The Free Village System of Jamaica," *Caribbean Quarterly* 10 (1964): 38–51.

23. R. W. Beachey, *The British West Indies Sugar Industry in the Late 19th Century* (Westport: Greenwood Press, 1978; original edition 1957), 166–168.

24. Richardson, *Economy and Environment in the Caribbean*, 230.

25. Gertrude Carmichael, *The History of the West Indian Islands of Trinidad and Tobago, 1498–1900* (London: Alvin Redman, 1961), 166–168.

26. Jack P. Greene, *The Intellectual Construction of America: Exceptionalism and Identity from 1492 to 1800* (Chapel Hill: University of North Carolina Press, 1993), 30.

27. Londa Schiebinger, *Plants and Empire: Colonial Bioprospecting in the Atlantic World* (Cambridge, MA: Harvard University Press, 2004).

28. Richard Drayton, *Nature's Government: Science, Imperial Britain, and the "Improvement" of the World* (New Haven: Yale University Press, 2000).

Chapter 2

The Colonial Office and Soil Conservation in the British Caribbean, 1938–1950

Lawrence S. Grossman

Concern about environmental degradation in the British Caribbean has a long history. The issue that clearly dominated officials' discussions about environmental problems during the colonial era was the state of the region's forests.[1] In contrast, widespread concern about soil erosion has had a much more recent history. Certainly, the topic of erosion was not new. Estates on Barbados were attempting to cope with soil loss in the latter half of the seventeenth century.[2] But the topic of erosion received only infrequent notice in official correspondence between the Colonial Office and its Caribbean colonies during much of the history of British control. The first British Caribbean-wide effort to control soil loss did not begin until the late 1930s.

This chapter explores the history of soil conservation efforts in the British Caribbean from the late 1930s to 1950, the era of soil conservation "mania" in the British Empire.[3] It argues that soil conservation efforts in the British Caribbean were not based on local initiatives made in response to locally perceived problems. Rather, the British Colonial Office in London and its agents in the Caribbean were the driving forces behind attempts to implement erosion control policies. The Colonial Office felt that resident officials in its Caribbean colonies—as well as peasants and estates there—failed to comprehend and appreciate the seriousness of the erosion problem, and thus it needed to make those in its colonies "erosion-conscious" through both directive and incentive. Moreover, the Colonial Office was not motivated by concerns related particularly to problems in the Caribbean. It stressed the need to implement soil conservation in the context of its concerns that the future of the entire British Empire was being threatened by environmental degradation and population growth. Finally, efforts to introduce soil conservation policies were not simply environmental initiatives. They reflected broader attempts by the Colonial Office to transform land tenure relationships, introduce more permanent forms of agriculture, and increase direct state intervention in and control over the peasant production process.

Although much research on the role of the British Colonial Office is available in relation to soil conservation in other regions of the empire, especially eastern and southern Africa, very little has been produced on the subject in relation to the British Caribbean.[4] Most research on the region's soil conservation efforts focuses on the case of Jamaica but ignores the critical role of the Colonial Office and only considers conservation efforts after 1950, thus failing to explore initiatives during the era of empirewide conservation "mania."[5] Similarly, although an extensive literature on the British Caribbean explores the relationship between the British Colonial Office in London and its colonies, such analyses in the context of environmental issues and policies are relatively rare in the literature, although Richardson's works on colonial forestry issues during the late nineteenth century are an important exception.[6]

This chapter first explores the context of the soil conservation issue in the British Empire. It then considers the British Caribbean response to pressures to ameliorate soil loss, highlighting the cases of St. Vincent and Jamaica. I select these two colonies for analysis because the Colonial Office viewed erosion problems there as being the most severe in the region.[7]

The Colonial Office and Soil Erosion

During the latter half of the 1930s, the British Colonial Office became increasingly concerned about soil erosion throughout the empire.[8] While a variety of influences contributed to the growth of empirewide interest in erosion, two were particularly prominent. First, the image of the devastating impacts of the Dust Bowl in the southern plains of the United States intensified worldwide concern about soil erosion. Second, officials in the Colonial Office were increasingly worried about the environmental impacts of rapid population growth.[9] To spur empirewide initiatives on this issue, the Secretary of State for the Colonies Sir W.G.A. Ormsby-Gore issued a circular despatch to almost all British colonies in January 1938 requiring them to report annually on the situation concerning the nature and causes of erosion in their territories, their plans to ameliorate the problem, and progress that they were making with regard to their soil conservation efforts.[10] Such annual reports were sent to the Colonial Office by its colonies, including those in the Caribbean, up until the late 1940s.

Articles began to appear stressing the empirewide significance of the problem, with such titles as "Erosion in the Empire," "Soil Erosion in the Colonial Empire," and "Dust Bowls of the Empire."[11] This newfound concern about erosion was also reflected in the changing priorities of the Colonial Advisory Council of Agriculture and Animal Health, which provided advice on agricultural issues to the Secretary of State for the Colonies. From its inception in 1929 until the mid-1930s, the focus of the Advisory Council was on commodity-based research and expanding tropical agricultural exports.[12] In the latter half of the 1930s, the issues of conservation of resources and soil erosion became increasingly prominent in the Council's discussions. The 1938 circular despatch from Ormsby-Gore dealing with soil erosion was based on advice from the members of this Council.

The person in the Colonial Advisory Council of Agriculture and Animal Health most responsible for pushing the agenda of soil erosion control in the British Empire was Sir Frank Stockdale, who served as Agricultural Advisor for the Secretary of State for the Colonies from 1929 to 1940. Stockdale was familiar with the Caribbean, starting his overseas career there with an appointment in 1905 as mycologist and lecturer in agricultural science in the Imperial Department of Agriculture in the West Indies. Stockdale had published extensively on the "evils" of soil erosion since 1923.[13] Another influential individual on the Council since 1930 was Professor Frank Engledow, the agricultural expert who accompanied the West India Royal Commission of 1938–1939 and authored the Commission's report on agriculture, which considered soil loss a serious problem in parts of the British Caribbean.[14] Also on the Council was Harold A. Tempany, who was Assistant Agricultural Advisor to the Secretary of State for the Colonies from 1936 to 1940 and then Agricultural Advisor from 1940 to 1946; he was equally committed to pressing the agenda of erosion control.

Stockdale's major concerns about erosion in the West Indies can be dated from the second half of the 1930s. Although he reported in 1931 that many people who visited Jamaica observed serious soil erosion there, his trip reports and discussions of his visits to the Caribbean in 1932 and 1933 at meetings of the Colonial Advisory Council of Agriculture and Animal Health rarely raised the issue of soil erosion.[15] In fact, his report on his visit during 1932 downplayed concerns about erosion in Jamaica, observing "the comparative freedom from soil erosion of the cultivations which have been pushed up the mountain sides."[16]

By the second half of the 1930s, however, he had changed his perspective. He declared, "Too little attention has been given in the West Indies to the evils of soil erosion or the need . . . of educative measures designed to weaning the inhabitants of the West Indies from shifting cultivation."[17]

Erosion and the Office of the Comptroller for Development and Welfare

Stockdale was soon to gain much greater influence over developments in the British Caribbean. In 1940, he was appointed Comptroller for Development and Welfare in the West Indies, a position that was created based on recommendations of the West India Royal Commission of 1938–1939. Based in Barbados, the Comptroller's mission was to advise administrators of the British Caribbean colonies on a wide range of development issues—including conservation of resources, agriculture, housing, labor conditions, education, and health care. The Comptroller visited the colonies to observe conditions, informed the colonies concerning what types of assistance programs he would support for funding under the Colonial Development and Welfare Act, aided them in developing long-range planning, and then made recommendations to the Secretary of State for the Colonies concerning which proposals for assistance should be funded. Stockdale served in this post from 1940 to 1945.

Assisting Stockdale were his expert advisors in several fields. The advisor for agriculture from 1940 to 1946 was A. J. Wakefield, who was given the title of Inspector General of Agriculture in the British West Indies. He served formerly as Director of Agriculture in Tanganyika, where soil erosion was a significant issue. Stockdale and Wakefield shared similar views not only about the urgent need to control erosion but also to change agrarian practices in the British Caribbean and modify land tenure in government-sponsored land settlement schemes. The latter two initiatives were closely related to their concerns about erosion.

The major change needed in British Caribbean agriculture, according to Stockdale and Wakefield, was the adoption of "mixed farming"—a model based on agricultural patterns in the United Kingdom and one that the Colonial Office emphasized should be utilized throughout the British Empire. Mixed farming involved a much more thorough integration of livestock raising and crop production than was characteristic of British Caribbean farming. It included the stall feeding of livestock, increased livestock manure production, application of manures on fields to improve yields, and rotational grass leys that would provide fodder for livestock. According to its proponents, mixed farming had numerous benefits, including reducing soil erosion, maintaining soil fertility, providing more regular, year-round opportunities for employment, and improving peasant nutrition.

Most importantly, the adoption of mixed farming would also result in a much more intensive and permanent form of agriculture for British Caribbean peasants. Many peasants engaged in shifting cultivation, which involved clearing and burning small forested plots often in steep, rugged hillsides, reaping harvests for a few years, and then fallowing the area for a number of years to permit tree regrowth while clearing and burning new forested plots in preparation for subsequent cultivation. Colonial officials frequently condemned the peasant practice of shifting cultivation, which they viewed as a major contributor to soil erosion.

Stockdale and Wakefield also attacked colonial administrators' commitment to providing freehold tenure in government-sponsored land settlement schemes. Both believed that granting freehold tenure to settlers after they finished paying for their lots would contribute to soil erosion because no effective government control over settlers' land-use practices would be possible. In this endeavor, Stockdale and Wakefield were relatively successful. In his review of land tenure issues in the Caribbean, Lewis noted that almost all British West Indian governments by the end of the 1940s offered settlements only on the basis of leasehold tenure.[18] The fear of soil erosion had far-reaching consequences.

Soil Erosion in the British Caribbean

The extent and significance of soil erosion in the British Caribbean in the late 1930s varied considerably among the colonies. The problem in specific places reflected a wide range of environmental, agronomic, demographic, and political-economic conditions. The environmental conditions of steep slopes and high rainfall found in many of the colonies increased the potential for erosion, but the impacts of such conditions were ameliorated where population densities were low and forests extensive, as in the case of Dominica. The types of crops grown and the agronomic practices employed were also critical. Some crops—such as cotton, grown extensively on St. Vincent and Montserrat, and bananas, the dominant crop of Jamaica—were clean-weeded, exposing the bare soil among the plants to the erosive power of the rain. In contrast, tree crops, such as nutmeg and cacao, dominant in Grenada, provided much better protection for the soil, as did sugarcane, which was widespread in Barbados and St. Lucia. Even crop disease could affect the potential for erosion; in Jamaica, for example, fear of Panama disease, a fungal infection that devastated the main commercial banana variety planted there, led farmers to abandon their infested fields after harvesting and replant in new lands free of the disease farther upslope on steep hillsides, leading to clearing of forests and soil erosion. Those new fields then became subject to Panama disease through the planting of infected suckers, forcing farmers still higher upslope.[19]

Inequalities in society, also extensive in the British Caribbean, affected the potential for erosion.[20] Reflecting continuities with the past of slavery, peasants tended to cultivate in marginal lands often on steeply sloping, small plots, whereas estates dominated the better lands in lower-lying areas with less steep slopes that were less susceptible to soil loss. Also, the nature of land tenure affected the extent of land degradation, a fact recognized by numerous officials within the region.[21] Many estates rented lands to peasants for short periods; given such insecure tenure, tenants had little incentive to conserve the soil. When plots lost fertility due to erosion, tenants could simply rent land elsewhere.

The Colonial Office and the Comptroller's office viewed the problem of soil erosion in the British Caribbean far more seriously than did the administrators and agricultural officials resident in the region. A sense of urgency about the issue in relation to the region was building in the Colonial Office.[22] In a review of colonial annual reports on soil conservation, members of the Colonial Advisory Council of Agriculture and Animal Health felt that "in regard to the reports from the West Indies . . . the information received tended to present a picture that was rather too favorable."[23]

Soil Conservation in the British Caribbean

Pressures from the Colonial Office and the Office of the Comptroller for Development and Welfare to deal with the perceived erosion "crisis" in the British Caribbean inspired a growing focus on soil conservation in the region. The actual pattern, timing, and intensity of initiatives employed varied considerably from colony to colony, but certain features in soil conservation programs were widespread.

The first step was typically an educational campaign to convince farmers of the need for erosion control and to explain possible changes in agricultural methods that could be implemented that would limit the problem. Campaigns involved public speeches, lectures, radio programs, and the distribution of leaflets and colored posters. Agricultural departments experimented with various methods of soil conservation on their own stations and also supervised efforts on demonstration plots located on farmers' fields to develop techniques that would be most effective—environmentally and economically— in controlling soil loss in specific environmental contexts. Efforts were directed at both peasant holdings and estates; although officials viewed erosion as being more serious on peasant holdings, they were also concerned about soil loss on estates. Agricultural departments also increased the size of their extension staff to enable more frequent contact with farmers to facilitate the adoption of conservation measures. Finally, specific soil conservation techniques were adopted for use on peasant farms and estates, the types utilized depending on the slope of the land and crops grown. In some cases, officials provided subsidies to farmers to encourage the adoption of conservation techniques.

The techniques that I had discussed elsewhere in relation to St. Vincent were widely explored throughout the region:[24]

1. Contour cultivation. Many peasants traditionally planted crops in a ridge and furrow system that was only partially aligned with the slope. Examples of crops planted in such a system included both food crops, such as sweet potato and dasheen, and export crops, such as cotton. Such misalignment could aggravate soil erosion. Extension agents focused on getting farmers to properly align their cultivation with the slope. To demarcate the actual contours in farmers' fields, extension agents would plant strips of grass or place sticks in the ground along the contour, which farmers could use as guides to follow when constructing systems of ridges and furrows.

2. Grass contour lines as soil barriers. Extension agents also encouraged farmers to plant grass barriers along the contour to trap sediment being washed downslope. These grass barriers were planted at varying vertical intervals, depending on the steepness of the slopes. In some cases in which the grass barriers were particularly effective, large terraces would build up behind them from the trapped soil.

3. Strip cropping. On long slopes, extension agents emphasized the need for farmers to plant alternating horizontal strips of clean-weeded crops (which made the ground beneath them susceptible to erosion) and soil-protecting crops, such as fodder grasses or sugarcane (which provided sufficient cover for the soil to limit the impact of rain). Stockdale and Wakefield viewed strip cropping as particularly valuable because they envisioned it as an integral part of mixed farming.

4. Bench terracing. Bench terraces were formed by digging soil out of the hillsides and creating a series of level benches down the slope on which to plant crops. Creating such terraces was much more complex and time-consuming than other forms of conservation adopted.

5. Drains. Extension officers suggested digging varying types of drains along the contour to control and trap water as it flowed downslope.

An example was the silt-trap drain, which was excavated along the contour and measured between 2 and 3 feet wide and between 2 and 3 feet deep.

Although numerous conservation techniques were examined and implemented, the simplest methods were most widely adopted. These included contour cultivation and contour grass barriers. However, even the success of these techniques varied over time. For example, proper maintenance of grass barriers was a widespread problem. In some cases in which fodder grasses were used for the barriers, uncontrolled grazing by cattle or theft of grass by livestock owners created breaches in the grass barriers that severely reduced their effectiveness. Proper long-term maintenance of barriers, particularly replanting areas where grass died or was stolen or eaten, was another problem.

Efforts at implementing soil conservation in the British Caribbean were funded by numerous grants made under the Colonial Development and Welfare Acts. Some grants were targeted specifically at soil conservation, whereas in other cases, the grants were for broad agricultural development programs, in which soil conservation was one component. Funding for soil conservation usually included support for experimental work and demonstration plots, an increase in the number of extension staff involved in erosion control efforts, and sometimes provision for subsidies paid to farmers as well.

Soil Conservation on St. Vincent and Jamaica

From the perspective of the Colonial Office, soil erosion in the British Caribbean was most serious on St. Vincent and Jamaica. A brief examination of these two cases reveals the high degree of variability among colonies in progress made in implementing soil conservation programs.

St. Vincent was clearly the most successful case of soil conservation in the British Caribbean. Between the mid-1940s and mid-1950s, the total length of all contour lines and barriers demarcated and planted in grass annually ranged from over 500,000 feet to approximately 1,000,000 feet.[25] Much of that progress can be attributed to the zeal of Superintendent of Agriculture C. K. Robinson. There were other reasons for the success of the Vincentian program compared to initiatives in the other islands. The conservation methods emphasized interfered minimally with existing agricultural patterns. Subsidies were widely employed to motivate adoption. The island's extension staff was expanded significantly to focus on educating peasants about soil conservation. St. Vincent's long experience with land settlement and associated intervention in peasant agriculture were also significant.

Stockdale was particularly impressed with the island's achievements. He observed in 1944, "Flying across the island of St. Vincent today whole stretches of land could be seen where conservation methods were being practiced, valley catchment areas preserved with contour lines of Khus-khus grass. . . . [I]t was really a pleasure to see what the agricultural people of St. Vincent were attempting to do."[26]

In contrast, conservation efforts in Jamaica were unimpressive during the period under review. Lack of progress was not due to lack of interest in the issue. Those officials most closely involved in the government's erosion control efforts—H. H. Croucher, the island's Agricultural Chemist, C. Swabey, its Forest Officer, and W. C. Lester-Smith, the Soil Conservation Officer from 1944 to 1947—published numerous reports as well as several articles on the subject of erosion control in the *Journal of the Jamaica Agricultural Society*.[27]

But instead of concerted action in farmers' fields, much of the conservation effort during this period was devoted to studying the problem. A consistent refrain from officials during this period was the need to gather more information about erosion problems and about the best methods of erosion control to suit the myriad environmental conditions throughout Jamaica before implementing an islandwide program.

Another problem was the nature of the strategies chosen. Although contour planting and grass barriers were utilized on the island, Lester-Smith placed great faith in strip cropping because the technique was critical to the success of mixed farming, a strategy that he fully endorsed.[28] Unfortunately, strip cropping proved unpopular because of the high labor costs involved and the amount of land that had to be removed from direct crop production to allow for the planting of contour grass strips used for fodder.

A major impediment to progress in controlling erosion was the unique structure of agricultural institutions on the island. In almost all cases in the British Caribbean, departments of agriculture did both experimental work and extension work. In contrast, these two functions were performed by separate institutions in Jamaica. The Department of Agriculture focused on research and experimentation. The role of extension, including that related to soil conservation, was performed separately by instructors of the Jamaica Agricultural Society.

The Jamaica Agricultural Society was established in 1895 by the Governor of Jamaica in an attempt to limit demands at the time to establish a separate department of agriculture. The Society received an annual stipend from the government, but it was an independent body. The majority of its members were peasants, who attended meetings at branches throughout the island.

In the context of soil conservation, insufficient finances and inadequate technical training of its extension staff limited the effectiveness of the Society's extension efforts. Also, conservation was only one of the Society's priorities in extension. In fact, Lester-Smith complained about the commitment of some of the Society's extension staff to the soil conservation effort.[29]

While St. Vincent was receiving praise by the middle of the decade, Jamaica was viewed as a disappointment. In 1945, Wakefield complained, "There has been and still is grave misuse, abuse and waste of land."[30] Educational campaigns, experiments, and demonstration plots were still the main achievements by the late 1940s. In 1948, L. Lord, who was the secretary of the Colonial Advisory Council of Agriculture, Animal Health and Forestry, commented while reviewing annual conservation reports from Jamaica that "the actual progress of soil conservation measures among cultivators is disappointingly slow—possibly because of lethargy on the part of cultivators but largely, apparently, because of the high cost per acre of the measures recommended."[31]

It was only in the subsequent decade that significant initiative in soil conservation was evident in Jamaica, particularly in the Yallahs Valley program. Facilitating efforts were the merging of the Jamaica Agricultural Society's extension staff into the Department of Agriculture in 1951 and a substantial increase in government funds available for the conservation effort.

Impacts of the Conservation Effort

In spite of his disappointment with efforts in Jamaica, Wakefield provided a positive assessment of the changes in the British Caribbean at the end of his tenure as Inspector General of Agriculture in the West Indies. He asserted,

> A major change of outlook has taken place in the West Indies in recent years in regard to the land. . . . [T]here was little, if any, public conscience as far as soil-conservation was concerned. The most severe and widespread examples of soil-erosion excited no comment. Now, a lively concern about the soil and its wastage is to be found in all classes. . . . In the course of five years, grass has come to be one of the most important crops in the West Indies.[32]

Stockdale and officials in the Colonial Office in London felt that much of the success that was achieved in relation to conservation and related social policies could be attributed to the tireless efforts of Wakefield. Stockdale asserted "that in consequence of the educative campaign which has been in force during the past few years and particularly since the appointment of Mr. Wakefield as Inspector General of Agriculture, there has been a marked change of outlook amongst West Indian agriculturalists in regard to the need for measures designed to effect soil conservation. It can now be said that the West Indian public is beginning to be 'soil conscious.' "[33] Officials in London also commented favorably on Wakefield's efforts; one noted that "Mr. Wakefield's missionary zeal is now producing results."[34]

As the decade progressed in the 1940s, reports from the colonies indicated a growing awareness of and concern about erosion. In fact, the emphasis on the erosion "menace" appeared contagious. For example, whereas officials on St. Lucia had not highlighted the erosion issue to the same extent as those on nearby St. Vincent, by the mid-1940s they too were swept up in the soil conservation mania. Swithin Schouten, the Agricultural Superintendent, proclaimed in his soil conservation report to the Colonial Office that "[t]hroughout the Colony of St. Lucia there is abundant and spectacular evidence of soil erosion."[35]

Certainly, the soil conservation effort in the 1930s and 1940s did not result in the radical transformation of agriculture hoped for by the Colonial Office and the Comptroller for Development and Welfare. Shifting cultivation remained, and mixed faming was not widely adopted. And in some cases where soil conservation techniques were initially adopted, their effectiveness over the longer term declined as proper maintenance of conservation structures was a continuing problem. Nonetheless, the Colonial Office and the Comptroller for Development and Welfare were responsible for creating an "erosion-conscious" populace and an administrative apparatus that facilitated future conservation efforts in the region.

Notes

I would like to thank the Wenner-Gren Foundation for Anthropological Research and the Summer Humanities Program at Virginia Tech for supporting this research. I also gratefully acknowledge the generous assistance provided by Peter Bursey at the Foreign and Commonwealth Office Library, Kate Manners at the archives of the Royal Botanical Gardens at Kew, the National Archives (Kew), the libraries at the Institute of Commonwealth Studies, Rhodes House (Oxford University) and the Natural Resources Institute (University of Greenwich, Chatham).

1. On forestry issues in the British Caribbean, see R. H. Grove, *Green Imperialism: Colonial Expansion, Tropical Island Edens and the Origins of Environmentalism, 1600–1860* (Cambridge: Cambridge University Press, 1995); J. Fairhead and M. Leach, *Science, Society and Power: Environmental Knowledge and Policy in West Africa and the Caribbean* (Cambridge: Cambridge University Press, 2003); and B. C. Richardson, *Igniting the Caribbean's Past: Fire in British West Indian History* (Chapel Hill: University of North Carolina Press, 2004).

2. D. Watts, *The West Indies: Patterns of Development, Culture and Environmental Change since 1492* (Cambridge: Cambridge University Press, 1987).

3. J. McCracken, "Experts and Expertise in Colonial Malawi," *African Affairs* 81 (1982): 101–116.

4. For an exception, see L. Grossman, "Soil Conservation, Political Ecology, and Technological Change on St. Vincent," *Geographical Review* 87 (1997): 353–374.

5. For example, see D. Edwards, *Small Farmers and the Protection of the Watersheds: The Experience of Jamaica since the 1950s* (Kingston, Jamaica: Canoe Press, University of the West Indies, 1995).

6. See B. C. Richardson, "Detrimental Determinists: Applied Environmentalism as Bureaucratic Self-Interest in the Fin-de-Siècle British Caribbean," *Annals of the Association of American Geographers* 86 (1996): 213–234; and B. C. Richardson, *Economy and Environment in the Caribbean: Barbados and the Windwards in the Late 1800s* (Kingston, Jamaica: The Press University of the West Indies, 1998).

7. F. A. Stockdale, "Soil Erosion in the Colonial Empire," *Empire Journal of Experimental Agriculture* 5 (1937): 281–297.

8. Grossman, "Soil Conservation, Political Ecology, and Technological Change on St. Vincent," 353–374.

9. D. Anderson, "Depression, Dust Bowl, Demography, and Drought: The Colonial State and Soil Conservation in East Africa during the 1930s," *African Affairs* 83 (1984): 321–343.

10. C.O. 323/1529/7, 1937, Agricultural: Soil Erosion in the U.S.A. C.O. is the letter code for Colonial Office documents held in the National Archives, Kew.

Henceforth, all Colonial Office documents held at the National Archives will be referred to as C.O.

11. C. G. Watson, "Erosion in the Empire," *East African Agricultural Journal* 2 (1936): 305–308; F. A. Stockdale, "Soil Erosion in the Colonial Empire," *Empire Journal of Experimental Agriculture* 5 (1937): 281–297; and Anonymous, "Dust Bowls of the Empire," *Round Table* 29 (1939): 338–351.

12. J. Hodge, "Development and Science: British Colonialism and the Rise of the 'Expert,' 1895–1945" (unpublished PhD dissertation, Queens University, Canada, 1999); and J. Hodge, "Science, Development, and Empire: The Colonial Advisory Council on Agriculture and Animal Health, 1929–43," *Journal of Imperial and Commonwealth History* 30 (2002): 1–26.

13. F. A. Stockdale, "Soil Erosion," *Tropical Agriculturalist* 61 (1923): 1–31.

14. F. L. Engledow, *West India Royal Commission Report on Agriculture, Fisheries, Forestry and Veterinary Matters* (London: His Majesty's Stationery Office, 1945).

15. C.O. 137/793/6, 1931, Jamaica: Land Settlement Schemes—Reports, minute by F. A. Stockdale, August 17, 1931.

16. F. A. Stockdale, *Report by Mr. F. A. Stockdale on His Visit to the West Indies, Bermuda, British Guyana, and British Honduras, 1932.* C.A.C. 128 (London: Colonial Office, 1932), 70.

17. C.O. 318/423/5, 1936, West Indies: Wimbush Forestry Report—Recommendations, minute by F. A. Stockdale, September 21, 1936.

18. C.O. 318/502/3, 1950, Caribbean Commission: West Indian Conference, Fourth Session—Documentation—Land Settlement. "Issues in Land Settlement Policy" by W. Arthur Lewis (1950).

19. C.O. 852/249/15, 1939, Economic: Soil Erosion—Annual Reports from the Colonies. "Soil Erosion in Jamaica" by G. G. Brinsley, Commissioner of Lands (1939).

20. See Grossman, "Soil Conservation, Political Ecology, and Technological Change on St. Vincent," 353–374.

21. See H. Croucher and C. Swabey, "Soil Erosion and Conservation in Jamaica, 1937" (Bulletin No. 17, Kingston, Jamaica, Department of Science and Agriculture, 1938).

22. See C.O. 852/249/19, 1939, Soil Erosion: West Indies.

23. Colonial Office, 1939, Minutes of the Forty-Fifth Meeting of the Colonial Advisory Council of Agriculture and Animal Health, November 28, 1939, 1 (source: Foreign and Commonwealth Office Library).

24. Grossman, "Soil Conservation, Political Ecology, and Technological Change on St. Vincent," 353–374.

25. Grossman, "Soil Conservation, Political Ecology, and Technological Change on St. Vincent," 353–374, at 366.

26. Colonial Office, 1944, Minutes of the Sixty-First Meeting of the Colonial Advisory Council of Agriculture, Animal Health and Forestry, July 28, 1944, in C.O. 996/1 Colonial Advisory Council of Agriculture, Animal Health and Forestry, Minutes of Meetings, 1944–1951.

27. See, e.g., Croucher and Swabey "Soil Erosion and Conservation in Jamaica"; and W. C. Lester-Smith, "Some Aspects of Soil Conservation for Jamaica," *Journal of the Jamaica Agricultural Society* 50 (1946): 162–168.

28. C.O. 852/1013/5, 1948, Soil Erosion: Jamaica. "Report of the Soil Conservation Officer for the Year Ended 31st March, 1946" by W. C. Lester-Smith (1946).

29. C.O. 852/1013/5, 1948, Soil Erosion: Jamaica. "Report of the Soil Conservation Officer for the Year Ended 31st March, 1947" by W. C. Lester-Smith (1947).

30. A. J. Wakefield, *Report of the Agricultural Policy Committee of Jamaica* (Kingston, Jamaica: Government Printer, 1945), 6.

31. C.O. 852/1013/5, 1948, Soil Erosion: Jamaica. Minute by L. Lord, May 11, 1948.

32. Cited in Sir J. Macpherson, "Development and Welfare in the West Indies, 1945–46," Colonial No. 212 (London: HMSO) in C.O. 318/490/1, 1947. C.D.W. Report 1945–1946.

33. C.O. 852/394/7, 1943, Soil Erosion: Annual Reports from the Colonies, 1943. Letter from F. A. Stockdale to Oliver Stanley, Secretary of State for the Colonies, July 13, 1943.

34. C.O. 852/543/6, 1944, Soil Erosion: Annual Reports from Colonies, 1944. Minute by L. Lord, June 24, 1944.

35. C.O. 852/1013/4, 1947, Soil Erosion: West Indies. Swithin Schouten "Memorandum on Soil Conservation in St. Lucia during the Years 1945–46," August 26, 1947.

Chapter 3

Domestic Food Production in Guadeloupe in World War II

Glenroy Taitt

The French West Indian colony of Guadeloupe was a plantation society whose economy on the eve of World War II was dominated by export agriculture: sugar and, to a lesser extent, bananas. Butterfly-shaped Guadeloupe comprises two islands: Grande-Terre and Basse-Terre. The former, being flat apart from a hilly enclave in the south known as Grands-Fonds, was well suited to sugarcane. Because of that island's more bustling economic climate, Guadeloupe's commercial capital Pointe-à-Pitre was located there. Basse-Terre, on the other hand, held the colony's administrative capital, which was also known as Basse-Terre. A mountainous chain, topped off by the Soufrière volcano, running along the north-south axis of Basse-Terre made a mockery of this island's name of "Low Land." Basse-Terre was therefore devoted to the secondary export crops such as bananas, coffee, vanilla, spices, and cocoa. However, two regions lay outside the orbit of these secondary crops. The east coast, especially the northeast with its rolling plains, though geographically part of Basse-Terre, was an extension of Grande-Terre, economically speaking; it belonged to the kingdom of sugar. The leeward coast because of its particularly rugged terrain had evaded the clutches of export agriculture.

Guadeloupean Society under Vichy

After its traumatic capitulation to Germany in June 1940, France was divided into a German-occupied sector and a much smaller unoccupied zone run by Marshall Pétain from the town of Vichy in central France. Vichy France, with National Revolution as its ideology and Work, Family, and Fatherland as its motto, existed from July 1940 until the liberation of France in August 1944. However, a section of the French military led by General Charles de Gaulle, rejecting the armistice, issued a call to resistance. Guadeloupe's immediate problem, therefore, was whether to recognize Vichy France or de Gaulle's London-based Free French alliance as the legitimate French government. Yet, ultimately, the colony had no choice in this matter. Despite the vote by the General Council, the colony's local parliament, in favor of the Free French, Admiral Georges Robert, the Commander-in-Chief of France's Western Atlantic naval force who had arrived in Martinique in September 1939, pledged loyalty to Vichy. To consolidate Robert's authority during the impending war, Paris had also appointed him High Commissioner to the French territories in the Western Hemisphere (Martinique, Guadeloupe, French Guiana along with St. Pierre and Miquelon, an archipelago off Newfoundland in Canada). In that latter capacity, the respective governors answered to him. Guadeloupe's Governor for most of the war was Constant Sorin, an even later arrival than Robert, having only taken up his position in April 1940.

Vichy rule in the French West Indies was autocratic, attempting to cleanse the society of what it regarded as 70 sordid years of republicanism.[1] Accordingly, Vichy's acolytes abrogated universal male suffrage, the republican system of justice, and what they regarded as the ungodly division of church and state. Foremost among Vichy's supporters were the local or Creole whites and the Catholic Church. The latter hailed the overthrow of the Third Republic with its overtones of anticlericalism. The local whites took up seats in the town halls and in a new, nominated Local Council, which replaced the fully elected, financially autonomous General Council. Nevertheless, any honest review of this traumatic period in Guadeloupe's history must admit that sections of the colored and, to a lesser extent, black population did support the regime as well, at least up to the end of 1942 when Germany invaded Vichy France. Vichy control of Guadeloupe lasted from 1940 to 1943. In May–June 1943, the black population rose up and, on the emotionally significant day of July 14—Bastille Day—the colony passed over to Free French control.

Blockade

Between 1940 and 1943 the French West Indies was under intense international pressure as Britain and the United States imposed a blockade around Martinique and Guadeloupe.[2] The blockade was not meant to strangle these colonies. Certainly, the United States did not adopt Britain's uncompromising stance on the embargo against the French West Indies. After all, a considerable degree of trade with the United States replaced trade with France. From January 1941 the U.S. Treasury made available US$600,000 a month, from the blocked accounts of the French government in the United States, to Guadeloupe and Martinique to purchase essential commodities. Instead, the quarantine was both a collar to hold the islands back from trading with the enemy as well as a lever to nudge the two colonies into the allied camp (and they pleaded repeatedly, though unsuccessfully, with Robert to change sides).

From 1942, Guadeloupe ceased trading with France, relying instead on nearby countries, even neighboring Martinique. The United States became Guadeloupe's major partner. Yet this alternative network was unable to provide Guadeloupe with its usual quantities of food. Imports of salted

Table 3.1 Guadeloupe: Some Major Food Imports, 1939–1945

Year	Salted fish/ Smoked fish (Tonnes)	Peas (Tonnes)	Rice (Tonnes)	Flour (Tonnes)
1939	1,804	851	8,140	6,952
1940	1,428	464	3,967	8,211
1941	792	501	3,558	11,227
1942	—	—	—	—
1943	—	—	—	—
1944	—	—	—	—
1945	877	522	3,148	9,609

Source: *Annuaire Statistique de la Guadeloupe* (*ASG*) (1949–1953): 124.

Table 3.2 Guadeloupe: Banana Cultivation, Production, and Exports, 1939–1945

Year	Cultivation (Hectares)	Production (Tonnes)	Exports (Tonnes)
1939	7,120	73,000	45,904
1940	6,200	68,000	22,887
1941	4,900	55,000	7,382
1942	—	—	—
1943	—	—	—
1944	—	—	—
1945	5,400	57,600	10,428

Source: *ASG* (1949–1953): 122 and 124; Renseignements statistiques demandés par lettre No. 77 A.E./3 du 12 novembre 1941 de l'Admiral Robert, Basse-Terre le 3 décembre 1941, Le Chef du Service de l'Agriculture, sous-série 7M, Liasse # 7M12240, Archives Départementales de la Martinique (hereafter cited as ADM), Fort-de-France.

fish, peas, and rice all declined by about one-half between 1939 and 1941 (see table 3.1). Records for 1942–1944 were unavailable, but in 1945 imports of salted fish and peas were up slightly, while rice imports continued to decline. Ironically, flour imports, no doubt from the United States (as in World War I), actually increased during the war, only to decline in 1945.

Export Agriculture

The banana sector underwent a significant reorientation during the conflict. The war all but eradicated the gains that bananas had made since commercial exploitation began in the 1920s. Exports dropped from 45,904 tonnes in 1939 to half that amount one year later, then they were slashed to a mere 7,382 tonnes by 1941 (see table 3.2). By 1945, the recovery had started, with exports showing a slight increase. Isolated from their principal export market, banana producers sharply reduced the amount of land under cultivation.

Sugar, on the other hand, continued like an unstoppable wave driven by the currents of history. Production actually rose in the first three years of the

Table **3.3** Guadeloupe: Sugar Cultivation, Production, and Exports, 1939–1945

Year	Cultivation (Hectares)	Production (Tonnes)	Exports (Tonnes)
1939	30,000	59,500	59,049
1940	—	61,300	59,818
1941	36,800	62,400	31,695
1942	—	69,600	—
1943	—	47,400	—
1944	—	28,400	—
1945	24,800	28,400	112,985

Source: *ASG* (1949–1953): 122–124.

war, only dropping considerably from 1943 (see table 3.3). On the other hand, exports declined then halted. Guadeloupe was only able to ship part of her 1941 harvest to North Africa instead of France. Thereafter Britain and the United States prevented her from sending any sugar overseas. So the rising quantities of sugar that the factories were producing piled up in warehouses. Indeed one of Robert's last acts in early July 1943 was to halt further sugar production in the French West Indies. When Guadeloupe passed over to Free French control, a part of the 1941 harvest, as well as all of the sugar from the 1942 and 1943 harvests were still in storage. In 1945 the extraordinary amount exported, 112,985 tonnes, represented the clearing of this massive surplus stock. Rum was also stockpiled in Guadeloupe, but here the situation was not as critical as with sugar because the alcohol was used to make petrol.

Domestic Agriculture

Domestic food production deals with a fairly wide range of agricultural commodities grown largely for consumption within Guadeloupe. Domestic food crops—root and leaf vegetables, pulses and cereals—included commodities such as cassava, yams, tannia, sweet potato, peas and beans, and corn. These crops were grown both for subsistence and for sale in the local markets. This type of agriculture was associated mainly with peasants who either owned land or acquired it under a sharecropping arrangement, but some peasants who already owned small parcels of land often took additional land from the factories under the sharecropping system. Alongside the peasants, there were *petit blancs* (lesser whites) and colored estate owners in Grands-Fonds who had taken up market gardening from the early 1900s.

Throughout the war, the government consistently supported domestic food production. In its initial response to the outbreak of fighting, the government issued a decree ordering all cultivators (except those called up for defense purposes), be they landowners or sharecroppers, to begin the cultivation of all idle lands.[3] This order extended even to sugar factories and rum distilleries that were to put an unspecified portion of their lands under domestic food crops. The penalty for noncompliance was confiscation of property. As the Governor indicated in his address at the start of an extraordinary session of the General Council, which was called to discuss the war, "through the intense development of domestic food crops" no one in Guadeloupe would go without food.[4] The government also sought to release state lands for domestic agriculture, at first in the communes—districts—of Capesterre, Trois-Rivières, and Goyave. Lands were to be allotted to residents who were married and had a family. Businesspeople, civil servants, and landowners were debarred from benefiting from this scheme.[5]

The unexpected fall of France in 1941 along with the subsequent blockade added a heightened sense of urgency to Guadeloupe's food security. Thereafter, the colony's attempt to grow as much of its food as possible became part of a wider policy of import substitution in the face of the deprivation of wartime: use of cotton seeds and coconut for making oil, fats, and soap; converting rum into petrol; and drawing salt from seawater. However, not surprisingly, politics became entangled in the genuine concern for alleviating hunger and hardship. According to a report on production by Devouton, Vichy's inspector in the Antilles, to Robert in June 1941, Sorin's aim in developing the resources of Guadeloupe was to "free it [Guadeloupe] partially from economic dependence on America."[6] Turning specifically to the colonial administration's policy of "intensification of domestic food cultivation," Devouton noted that results were already visible with the cultivation of peas and beans, corn, sweet potato, and various other root crops.

Cassava was particularly important in the government's strategy. According to Devouton, the administration was also trying to improve the procedure for making cassava flour, hoping thereby to incorporate a percentage of cassava flour in the making of bread in order to decrease the importation of American flour. Toward the end of 1941, the government stipulated that cassava flour had to be mixed with wheat flour for making bread.[7] But contrary to the government's hopes the measure failed, according to the Director of Agriculture. The latter said that the opening of this new market created a scarcity of cassava, which led to a rise in price from 3 francs a bucket in 1940 to 7 francs, then to 10 francs 20 centimes, even 25 francs a bucket at the most critical moment.[8] He said that, undoubtedly, the rise in price led to an increase in cassava cultivation but, ironically, it also made the bakers use less cassava flour in the making of bread. In October 1942, he noted, the government withdrew the order to use cassava flour in bread.

Attempts were also made to cultivate rice, large amounts of which were imported each year. Guadeloupe was not a rice producer although the colony—like Trinidad and British Guiana—had a sizable Indian population. Instead, it imported rice from Suriname. Writing to the French Ambassador in Rio de Janeiro, in February 1942, Sorin referred to the experiments conducted the previous year with rice obtained from Brazil.[9] In October 1941, seven varieties of rice were planted in Petit Bourg in land that, previously swampy, had been partly drained but was capable of being irrigated: *matao branco, cacho de duro, catete, honduras, ponte prete, amerlao,* and *aguhla branco.* The last two, he said, had given the best results. Paddy received from the latter already represented 65 times the amount sown. Since Sorin was desirous of expanding the trials, he was asking the Ambassador to dispatch 1 tonne each of *aguhla branco* and *amerlao.* Regrettably, further documentation was not forthcoming on this novel experiment.

In its campaign to intensify domestic food production, the colonial administration relied on several measures: exhorting the populace through radio broadcasts, talks, written appeals, distributing seeds and plants, and by making land available through forestry concessions. Following the precedent set before the war, the government again made state lands in the forests available in small parcels for domestic food production (concessions were also offered for the cultivation of oil-yielding plants, to get around the shortage of imported lubricants as well as for reforestation). Details of a concession in 1942 revealed that the government was offering forested areas for a duration of four years.[10] While in the prewar period the recipients had obtained these concessions free of charge, subsidized by the General Council, they now had to pay 25 francs per hectare, as a contribution to the cost of dividing the land into lots, and 10 francs per hectare as an annual lease fee. However, the Director of the Agricultural Service Alexandre Buffon later criticized the policy of granting forestry concessions, both before and during the war. In July 1945, Buffon admitted that only a small proportion of the land that had been allocated over the years had been occupied, with an even smaller number being fully exploited.[11] In most cases, the land was abandoned after having been cleared.

Moral suasion was the main weapon that the government used to encourage the populace to intensify food production. "Return to the land" was a strong theme in the Vichy government, and in Guadeloupe Sorin had a similar crusade. A perfect example of this is the "Appeal of Governor Sorin to the Agriculturists of Guadeloupe" in November 1941.[12] Sorin began with one of Pétain's favorite slogans, "A field which is lying fallow, is a piece of France which dies." He then went on,

> Do you therefore want France to die, YOU WHO STILL HAVE LAND LYING FALLOW AT THE PRESENT TIME [*sic*] in this very fertile Guadeloupe. . . .
> Are you forgetting your important duty towards the earth which God has given you? Don't you know the grandeur and the beauty, the joy of that duty?
> Our MARSHAL, reminds you of it every day. . . .
> The MARSHAL has for you, Agriculturists and Peasants, the greatest esteem since he knows that it is you who will once again make France rich, make Guadeloupe rich.
> He knows, as we all do, that if it is God who makes the plants grow, when you cultivate, you "help God . . ."
> Collaborators with God—What more beautiful title can you want?

Noticeably, the payment of bonuses for cultivating selected food crops, a common prewar measure, was not part of the government's policy during the

Vichy years. For ideological reasons, though, the Vichy government would not have entertained the notion. Given those references to love, joy, perseverance, and God in Sorin's address, only a heretic could have handed over a sackful of francs to the peasants to grow domestic food crops. Indeed, according to Lucien Degras, former Director of Research at the National Institute for Agronomic Research (INRA) in Guadeloupe, since Vichy encouraged people to love the land, paying the populace to plant food would have been an act of profanity.[13] After the downfall of the sanctimonious Vichy regime, the payment of monetary incentives resumed. Under Free French control, the colony resorted to bonuses in January 1945.[14] In recommending payment of bounties, the General Council noted that prices for domestic food crops had fallen because of competition from imported food. The maximum payable per crop ranged from 500 francs a hectare for corn to 1,200 francs a hectare for onions. The minimum area that had to be cultivated to qualify for a bonus ranged from 10 ares—one-tenth of a hectare—in the case of garlic and onion to 100 ares in the case of yam.

Marketing of domestic food crops was another tool that the government failed to consider. Instead, the government concentrated on marketing food from abroad. Imports from the United States went first to Martinique where they were divided between the two colonies, an insensitive move given the long-standing rivalry between them (the people of Guadeloupe felt that Martinique took food at their expense). In Guadeloupe, the mayors took a census of their populations to allow the authorities to allocate foodstuffs equitably to each commune, and the government distributed the food through two or three selected merchants in each commune, who then sold to the retailers.

Nevertheless, the government's campaign appeared to have had some success. According to an unsigned newspaper article in February 1943, the Basse-Terre market was said to have been well supplied with domestic food crops.[15] Housewives could expect to find a variety of food crops, though at high prices. The article attributed the improvement to the efforts of the Agricultural Service, which had been making available seeds and plants of all kinds as well as the suppression of predial larceny.

Sugarcane versus the Sweet Potato

Throughout the war Guadeloupe's sugar industry was largely uncooperative, making only a token contribution to the campaign to intensify domestic food production. Even during the embargo, when life was exceedingly difficult for the majority in Guadeloupe, the industry made only halfhearted efforts to produce food for local consumption. Early in the war, the government asked the factories and distilleries to employ a small portion of their land to grow domestic food crops. By this means, according to Devouton, 800 hectares were said to have been cultivated in 1940, with 1,400 hectares being estimated for 1941. Figures released by the Agricultural Service revealed that in 1940 the principal factories and distilleries had altogether planted 836.75 hectares in domestic food crops: cassava, sweet potato, peas and beans, corns, and other miscellaneous food crops.[16] According to these statistics, emanating from the factories themselves or the police, the factories had contributed some 606 hectares while the distilleries were responsible for a further 230 hectares. This total of some 836 hectares was negligible considering that Guadeloupe then had approximately 30,000 hectares under sugar.

An intelligence report by the police in Sainte-Rose pointed to the different attitudes of the two factories in the commune.[17] The Comté de Lohéac was said to be cultivating domestic food crops at the expense of sugar. Out of 900 hectares of arable land, 90 hectares was under domestic food crops. Cassava and yam in particular were the domestic food crops most widely grown, and the factory had even set up a cassava factory, making biscuits and flour. On the other hand,

> [t]he "Bonne Mére" [sic] factory is not making any effort to intensify its domestic food crop production which would play a large part in feeding the workers, especially since it is customary that the domestic food crops grown are sold to the workers, in the factory's shop. Although the figures given by the offices seem rather high—100 hectares out of 2.500 hectares of arable land—an assessment made by trained officers would show that almost nothing is being done, except for sugar cane cultivation.

Well aware of the industry's inflexible attitude, the authorities contemplated more decisive measures. In January 1942, Sorin spoke of the stubbornness of some factories in a letter to the Governor of Martinique:

> [T]he decree of 15 May 1941, modified on 19 June, obliging the large landowners to plant 5% of their lands in vegetables and ground provisions has become inadequate. The decree of 19 June, permitting the substitution of pasture lands for domestic food crops, has given those so inclined a way out which they have abused. . . . I even think it is necessary to raise to 10% the proportion of lands to be cultivated in vegetables and ground provisions and to extend it to arable land owned by the distilleries.[18]

In a secret telegram to Robert in June that year, Sorin revealed that since the factories did not see the need to refocus, he was considering issuing a decree reducing cane cultivation by 25 percent and having them devote the land thereby made available to domestic food crops, cassava, and oil-bearing plants.[19] By April 1943, Sorin had raised the quota of lands for domestic agriculture to 20 percent.

Eugène Plumasseau's novel *Ma part d'héritage*, which depicts the life of the sharecropper in Guadeloupe in World War II, shows how one factory cynically exploited the government's edict to set aside land for either domestic food production or animal rearing. Ostensibly a work of fiction, *Ma part d'héritage* is based on the Beauport factory in the north of Grande-Terre. In the novel, Plumasseau describes how the factory abruptly terminated the tenancy contracts of some of its sharecroppers in order to turn into a pasture the land previously allocated to them.[20] As a preamble to the harsh news that they were going to be set adrift, the director of the factory told the sharecroppers that the factory had to make them part of the decision to diversify the activities of the company. Like Sorin, Plumasseau was showing that the factories were on the lookout for any escape hatch freeing them from the obligation to cultivate domestic food crops.

In light of their intransigence, sanctions against the factories and distilleries were discussed in several items of correspondence between Robert and the three governors in the Caribbean. In a secret letter that he wrote to the Governor of Martinique, and which was also sent to the governors of Guadeloupe and French Guiana, in February 1943 on the subject of the "re-adaptation of the local economy," Robert spoke of the recalcitrance of the large- and medium-size landowners.[21] Since persuasion had not worked, the Admiral felt it was time for coercive measures: issuing of contracts to the landowners with stipulations as to quantity and type of domestic food crops to be grown, setting of deadlines and giving priority to domestic food crops in the allocation of labor. Robert was also proposing "rapid and exemplary sanctions." If successful, the readaptation that Robert was proposing would have humbled the sugar industry, historically the linchpin of the colonial society. Writing to Sorin in April, however, Robert revealed that since the existing legislation did not allow for the enforcement of the policy he had envisaged, he had asked the government to extend his powers so that he, in turn, could amend the law accordingly.[22] As such, he said, he was unable to approve the penal sanctions that Sorin was proposing for infractions of the policy.

The Statistical Record and Voices from Grands-Fonds

Incomplete as they are, the available statistics for domestic food crops still reveal an intriguing story (see table 3.4). A steady, though modest, rise in the amount of land under domestic food crops is evident between 1939 and 1941: from 10,000 hectares to 13,500 hectares.[23] Land under cassava rose as

Table 3.4 Guadeloupe: Sugar, Banana, and Domestic Food Crop Cultivation, 1939–1945

Year	S (Ha)	B (Ha)	Dfc (Ha)	Ca (Ha)	Co (Ha)
1939	30,000	7,100	10,000	2,000	150
1940	—	6,200	12,500	2,500	200
1941	36,800	4,900	13,500	3,500	200
1942	—	—	—	—	—
1943	—	—	—	—	—
1944	—	—	—	—	—
1945	24,800	5,400	6,500	1,600	—

Note: S = Sugar; B = Bananas; Dfc = Domestic food crops; Ca = Cassava; Co = Corn; Ha = Hectares.
Source: ASG (1949–1953): 122; Renseignements statistiques demandés par lettre No. 77 A.E./3 du 12 novembre 1941 de l'Admiral Robert, Basse-Terre le 3 décembre 1941, Le Chef du Service de l'Agriculture, sous-série 7M, Liasse # 7M12240, ADM.

well, from 2,000 hectares to 3,500 hectares. The statistics indicate a small extent of land under corn, but it was a significant amount as this was the first time that corn had been listed separately, the peasants having taken up corn cultivation in the early 1930s, predominantly in the leeward coast of Basse-Terre. So clearly the government's campaign to intensify domestic food production had succeeded, at least to an extent. For it cannot be denied that there were flaws in the program. The government's support was just one of several factors that, collectively, were responsible for the expansion. The shortage of imported food too provided a strong incentive to augment the domestic food supply. In seesaw fashion, the quantity of land under domestic food crops rose when imported food declined drastically. Furthermore, the extension in domestic food crop cultivation also coincided with the decline in land under bananas, suggesting that land was being switched from bananas, because exports plunged, to domestic food crops. There was therefore an interplay between, first, domestic food production and imported food and, second, between domestic and export agriculture.

Sugar and domestic food crops shared a relationship as well. The additional 3,500 hectares under domestic food crops is far too modest a sum given the critical shortage of imported food in Guadeloupe. In the colony's quest for self-reliance, much more land should have been devoted to domestic food crops. Although there may have been an underreporting of statistics for fear that the government would commandeer food, as happened in Martinique, the answer lies elsewhere. Possibly, the sluggish increase in land under domestic food crops was due to the intransigent attitude of the sugar industry. The mulish expansion of sugar between 1939 and 1941 stifled further growth in the domestic food sector. In Basse-Terre, land was switched from bananas to domestic food crops, but a similar diversion failed to materialize in the sugar zone.

The peasant zones—Grands-Fonds and to a lesser extent the leeward coast of Basse-Terre—were the areas that fed Guadeloupe throughout the war.[24] For decades, Grands-Fonds had been regarded as the breadbasket of Grande-Terre. The war was a particularly dynamic period for Grands-Fonds as its domestic food crops were in even greater demand. The factories in Grande-Terre: Gardel, Courcelles, Ste-Marthe, Blanchet, Beauport, and Darboussier all sent caravans of oxcarts to Grands-Fonds, to obtain food for their wage laborers. However, during wartime the peasants stopped leaving their land fallow for a long time. While this allowed them to reap even more during those critical years, it exhausted the soil, so compromising Grands-Fonds' future.

While the wartime was indeed difficult for the people of Guadeloupe, ironically it was rather favorable to the inhabitants of Grands-Fonds.[25] They no longer had to go down to Pointe-à-Pitre to sell their produce since the market came to them: people arrived with donkeys and oxcarts from neighboring areas, even from as far as the southern town of Basse-Terre. Many of those who came to buy were retailers who, in turn, sold over the produce in the markets outside. These retailers also brought in commodities that the region did not produce such as salt, lard, and rice. However, once the war ended, the market retreated from their doorstep. One informant remembered those years as a time when he earned a lot of money from the cultivation of domestic food crops since he sold practically all that he planted.

Conclusion

World War II was a time of great social and economic upheaval in Guadeloupe. Traumatized by the unexpected fall of the mother country, the country found itself blockaded by the allies. Yet the war was also a period of opportunity for the colony that, cut off from its traditional overseas suppliers, was forced to rely on its own resources. In the consequent drive for self-reliance, the government ran a campaign to intensify domestic food production. The few available statistics together with anecdotal evidence indicate a rise in domestic food crops during the war. However, the growth was not as pronounced as expected because the sugar industry made only token concessions. There was therefore a double interplay between domestic food production and export agriculture as well as between the former and imported food. In Guadeloupe's outward-looking economy, the domestic agricultural sector was not autonomous.

Notes

1. See Eric T. Jennings, *Vichy in the Tropics: Pétain's National Revolution in Madagascar, Guadeloupe and Indochina, 1940–1944* (Stanford: Stanford University Press, 2001), especially chapter 4, which offers a good discussion of the sociopolitical changes in Guadeloupe under Vichy rule.
2. See Fitzroy André Baptiste, *War, Cooperation, and Conflict: The European Possessions in the Caribbean, 1939–1945* (New York: Greenwood Press, 1988) for a discussion of the international diplomacy involved.
3. *Journal Officiel de la Guadeloupe* (*JO*), September 14, 1939: 822.
4. *JO*, September 21, 1939: 836. All translations have been done by this author.
5. *JO*, October 19, 1939: 953.
6. Rapports Devouton as production Guadeloupe et Martinique, Politique de production suivi par le Gouverneur de la Guadeloupe, June 3, 1941, sous-série 7M, 7M11680, Archives Départementales de la Martinique (hereafter cited as ADM), Fort de France.
7. *JO*, December 30, 1941: 1489–1490.
8. Alexandre Buffon, "Farine de manioc et panification," *Revue agricole*, n.s., 1, no. 2 (September 1944): 28–31.
9. Sorin to the French Ambassador in Rio de Janeiro, Brazil, February 5, 1942, série continue (hereafter cited as SC) 3995, Archives Départementales de la Guadeloupe (hereafter cited as ADG), Bisdary.
10. *JO*, August 1, 1942: 811–812.
11. Buffon, "Le problème des terres," *Revue agricole*, n.s., 2, no. 4 (July 1945): 100.
12. *Hebdomadaire de la Guadeloupe* (*HDG*), November 29, 1941: 1.
13. Lucien Degras, personal interview with the author, December 1, 1993.
14. Minutes of the General Council, Second Ordinary Session for 1944, sous-série 1N, 1N171, ADG, 341–354; *JO*, February 24 1945: 179.

15. *HDG*, February 20 and 27, joint issue (1943): 1.
16. Dossier Production Agricole, Service de l'Agriculture, Production Agricole 1939–1943, Sous-série 7M, Liasse # 7M10546/C, ADM.
17. References: Notes No. 318 and 366/2, Détachement des 24 juin 1942 et 22 novembre 1943, Gendarmerie Nationale, Détachement de la Guadeloupe, Section de Pointe-à-Pitre, Brigade de Sainte-Rose, Documents de la Deuxième Guerre Mondiale à la Guadeloupe, ADG. These documents that were consulted in 1993 were no longer available in a subsequent visit in 2004.
18. Sorin to the Governor of Martinique, January 2, 1942, SC 6193, ADG. In Martinique some factories avoided planting domestic food crops as well; see M. Horowitz, *Morne-Paysan, Peasant Village in Martinique* (New York: Holt, Rinehart and Winston, 1967), 86.
19. Sorin to Robert, telegram, June 23, 1942, sous-série 7M, 7M10546/C, ADM.
20. Eugène Plumasseau, *Ma part d'héritage* (Pointe-à-Pitre: Imprimerie G. Alcindor, 1982), 144. This is apparently an extremely rare book, a copy of which I consulted at the Médiathèque Caraïbe Bettino Lara in Basse-Terre, Guadeloupe, in January 2006.
21. Robert to the Governor of Martinique, February 2, 1943, sous-série 7M, 7M12229, ADM.
22. Robert to Sorin, April 14, 1943, sous-série 7M, 7M12229, ADM.
23. Other figures provided by the Director of Agriculture showed that 8,000 hectares and 9,025 hectares of land were planted in domestic food crops in 1941 and 1943, respectively. These figures would have indicated a reduction in the amount of land under domestic food crops between 1939 and 1945.
24. George Lawson-Body, "Stratégies paysannes dans la Guadeloupe en transition vers le salariat: des habitations marchandes-esclavagistes aux communautés paysannes libres dans l'espace des Grands-Fonds" (doctoral thesis, Université Paris 7, 1990) as well as personal interview with the author, December 2002 and also December 1993. A historian, Lawson-Body, has conducted extensive research on the Grands-Fonds region.
25. Samson Pierre-Victor, personal interview with the author, January 9, 2006; Apollinaire Pédurand, personal interview with the author, January 12, 2006. Pierre-Victor and Pédurand, born in 1918 and circa 1923, respectively, are inhabitants of Grands-Fonds, who grew domestic food crops during the war.

Chapter 4

Cuba's Farmers' Markets in the "Special Period," 1990–1995

Rebecca Torres, Janet Momsen, and
Debbie A. Niemeier

Introduction

The end of the Cold War and the collapse of the Soviet Union forced Cuba to diversify its trade links and to produce more goods domestically. In spring 1990, Cuba announced a "Special Period in Peacetime" in which food self-sufficiency was to be paramount.[1] Much land previously used for export crops, especially sugar, was turned over to production for domestic consumption, and there was a return to nonmechanized agriculture using mainly organic inputs. By 1992 Cuban trade with Eastern bloc countries had fallen to 7 percent of its 1989 levels.[2] The U.S. trade embargo was continuously tightened, culminating in the Helms-Burton Act in 1996 under which the United States threatened to punish third countries trading with Cuba.

During Cuba's Special Period the Cuban government opened free enterprise farmers' markets (*agromercados*) as one of a series of steps designed to mitigate the nation's growing food shortage.[3] Despite an earlier failed experiment with "free" farmers' markets from 1980 to 1986[4] the new markets were established in an attempt to stimulate production, undercut the flourishing black market, and make more food available at lower prices.[5] Within a year of the program's commencement in 1994, there were 211 markets operating in the country—with 33 in the capital city alone.[6]

This chapter looks at the operation of the Cuban farmers' markets during the Special Period, particularly comparing the participation and contribution of the collective and private farming sectors. We present data collected from these markets in 1995, through a cross-sectional survey of 150 vendors in 10 Havana City farmers' markets. After a brief review of the restructuring of the Cuban food system and agricultural production during the Special Period, we focus on sources of goods, product offerings, prices, and access to inputs.

The Cuban Food System

Three years after the 1959 Cuban Revolution, Cuba introduced a rationing system that ensured that basic needs could be met for the whole population. This system supplied a low-cost highly nutritious diet which made the Cuban population the best fed in Latin America and the Caribbean.[7] Post-1989 economic problems led to supply shortfalls resulting in vitamin deficiency diseases, as well as a drop in the average per capita caloric and protein intake of over 30 percent by the early 1990s.[8] Faced with growing social unrest culminating in the massive 1994 raft and small boat exodus, the Cuban government initiated a number of steps designed to assuage the growing food crisis. The most prominent of these was the October 1994 approval of free enterprise farmers' markets.

There is wide recognition that without the markets the population's food requirements simply could not be met. Despite what are considered to be high prices by Cuban standards, the markets enabled people to purchase food that was unavailable through the ailing national ration system. Those Cubans having access to dollars, either through remittances from exiled family members, employment in the tourism industry, or association with other foreign joint venture enterprises, benefited most from the existence of the markets.[9]

Participation in the *agromercados* was quickly dominated by private producers, and within a month their participation had climbed toward the 1994–1995 average of 93 percent of all market suppliers (331,752 total by July 1994). Despite having significantly smaller landholdings (averaging 11.7 hectares)[10]

Figure 4.1 Exterior View of One of the 10 City of Havana Markets Represented in the Survey Sample

Source: Photograph by Rebecca Torres.

than their state counterparts, by June 1995 private producers' portion of market sales reached 92 percent (72,172.5 million pesos).[11] It is estimated that these markets provided approximately 25–30 percent of all agricultural products sold in the country,[12] an estimated one-third of the caloric requirements of the Cuban people[13] and as much as 60 percent of the caloric intake of the population of the City of Havana (see figure 4.1).[14]

Historically the Cuban "nonstate" farming sector[15] has consistently performed better than the state farms, as measured by both quantity and quality of output.[16] On approximately 20–25 percent of arable land, the nonstate farming sector produces over one-third of the agricultural output accounted for in official statistics.[17] The nonstate sector has also been an important long-term source of key food crops—providing 52 percent of fruits, 61 percent of vegetables, and 35 percent of all roots and tubers.[18] The Cuban government generally favors state and collective farms in the distribution of agricultural services, inputs, and facilities. This creates the paradox, noted in many studies, where the private independent farms, despite input restrictions are the most productive.[19]

Agricultural Production in the Special Period

Between 1989 and 1992 imports of agricultural inputs dropped dramatically, with petroleum falling by 53 percent, fertilizer by 77 percent, animal feed by 70 percent, and pesticides by 63 percent.[20] Both the sugar- and nonsugar-producing sectors were affected by this rapid decline in inputs, but sugar, as Cuba's principal export crop and an important source of desperately needed hard currency, retained priority access to the limited pool of such resources. By the end of 1993, the nonsugar agricultural sector was operating with only 20 percent of the material inputs it received in 1989.[21]

The collective state farm system dominated Cuban agricultural production through 1993, with the state controlling 82.3 percent of all land resources.[22] Before the Special Period, Cuban agriculture had already experienced problems with low productivity,[23] inefficiency, poor management,[24] lack of labor incentives, poor worker discipline,[25] high production costs,[26] and corruption. The combined effects of a relatively inefficient and unproductive state farming sector, labor shortages, and the loss of inputs and resources associated with the Special Period plunged Cuba into a deep agricultural crisis. Domestic food production dropped from 1.5 million MT in 1991 to 920,000 MT in 1994.[27]

Faced with this agrarian crisis, the Cuban government took several steps to provide a basic food safety net for the Cuban people. Among these were the National Food Program (1989),[28] which emphasized noncane agriculture and resulted in the implementation of a series of strategic investments in irrigation, refrigeration, and transportation.[29] Another measure designed to boost domestic food production was the creation of UBPCs (Unidades Básicas de Production Cooperativa/Basic Units of Cooperative Production), which granted agricultural workers usufruct rights to state farmland for collective production purposes.[30] The government also began to distribute usufruct rights to unused state farmland to individual collective farm workers (Resolution 357/93) for self-provision and in some cases, for sale for profit.[31] There was an emphasis on self-provisioning—encouraging food production by cooperatives, state enterprises and families, often through the bourgeoning urban gardening movement. Most urban garden production was for subsistence because of small volumes, and marketing and transportation difficulties, although sales were technically permitted.[32] These measures were complemented by new state-driven foci on "sustainable" or "alternative" agriculture production as a means of overcoming input shortages and labor mobilization programs designed to address a continuing chronic shortage of agricultural workers.[33] Creation of the farmers' markets in October 1994 was probably the most radical measure taken by the Cuban government in the Special Period.

Since the revolution the structure of Cuban agriculture has evolved to encompass a number of very distinct forms. These include the traditional socialist state collective farms; the more recent UBPCs, consisting of state land farmed by former state farm workers for collective purposes (described earlier); CPAs (Cooperativas de Producción Agropecuarias/Agricultural Production Cooperatives), formed by individual farmers who voluntarily pool their land into permanent collective ownership and production; CCSs (Cooperativas de Crédito y Servicio/Credit and Service Cooperatives), independent farmers who have loosely organized to facilitate access to state-controlled resources although land tenure and production remain private; independent or "dispersed" private farmers who cultivate individual private plots; and finally family or individual gardens on private property or usufruct *parcels* for subsistence consumption and, in rare cases, market sale.[34] All forms of agriculture, with the exception of the family gardens, are expected to deliver a quota to the state food system, *Acopio*. Although private farmers are able to retain a higher percentage of their production, they have very limited access to state-provided inputs.

The various forms of agricultural production are classified as either "state" or "nonstate" in Cuban official statistics. Historically, the state category has included collective farms while the nonstate category comprised cooperatives—including CPAs and CCSs—and dispersed independent farmers. This method of classification has diminished utility now that most state land has been converted into UBPCs, which are considered to be nonstate. For example, utilizing this classification, it was estimated that by the end of 1994, 66 percent of the 6,741,000 hectares of arable land was controlled by the nonstate sector when, in fact, approximately 86 percent of the arable land was controlled by state-managed collectives.[35] Additionally, the state/nonstate dichotomy does not accurately reflect the degree of state intervention and control of resources inherent in all forms of agriculture—particularly with respect to the collective UBPCs and CPAs. Another Cuban statistical classification identifies the "Socialist Sector," as including state farms and CPAs, and the "Private Sector," comprising CCSs and dispersed farmers. For the purposes of this chapter, we utilize a classification based on collective versus private production to interpret survey results.

Collective production refers to production in which land is communally owned and benefits are distributed collectively. This includes UBPCs, CPAs, and EJTs (Ejército Juvenil de Trabajo, the youth farm programs) farms and comprised 16.3 percent of the survey respondents. The term "private" refers to land that is owned and farmed by individuals or families to whom earnings directly accrue. For the *agromercado* survey data, this category included CCSs, independent farms, and family gardens, accounting for 83.7 percent of survey respondents.

In reality, no dichotomous classification adequately captures the varying degrees of state intervention in the different forms of Cuban agricultural production. According to Puerta and Alvarez, "In essence, all four forms of production [state farms, CPAs, CCSs, and dispersed farmers] are subject to the power of the state, whose interference decreases (but does not end) from State farms to dispersed farmers."[36] The more recent UBPCs would logically follow state farms with respect to level of state intervention. As Puerta and Alvarez suggest, it is perhaps more accurate to view state intervention in agricultural production as a continuum, with state farms representing the strongest state presence, and individual dispersed farmers representing the least. In the remaining sections of the chapter, we use the collective-private distinction in our examination of product offerings and sales, and access to inputs, as revealed by the *agromercado* survey.

Havana Farmers' Markets in the Special Period

The *agromercado* survey was administered to 150 market vendors in 10 of the 33 City of Havana Province markets during five days between July and September 1995 after they had been in operation for almost a year. The survey was conducted on both weekdays and weekends to capture broadly representative consumer and vendor behavior. The selected markets were chosen to reflect a geographic balance between inner-city and suburban markets in western, eastern, and southern regions of the city as well as the wide size range of the Havana markets. In addition to the survey, we interviewed representatives of different Cuban government agencies and organizations and paid visits to state farms, cooperatives, and urban gardens.

Geographical Sources of Vendors in Havana's Markets

While vendors came from 60 different locations in 41 municipalities scattered throughout Cuba, the overwhelming majority (91 percent) were from the City of Havana and its surrounding province. Sixty-three percent of vendors identified themselves as producer representatives. Only 32 percent reported themselves to be farmers/producers. Since farmers selling directly through the markets are permitted by law to have one representative, it is impossible to determine precisely how many vendors are illegal intermediaries (representing more than one farmer). The fact that 68 percent of vendors reported living within the City of Havana, while only 26.4 percent of market produce came from the city, suggests a high incidence of intermediary participation in the farmer's markets. This regional concentration was particularly strong for representatives, 73 percent of whom were from Havana Province, in contrast to 52 percent of farmers/producer vendors. At the municipal level vendors appeared to favor markets in their home municipality. However, the larger markets, including Cuatro Caminos, Havana's largest market, attracted vendors from many areas.

Product Offering, Sales, and Prices

As table 4.1 illustrates, the Havana farmers' markets sold a wide range of fresh produce with 63 different products offered by sampled vendors. Approximately 57 percent of the products observed on the survey day were fresh fruits (45.0 percent) and vegetables (12.5 percent). Other types of products included flavorings and garnishes (fresh spices, onions, and garlic), *viandas* (high carbohydrate tubers and fruits), meats, legumes, grains, and flowers. Sixty-five percent of observed products could be classified as "perishable." The most frequently offered products were dietary staples such as avocados, bananas, garlic, sweet potatoes, rice, and beans. An absence of imported produce combined with seasonal constraints dictated a noticeable shortage of winter crops such as tomatoes, lettuce, standard onions, carrots, and oranges. Also absent were officially restricted items such as fresh dairy products, beef, sugar, coffee, potatoes, fish, and poultry.

Table 4.1 Percentage of Market Products by Production Sector (Observed and Reported Frequency of Offering)

		Organization	
Product	Total (%)	Collective (%)	Private (%)
Fresh fruit	45.0	17.6	82.3
Vegetables	12.5	13.0	87.0
Flavors and garnishes	14.3	11.8	88.2
Root crops	10.0	16.7	83.3
Meats	4.5	6.3	93.7
Legumes	5.3	21.1	78.9
Grains	5.0	27.8	72.2
Flowers	3.4	None	100.0
Total product supply	100.0		
Market supply by production sector		15.7%	84.3%

Source: Authors' survey data, 1995.

According to the survey the private sector supplied approximately 70 percent of total market volume, accounting for about 71 percent of the value of sales. CCSs made the greatest contribution to market volume, supplying 46 percent of all products sold, but their sales value (33 percent of the total) was exceeded by private independent farmers, with 36 percent of total market sales value on only 23 percent of total volume. The average private vendor market volume was significantly lower at 296 kilograms than the average volume reported by the collective respondents (562 kilograms). Additionally, collective vendors, on average, experienced significantly greater sales (4,399 pesos) than did their private counterparts (2,400 pesos). This suggests that the private vendors may tend to sell slightly higher priced products (8.11 pesos per kilogram) than the collective vendors (7.83 pesos per kilogram).

The mean price of products offered by independent farmers was the highest, averaging 16.4 pesos per kilogram. Family gardeners had the cheapest offerings at an average of 9.3 pesos per kilogram. A comparison of mean prices offered by the collective (12.5 pesos per kilogram) and private sectors (13.7 pesos per kilogram) revealed little difference. The higher product prices of private independent farmer offerings were balanced by the lower prices of CCS and family gardener offerings. This result negated the common belief in Cuba that the private farming sector (i.e., CCSs and private independent farmers) generally charged significantly higher prices. It also ran counter to the Cuban government's expressed objective that government-owned collective farms should serve the function of depressing mean market prices by offering their products at lower prices.

However, there was a notable variation in mean product prices across markets. Discounting meats, all of which came from a single market, Regla, an inner-city market had the highest mean price with 20.3 pesos per kilogram. Examining just those markets within Havana, there were significant differences in average market prices (analysis of variance [ANOVA]: $p < 0.01$). All of these prices, given that the sample was limited to Havana, were likely considerably higher than what would have been found in other regions of the country.[37]

A comparison between Cuban retail and Mexican wholesale prices during this time period reveals that many Cuban product prices were relatively inexpensive. For example, Cuban sweet potato retail prices averaged only US$0.10 per kilogram compared to Mexico City and Monterrey wholesale prices, which were approximately US$0.90 per kilogram. *Yucca* or manioc prices were also much lower in Havana, at approximately US$0.12 per kilogram compared to Mexican wholesale terminal prices, which ranged between US$0.45 and US$0.50 per kilogram. Other Havana prices, such as those for pork, avocados, and bananas, were comparable with those of Mexico. For green onions and limes Havana prices were higher than Mexican prices. Since both these products were out of season at the time of the survey and, in the absence of any imports, or off-season production (as in Mexico), prices were understandably high. This comparison of Havana, Mexico City, and Monterrey prices challenges the commonly held assertion in Cuba that market prices were unreasonably high. It could be argued, to the contrary, that many

Havana prices were unrealistically low by world standards. Nevertheless, with the average government salary pegged at US$10 a month,[38] the products remained out of reach for many Cubans, particularly those without access to U.S. dollars.[39]

Differences in Access to Inputs, Infrastructure, and Services

Land Resources

Havana farmers' markets were served primarily by small farming operations. Forty-four percent of farms supplying the vendors were less than 7 hectares in size. All of these were privately operated, either by independent farmers and family gardeners or by cooperative CCSs. Larger farms of more than 28 hectares, represented 23.5 percent of all the landholdings in the sample. All the collective farms in the sample—the CPAs and UBPCs—fell into this category. Nineteen percent of the farms supplying the market were between 7 and 14 hectares, with most (69 percent) being independent farming operations.

The large UBPCs accounted for 42.5 percent and CPAs another 42 percent of all land supplying the farmers' markets. By contrast, private independent farms supplying the markets accounted for only 7.6 percent of the total land resources represented in the market survey. Similarly CCSs controlled only 6.3 percent of the landholdings. The mean farm size of collective sector suppliers, at 329.54 hectares, was significantly greater than that of private farms, which average 12.72 hectares (t-test: $p < .001$). Finally, it is notable that the survey's 15.5 and 84.5 percent division between the private and collective sectors, respectively, closely approximated the Cuban government's published statistics (14 percent versus 86 percent).

Small farm contribution to market sales volume was disproportionately high relative to landholdings. The smallest farms (0–7 hectares) supplied an average of 214 kilograms per hectare to their vendors. By contrast, the largest farms (> 28 hectares) provided an average of only 7.5 kilograms per hectare. Differences in the mean volume of market sales per hectare by farm size are highly significant (ANOVA: $p = .01$), reflecting both the more intensive operations of small farms and the inherent inefficiencies of collective agriculture on large tracts of land.

Despite having significantly less access to land than their collective counterparts, the private sector provided a disproportionate amount of the products sold at the farmers' markets. From only 15 percent of the landholdings, the private sector supplied 71 percent of the sales value and 70 percent of the volume of all products sold in the farmers' markets. While the private sector's significantly greater land-use intensity—0.95^{40} versus 0.88 for the collective sector (t-test: $p = .008$)—may, in part, contribute to the private sector's greater participation in the markets, the difference is more likely attributable to a combination of the private sector's higher productivity and its ability to divert production away from the national food distribution apparatus.

Inputs

Forty-nine percent of survey respondents indicated that their yields (or those of the farms supplying their products) had been significantly affected by lack of fertilizer, herbicides, or insecticides. Chemical fertilizers were reportedly utilized by half of the farms supplying the market vendors. Animal manure was also widely used, with 47.9 percent of the farms reporting its application. Employing the collective/private dichotomy, 46.7 percent of collective farms reported applying biofertilizers compared to only 13.6 percent of private sector production units (t-test: $p < 001$). Many UBPCs and CPAs did, however, report having workshops/laboratories capable of producing their own biofertilizer requirements. There was no significant difference across the collective-private distinction in terms of type of fertilizer used. While a shortage of fertilizer appeared to affect all sectors of Cuban agriculture, private farmers and their market representatives perceived a greater yield loss than did their state/collective counterparts. Smaller, private sector farms reported similar access to chemical fertilizers for market production as did larger state-supplied collective farms. However, private producers reported far less access to biofertilizer alternatives than did collective growers. As a group, private farmers expressed greater dissatisfaction with the impact of input constraints on their production. Given that there were no legal outlets for private farmers to obtain fertilizer for market production, it is likely these inputs were obtained through the black market by diversion of government supplies provided to collective farms.

Despite a critical shortage of agricultural chemicals in Cuba, chemical application of herbicides and pesticides was the most popular form of weed and pest control. Thirty-six percent of those vendors surveyed reported relying entirely upon chemical weed and pest control. Twenty-three percent indicated use of both chemicals and some form of biological control, while only 7 percent reported relying upon biological control alone. One-third reported using no weed or pest control, despite accounts of severe crop losses due to pests and diseases. This was a strong indicator of the severe deficits in Cuba's agricultural inputs and labor supply.

Product Transport

All Cuban transportation services were severely affected by Special Period constraints. Severe shortages of fuel and vehicle spare parts, combined with poor road maintenance, had left the Cuban transportation system in a serious state of deterioration. Inadequate transport may partially explain the concentration of sources of market supplies (72 percent) from the nearby City of Havana and Havana provinces. It would appear that the friction of distance exceeded the "pull" of pricing and tax incentives to bring products to Havana markets.[41] Market domination by intermediaries was noted and may be attributable, in part, to transportation constraints; individuals with access to vehicles and fuel had the opportunity to exploit those producers having only limited means by which to transport products to market.

Conclusion

In light of the closure of the earlier MLCs (Mercados Libres Camposinos/free farmers' markets) in 1986, the decision to experiment once again with "free" markets was an ambivalent one, and many questioned the viability and longevity of these new farmers' markets. Over a decade later the markets continue to function regardless of continuing state pressure—including occasional market closures, market raids, blocking farmers' access to markets, and government disaffection for "middlemen" and farmers who have "enriched" themselves.[42] The farmers' markets have survived; the variety of products offered has improved;[43] prices have gone down;[44] and agricultural production appears to have been stimulated.[45] Despite these improvements, market products still remain out of reach of the average Cuban.[46] In an attempt to lower food prices, in 1999 the Cuban government opened a series of small agricultural markets with fixed maximum prices (Mercado de Productos Agrícolas a Precios Topados/fixed price agricultural market) offering products supplied primarily by state farms, UBPCs, and CPAs.[47] By 2001 there were over 2,455 of these *topados*. The generally low and inconsistent quality and lack of variety of goods in these small markets have prevented them from being truly competitive.[48] However, they have served to increase the "food options" available to lower-income families, and the *agromercados* appear to have also placed downward pressure on black market prices.[49] In combination these markets have had a significant positive impact on Cuban food consumption, with per capita caloric intake, rising more than 40 percent since 1994.[50] Today, most Cuban families are able to meet their minimal nutritional requirements by supplementing government rations with food purchased at the farmers' markets, and these markets continue to provide an estimated third of the Cuban diet.

The farmers' markets have been a triumph for the small remaining number of private Cuban farmers who, in the 1995 study, supplied over 80 percent of market offerings. They have earned windfall profits, and by demonstrating superior performance in comparison with their collective counterparts, they have vindicated decades of struggle to maintain their independence. Private producers in Cuba now enjoy the highest incomes in the agricultural sector, earning considerably more than their state farm counterparts.[51] Ironically, because of this economic success, the private farming sector and the markets it supplies remain vulnerable to criticism, resentment, and pressure from the state.[52] Nevertheless, the tenacity exhibited by Cuba's private farmers, combined with the critical role the markets play in feeding the nation's population, should allow their continued survival.

Acknowledgments

This research was made possible by a University of California, Davis, Transportation Center Fellowship. We should also like to thank Ana Eskridge for her services as a research assistant.

Notes

1. Jean Stubbs, "Women and Cuban Smallholder Agriculture in Transition," in Janet Momsen (ed.), *Women and Change in the Caribbean* (London: James Currey, 1993), 219–231.

2. Carmen Diana Deere, "Cuba's National Food Program and Its Prospects for Food Security," *Agriculture and Human Values* X, no. 3 (1993): 35–51.

3. Other economic reforms included attracting foreign direct investment, authorizing the use of the U.S. dollar, legalizing limited self-employment, and promoting tourism.

4. Jonathan Rosenberg, "Cuba's Free Market Experiment: Los Mercados Libres Campesinos, 1980–1986," *Latin American Research Review* 27 (1992): 51–89. See also Jeffery H. Marshall, "The Political Viability of Free Market Experimentation in Cuba: Evidence from *Los Mercados Agropecuarios*," *World Development* 26 (1998): 277–288.

5. Laura J. Enríquez, "Economic Reform and Repeasantization in Post-1990 Cuba," *Latin American Research Review* 38 (2003): 202–218.

6. Susana Lee, "El Sí y el No de los Precios y los Resultados de una Inspección," *Granma*, Saturday, April 1, 1995.

7. Medea Benjamin, Joseph Collins, and Michael Scott, *No Free Lunch: Food and Revolution in Cuba Today* (San Francisco: Food First, 1984).

8. Peter M. Rosset, "A Successful Case Study of Sustainable Agriculture," in Fred Magdoff, John Bellamy, and Frederick H. Buttel (eds.), *Hungry for Profit: The Agribusiness Threat to Farmers Food and the Environment* (New York: Monthly Review Press, 2000), 203–214. In addition, Koont reported that by 1993 the food consumption of an average Cuban citizen was well below FAO-recommended daily minimums. Sinan Koont, "Food Security in Cuba," *Monthly Review*, January 2004, http:/www.findarticles.com/cf_0/m1132/8_55/112411336/print.jhtml (accessed April 27, 2004).

9. Dalia Acosta, "CUBA ECONOMY: Foreign Exchange Bureaus Booming," Interpress Service, October 24, 1995.

10. Víctor Figueroa and Luis A. García, "Apuntes Sobre la Comercialización Agrícola no Estatal," *Economía y Desarrollo* 83 (1984): 34–61.

11. Dirección Provincial de Comercio, "Acerca del Mercado Agropecuario en Ciudad de la Habana. Informe de mercado acumulado hasta Junio del 95," Havana, July 10, 1995.

12. The City of Havana marketing authorities reported that in June 1995 the markets supplied 44.05 pounds per capita to the city's population. After less than a year of operation the markets were estimated to account for between 25 and 30% of the total Cuban consumer food sales.

13. William A. Messina, Jr., "Agricultural Reform in Cuba: Implications for Agricultural Production, Markets and Trade," *Cuba in Transition* (1999): 441.

14. Cuban economist Nova González, cited in Messina, "Agricultural Reform in Cuba," 438.

15. The *state/non-state* dichotomy is commonly used in Cuban agricultural reporting and statistics. The nonstate sector comprises independent farmers, the cooperatives (Credit and Service Cooperatives [CCSs] and the Agricultural Production Cooperatives [CPA]), while the state sector encompasses the large state collective farms.

16. Nancy Forster, "Cuban Agricultural Productivity," in Irving Louis Horowitz (ed.), *Cuban Communism* (New Brunswick and London: Transaction Publishers, 1989), 235–255.

17. Carmen Diana Deere and Mieke Meurs, "Markets, Markets Everywhere? Understanding the Cuban Anomaly," *World Development* 20, no. 6 (1992): 825–839. See also Armando Nova, *Cuba: Modificación o Transformación Agrícola?* (Havana: Instituto Nacional de Investigaciones Económicas, 1994), 62. The only official measures of production volumes are records of produce that passes through the *Acopio* state distribution system (not including production withheld for self-provision, barter, and private sale). Production levels of the nonstate sector are likely far greater than is reflected in national statistics. There is also evidence that nonstate farms outperform the state agricultural production sector. See José Alvarez and William A. Messina, Jr., "Cuba's New Agricultural Cooperatives and Markets: Antecedents, Organization, Early Performance and Prospects," *Cuba in Transition* (1996): 175–195.

18. Nova, *Cuba*, 63.

19. Ricardo Puerta and José Alvarez, "Organization and Performance of Cuban Agriculture at Different Levels of State Intervention" (International Working Paper Series IW93014, Gainesville, FL, Institute of Food and Agricultural Sciences, 1993), 38–41.

20. See J. Oramas, "New Approach to Cuba's Foreign Trade," *Granma International*, September 29, 1993.

21. Oscar Everleny, *Cuba: Apertura del Mercado Agropecuario. Evaluación Preliminar* (Havana: Centro de Estudios de la Economía Cubana, 1995), no. 1.

22. José Alvarez and Ricardo Puerta, "State Intervention in Cuban Agriculture: Impact on Organization and Performance," *World Development* 22 (1994): 1663–1675.

23. See Armando Nova, *Mercado Agropecuario: Problemática Actual* (Habana: Instituto Nacional de Investigaciones Económicas, 1995), 3.

24. See Forster, "Cuban Agricultural Productivity," 239, 251–252. Also see Rodríguez, *Los Cambios en la Agricultura Cubana*, 4.

25. See Carmen Diana Deere, Niurka Pérez, and Ernel Gonzales, "The View from Below: Cuban Agriculture in the 'Special Period in Peacetime,'" *Journal of Peasant Studies* 21, no. 2 (1994): 194–234.

26. Nova, *Mercado Agropecuario*, 3.

27. Agiris Malapanis and Mary-Alice Waters, "Agricultural Markets Raise Expectations That Food Scarcities May Ease in Cuba," *Militant*, January 21, 1995.

28. For a detailed analysis of Cuba's food program see Carmen Diana Deere, "Socialism on One Island? Cuba's National Food Program and Its Prospects for Food Security" (ISS Working Paper No. 124, 1992).

29. Deere, "Socialism on One Island," 1–50; Deere and Meurs, "Markets, Markets, Everywhere," 825–839.

30. Deere, Pérez, and Gonzales, "The View from Below." 194–234.

31. Deere, Pérez, and Gonzales, "The View from Below."

32. Personal communication with farmer during visits to urban gardens in Havana, 1995.

33. See Peter Rosset and Medea Benjamin, *The Greening of the Revolution: Cuba's Experiment with Organic Agriculture* (San Francisco: Global Exchange, 1995).

34. *Consejo de Administración de La Provincia de la Ciudad de la Habana*, interview, 1995.

35. Interview by Rebecca Torres with Cuban economist and agricultural expert Armando Novas, Havana, 1995.

36. Puerta and Alvarez, "Organization and Performance of Cuban Agriculture at Different Levels of State Intervention," 11.

37. José Alvarez, "Rationed Products and Something Else: Food Availability and Distribution in 2000 Cuba," *Cuba in Transition* (2001): 305–322.

38. Susan Archer, *Caribbean Basin Market Development Reports: How Cubans Survive*. USDA Foreign Agricultural Service Global Agricultural Information Network Report #C13006, July 11, 2003.

39. Archer, *Caribbean Basin Market Development Reports*, calculated that a basic market basket for a four-person family cost 563 CP (Cuban peso) (after rations) while the average family wage was only 524 CP.

40. Calculated by dividing a category's total landholdings by hectares planted. A result of 1 represents 100% land-use intensity.

41. The 5% Havana "farmers' market sales tax" is lower than in other regions and serves as an inducement to bring produce to Havana. Other places outside of Havana have taxes reportedly as high as 15% (Philip Peters, *The Farmers Market: Crossroads of Cuba's New Economy* [Arlington: Lexington Institute, 2000], 5). An additional incentive to market produce through Havana markets is the higher prices that generally prevail in those markets.

42. See Marshall, "The Political Viability of Free Market Experimentation in Cuba," 277–288; Peters, *The Farmers Market*.

43. Peters, *The Farmers Market*; Alvarez, "Rationed Products and Something Else," 305–322.

44. Juan Carlos Espinosa, "Markets Redux: The Politics of Farmers' Markets in Cuba." *Cuba in Transition* (1995): 51–73.

45. Marshall, "The Political Viability of Free Market Experimentation in Cuba," 277–288; Messina, "Agricultural Reform in Cuba," 441.

46. Peters, *The Farmers Market*; Alvarez, "Rationed Products and Something Else," 305–322; Archer, *Caribbean Basin Market Development Reports*.

47. Prices are generally fixed at approximately 25–30% lower than the *agromercados* (Peters, *The Farmers Market*, 10).

48. Alvarez, "Rationed Products and Something Else," 305–322; Archer, *Caribbean Basin Market Development Reports*.

49. Nova González, cited in Peters, *The Farmers Market*, 5.

50 Oxfam America, "Cuban Farmers Doing More with Less," *Organic Consumers Association*, July 20, 2001, http://www.organicconsumers.org/Organic/cuba081701.cfm (accessed April 27, 2004).

51. See Carmen Diana Deere, Ernel Gonzales, Niurka Pérez, and Gustavo Rodríguez, "Household Incomes in Cuban Agriculture: A Comparison of State, Cooperative, and Peasant Sectors," *Development and Change* 26, no. 2 (1995): 209–234. In August 2006 Juan Forero reported that there were currently 300 farmer's markets throughout the country selling high-quality produce. Juan Forero, "Cuba Perks Up as Venezuela's Lifeline Foils US Embargo," *New York Times*, August 4, 2006, 1 and 3.

52. Enríquez, "Economic Reform and Repeasantization in Post-1990 Cuba," 202–218. See also Juan Ferero, "Cuba Perks up as Venezuela's Lifeline Foils US Embargo," 3, reporting that by 2006 farmers' markets had turned some farmers into venture capitalists earning net profits of US$3.00 a day (http://www.nytimes.com/2006/08/04/world/americas/04Cuba.html?ex= 1312344000en=7718d0ea3677005d&ei=5088&partner=rssnyt&emc=rss).

Part II

Policy, Planning, and Management

Chapter 5

Land, Development, and Indigenous Rights in Suriname: The Role of International Human Rights Law

Ellen-Rose Kambel

I do not think anybody can say: "this land is mine." Only God can say: "this is mine." What I want to ask the Minister is: "where is the paper of the government that says that [the land] is yours?" His answer is going to be: "first, 'the law is the law' and second, 'without law there is no order' [. . .]" That's what they will say, but I still want to ask this question.

Indigenous villager from Galibi. Personal
communication, March 4, 1999

Introduction

Suriname is the only country in the Americas that has not legally recognized the collective rights of indigenous and tribal peoples to the lands and resources they have occupied and used for centuries. According to Surinamese legislation, the state owns all land and natural resources and only those who can show titles that derive from the state, may claim ownership rights. Since indigenous peoples and maroons[1] do not possess such titles, they may only claim certain "entitlements" that are subject to the general interest.

In 1995, after the Surinamese government agreed to grant 3 million hectares of forest to Asian logging companies, indigenous and maroon leaders convened a Gran Krutu (Great Gathering) where they claimed the right to self-determination and demanded that the state recognize their collective ownership rights to their ancestral territories and natural resources. Their claims were explicitly linked to international human rights instruments protecting the rights of indigenous and tribal peoples. These instruments reflect the increasing recognition among states and intergovernmental organizations, such as the United Nations (UN) and the Organization of American States (OAS), that the root cause of most of the social and economic problems experienced by indigenous and tribal peoples is related to their inability to maintain some form of control over the lands and resources they have occupied and used for generations. Disturbing the intimate connection between indigenous lands and their ways of life, through large-scale mining or logging operations, may amount to a number of human rights violations, including the rights to life, culture, and property.[2]

Despite the often-heard criticism of human rights law as ineffective or Eurocentric,[3] this chapter seeks to show that human rights law can play an immensely important role for historically marginalized groups. By providing a legitimate platform for discussion (*"a site of struggle"*), human rights law has opened up the Surinamese national discourse to allow indigenous perspectives on land, development and cultural identity.[4] These are perspectives that challenge the hegemony of legal centralism (the notion that the state is the sole source of law) as well as the long-standing practice of state-planned, top-down development.[5]

The chapter starts out with an introduction of the national context. This is followed by an overview of the colonial land policy and the introduction of development planning during the 1950s that led to increasing pressure on indigenous and maroon territories. I will then discuss the dominant theory ("the conventional story") that the state owns all land in Suriname, which despite little historical or legal evidence, has gained widespread authority in Suriname. The chapter concludes with the way indigenous peoples and maroons have started to use human rights law.

The National Context

Despite its location on the South American mainland, where it is bordered by French Guiana, Guyana, and Brazil, Suriname, a former Dutch colony, is historically, politically, culturally, and also given its size, closer to and often seen more as belonging to the Caribbean.[6] Colonial politics have resulted in a highly varied ethnic population. Unlike most Caribbean states, however, but similar to Guyana and French Guiana, there is a sharp division between the narrow strip of land that runs along the Atlantic coast (the former plantation area, also known as the coastal area), which includes the capital Paramaribo, and the hinterland, or interior, which is hilly, traversed by large rivers and for 90 percent covered with tropical rainforest.

The coastal area is inhabited by the vast majority of the population (approximately 490,000) and is home to the three largest ethnic groups: the Creoles, who are the descendants of African slaves;[7] the Hindustanis (East Indians), whose forebears were recruited in India to work as contract laborers on the plantations after slavery was abolished in 1863; and the Javanese, who were brought to Suriname from the Indonesian island of Java, also as indentured laborers. To some extent, all ethnic groups have maintained something of their cultural roots, including language, religion, food, and dress. While intermarriage is more common today, ethnic background is still what determines the social network of most urban residents.[8]

The interior is home to four indigenous peoples and six maroon tribes, spread over some 230 communities. According to the 2004 census, the total number of indigenous and maroon persons living in Suriname is 18,037 (or 3.7 percent of the total population) and 72,553 (14.7 percent), respectively.[9] This means that indigenous and tribal peoples now make up almost 20 percent of the population.

Colonial Land Policy (1650–1945)

The Dutch colonial administration did not undertake any efforts to codify indigenous or maroon customary law or set up indigenous or maroon courts of law in Suriname, as they did in the East Indies. This is probably because the Dutch showed little economic interest in the lands that were inhabited by indigenous peoples and maroons. The only area that was considered profitable was the coastal strip where plantations were established and tropical cash crops were produced for export. Here, the Dutch were governed by laws they had brought with them. The slaves and other immigrants were subjected to other, much harsher, laws but that were nevertheless regarded as European law. After the abolition of slavery in 1863 the Dutch gradually left the colony as agriculture was no longer profitable. The coastal area then became dominated by a new elite of light-colored Creoles who largely shared or aspired to share Dutch culture, including Dutch legal codes that were copied and applied virtually verbatim in the settler colony.

At least until the 1950s, the interior was the domain of indigenous peoples and maroons whose status may be described as self-governing autonomous nations or "states within a state." Here, the Dutch legal system had little relevance, and maroons and indigenous peoples governed themselves. The autonomous status of maroons was based on formal peace treaties that were concluded with the colonial administration during the eighteenth and nineteenth century. From that point neither the maroons nor the indigenous peoples were considered to be really part of Surinamese society.[10]

The sharp division between the settled coastal area and the interior gradually began to blur during the mid-nineteenth century, as the maroons became more involved in the economic pursuits of the colony. The decline of the plantation system after the abolition of slavery encouraged the emergence of other types of resource exploitation such as gold, bauxite, and natural rubber, which were located further inland, notably in indigenous and maroon territories. These activities necessitated new legislation, and the majority of the resource laws that are currently in force still rely heavily on these early texts. Importantly, the new laws included savings clauses, provisions that exempted indigenous and maroon lands from the areas allocated for logging or mining. Such provisions were an expression of the Dutch colonial land policy dating back to the seventeenth century that recognized native titles in North America and the West Indies.[11] We still find them in the Surinamese legislation today, albeit watered down with provisions that recognize indigenous and maroon rights only "as far as possible," or "if not against the general interest."[12]

Development Planning (1945–1975)

After World War II, development planning became one of the main ideological forces behind resource regulation and further increased the pressure on indigenous and maroon territories. Ten and Five Year Plans funded by the Dutch focused primarily on large infrastructure projects, which led to the "opening up" of the until then fairly isolated indigenous and maroon territories. Other projects caused the forced relocation of thousands of maroons and posed serious threats for the survival of indigenous communities.

The Brokopondo Project (1960s)

By far the largest development project ever carried out in Suriname was the construction of a hydroelectric dam and an artificial lake in order to generate electricity for an aluminum smelter. The agreement between the U.S. company Alcoa and the Surinamese government provided that Alcoa would finance the dam and the smelter. For their part, the government would organize the relocation of 5,000 Saramaka maroons whose territory was to be flooded. Compensation to the Saramaka was only provided for the houses and fruit trees that they lost due to the flooding, but not for the land. The Head of the Department of Administration and Decentralization, Law Professor A. J. A. Quintus Bosz, felt that this was legally not required as the Saramaka held no title to land.[13]

The West Suriname Project (1970s)

The West Suriname Project also entailed the construction of a hydroelectric dam and bauxite mining which would be centered on a new city (Apura). When bauxite prices dropped and a military regime took over in the 1980s, the West Suriname project was shelved. The plans are currently back on the agenda however, and negotiations are currently underway between the government and two of the largest mining companies in the world. If approved, an area twice the size of the lake that was created in the 1950s will be flooded.[14]

Although the West Suriname plan was never fully executed, the agricultural plots of the local indigenous communities were bulldozed to make way for the new city. After protests, the communities were offered a compensation of 500 guilders, which they turned down. Instead, they demanded a legal title to an indigenous territory. The position of the government, voiced by the Advisory Commission on Entitlements to Lands in the Interior, which was chaired, again, by Professor Quintus Bosz, was that the West Suriname project had already been approved and that the Amerindians had no rights, only entitlements to the land.[15]

The Conventional Story

Professor Quintus Bosz maintained that the state had always "privately" owned the land in Suriname and only those who could show titles that were once issued to them by the state could claim any rights to land ("the domain principle"). As indigenous peoples and maroons did not possess these titles, they could not claim to have any rights, only "entitlements." With regard to these entitlements, Quintus Bosz held that the state only needed to take account of them as long as they were compatible with the "national interest." Over time, Quintus Bosz's views have assumed authoritative status, and to date his writings are mandatory texts in law schools.

Legal and historical analysis shows however that the state never acquired property rights over lands that were historically occupied and used by indigenous peoples.[16] These rights were recognized since the first European settlement and were included in the savings clauses discussed above. In fact, the domain principle was not formally introduced in the legislation until 1982 and this was probably directly related to the position of Quintus Bosz himself. As a Dutch law professor in a colonial setting, his opinions were beyond questioning and his publications were the primary source of knowledge about Surinamese land legislation. Similarly, the idea that the state owns all natural resources, which is currently enshrined in the Constitution, was introduced during the military regime in 1986–1987 and has never been the subject of national discussion, not by the National Assembly that was inoperative at the time, and much less by indigenous peoples and maroons who were then caught up in an interior war.[17]

Nevertheless, the notion that the state owns all land and all natural resources in Suriname is widely shared in Paramaribo, among legal practitioners and the public in general. I suggest that this is related to three factors: the ideology of legal centralism, the economic interests of the urban elite, and the national development ideology.

The Ideology of Legal Centralism

The idea that there is and there should only be one legal order in Suriname goes back to the policy adopted by the Dutch colonial government at the end of the nineteenth century to refrain from recognizing customary laws of the "Natives," which, as indicated above, were different from Dutch practice in the East Indies. Instead, the colonial government in Suriname maintained what have been termed "foreign relations" with maroon and indigenous traditional leaders, recognizing the latter's authority to govern over a territory that was more or less considered their own. It was precisely when the government ceased to respect the authority of the traditional leaders and started issuing land and resource titles to third parties without their consent, that the land rights issue *became* an issue.

Economic Interests of the Urban Elite

The reluctance on the part of the urban population to grant indigenous peoples and maroons greater control over natural resources can be explained in part by the economic interests of urban elites. As discussed above, the area south of the plantation zone was long considered irrelevant to the Dutch.

Only when gold, bauxite, and natural rubber were discovered at the end of the nineteenth century and foreign companies were attracted to exploit these resources did the Dutch develop an interest for the interior. After gaining autonomy from the Dutch in 1954 and attaining full independence in 1975, the Surinamese state was governed by members of the Creole, Hindustani, and Javanese Surinamese middle class, who, through patronage networks, were able to control Suriname's natural resources.[18]

Economic interests go a long way toward explaining why the conventional story is so readily accepted by urban elites. The resistance to allowing indigenous peoples and maroons to exert greater control over the natural resources within their territories is not limited to the urban elite but is also widely shared in the coastal area, cutting across class and ethnic differences. In my view, the national development ideology in which the state is seen as the primary driving force of "development" and where natural resources are perceived as the means to achieve progress and modernity provides an important explanation of why urban Surinamers, regardless of ethnic background or economic class, are so willing to accept the conventional story. Racist attitudes toward indigenous peoples and maroons, who are perceived as backward and underdeveloped, only reinforce this ideology.

Ethnicity and the National Development Ideology

Historian Peter Meel mentions two myths that, in his view, contain notions of "genuine nationalism" in Suriname.[19] The first is the myth of the unfulfilled promise or the inverted El Dorado myth. With all of Suriname's natural endowments, or so the myth goes—the rich and fertile coastland, the lush forests of the interior where timber and gold reserves are simply waiting to be discovered—it will be just a matter of time before Suriname achieves true prosperity. The second myth is what Meel calls the "*mamio* (patch work quilt) myth," the idea that Suriname consists of a unique variety of ethnic groups where "unity in diversity" produces peace and harmony.[20]

What is problematic about the *mamio* myth is that claims based on ethnicity run the risk of becoming labeled "antinationalist." Land rights claims by indigenous peoples and maroons, which are *explicitly* based on the right to maintain their ethnic identity and which are aimed at achieving greater control over the country's natural wealth, are thus easily considered to be a threat to the perceived ethnic harmony and national unity. In reality, of course, the allocation of resource rights has always been linked to ethnicity in Suriname.

During the colonial period, the Dutch instituted a policy that allowed only Creoles to work on the gold, timber, and rubber fields, while Javanese and Hindustanis were given plots of land in the coastal region to encourage them to become farmers.[21] After 1954, and particularly after 1975, land and resource rights became an important instrument in the patron-client networks of the coastal residents.[22] It is now generally accepted in Suriname that you must have "connections" to obtain a land title. And since the patronage networks operate largely along ethnic lines, land and resource rights are also allocated on the basis of ethnicity. Yet, to recognize land rights of indigenous peoples and maroons because of their cultural attachment to the land is seen as disturbing the ethnic balance and even seen as a threat to national integrity.[23] This can be explained if we take account of the way indigenous peoples and maroons have been and, to a large extent, still are perceived by urban residents as a kind of remnants of the stone age who need to be "developed" or brought into the modern era and who are incapable of managing, let alone controlling the country's natural riches. For example, a government official working for the Forestry Service stated,

> [I]t depends on what the government chooses as [a] development model. I think it will cause a delay if they opt for a bottom-up model. We can't do that now. Suriname needs rapid development. And only when we have achieved a certain level, then we can give [natural resources] to [indigenous peoples and maroons]. In Suriname the majority of the resources are unused. There are huge forests. It is inconceivable that those forests would be intended only for some 50,000 people. They would not be able to exploit them.

This is a variation on the same theme that I have heard time and again in conversations with "ordinary" citizens in Paramaribo: "Amerindians don't do anything with the forest, so why should we give them land rights?" The fact that these views are embedded in "the law" provides the ultimate justification for maintaining and even openly expressing such views.[24]

"Indigenous and Tribal Peoples Have Human Rights Too": Resisting the Conventional Story

The increasing pressure on indigenous and maroon territories during the 1990s led to greater mobilization of indigenous peoples and maroons who explicitly started to invoke international human rights law to demand legal recognition of their rights to land and resources. An important turning point was the organization of the Gran Krutu in 1995. This was the first gathering of nearly all maroon and indigenous leaders in Suriname, organized by themselves and without the presence of the government. The leaders complained about the lack of respect on the part of the government, testified among others by the complete absence of any reference to indigenous peoples and maroons in the Surinamese constitution or other Surinamese laws. At the end of the meeting, the Charter of the Indigenous Peoples and Maroons in Suriname was adopted. The Charter was formulated as a response to the threat of our collective rights: "the right to be recognized as distinctive indigenous and tribal peoples, the right to self-determination, self-government, and self-development, our right to undisturbed enjoyment of our culture and traditions, our right to live in our territories and use and exploit the natural resources on and in them, our right to participate in decisions regarding our territories, our right to maintain a healthy environment that offers guarantees for a continuation of our traditional lifestyles in our free will, our right to our intellectual possessions, knowledge and experiences" (article 1).

The Charter underlined the importance of the natural environment to indigenous peoples and maroons and considered the large-scale exploitation of natural resources "a restriction of our right to life, as a crime against our peoples and against humanity." The text of the Charter rests heavily on international human rights language and directly relates the rights of indigenous peoples and maroons to international standards by referring to UN and OAS instruments and resolutions adopted by indigenous and tribal groups elsewhere in the world.

A year later, one of the leaders stated that the claim for self-determination was not to establish separate states but to create better living conditions for indigenous peoples and maroons and since the distinctive culture of indigenous peoples and maroons was connected to the land, he argued that their land rights had to be recognized.[25] Another participant pointed out that important changes had occurred in the interior, in particular that the indigenous peoples and maroons had become aware of the fact that "the world has shown that indigenous and tribal peoples have human rights too."[26]

The snowballing effect of the global indigenous rights movement has proved difficult to bring to a standstill. With the support of human rights and environmental organizations, maps of indigenous and maroon territories have been produced, based on the international standard that indigenous and tribal peoples have rights to the lands and resources they *traditionally occupy and use*, indicating their hunting and fishing areas as well as spiritual sites. Also, community-based training programs and research projects have raised awareness of the rights indigenous peoples and maroons enjoy internationally.

International Human Rights Procedures

In addition to these local and national efforts, indigenous and maroon organizations have also started to voice their concerns at the global level. In 2003, a detailed report about the human rights situation of indigenous peoples and maroons in Suriname was submitted to the UN Committee on the Elimination of Racial Discrimination (CERD), which subsequently issued various decisions and recommendations.[27] In 2005, CERD expressed its deep concern about information alleging that Suriname is actively disregarding the CERD's recommendations by authorizing additional resource exploitation and associated infrastructure projects that pose "substantial threats of irreparable harm to indigenous and tribal peoples, without any formal notification to the affected communities and without seeking their prior agreement or informed consent" and urged Suriname to

> [e]nsure legal acknowledgement of the rights of indigenous and tribal peoples to possess, develop, control and use their communal lands and to participate in the exploitation, management and conservation of the associated natural resources.[28]

Further, in 1997 and 2000, two cases were filed by maroons against the Surinamese government with the Inter-American Commission on Human Rights. One case was submitted by Saramaka maroon leaders who argued violation of their human rights because of Suriname's refusal to recognize their land rights and issuing logging concessions to Asian companies without their consent.[29] This case was recently submitted to the Inter-American Court of Human Rights for a binding judgment. The other case was filed by the survivors of a massacre committed by the National Army, killing 43 maroons at the community of Moiwana. Although land rights were not the main focus of the latter case, the Inter-American Court found that Suriname had violated the right to property of the maroon community who had fled to neighboring French Guiana where the majority remains today. By not recognizing the maroons as the "legitimate owners of their traditional lands" and depriving them of the right to the use and enjoyment of those lands, the Inter-American Court found Suriname in violation of the American Convention on Human Rights and ordered the state to "adopt such legislative, administrative, and other measures as are necessary to ensure the property rights of the members of the Moiwana community in relation to the traditional territories from which they were expelled and provide for their use and enjoyment of those territories. These measures shall include the creation of an effective mechanism for the delimitation, demarcation and titling of said traditional territories."[30] Importantly, the court confirmed in its jurisprudence that indigenous and tribal peoples' rights to their lands do not derive from grants or recognition by the state but arise from their own customary laws, traditions, and forms of land tenure.[31]

Conclusion

While Suriname has ignored the recommendations of CERD, this was impossible with the decision of the Inter-American Court in the Moiwana case, which has binding legal effect. The government has assured that it will fully comply with the court decision and has established various committees to implement the decision.[32] Among others, a Presidential Committee on Land Rights was installed, which is mandated to address the land rights issue of the Interior. In the case of the Saramaka maroons, the Minister of Justice announced that the government would comply with all of the Commission's recommendations, among others, to remove all legal obstacles to recognize the collective land rights of the Saramaka people.[33]

Public opinion among urban residents and legal practitioners also seems to be undergoing a subtle shift as the discussion over indigenous and maroon land rights is gaining momentum. In an unprecedented move, at a meeting of the Surinamese Jurists Association, a prominent Surinamese jurist publicly denounced the theories of Quintus Bosz as unfounded,[34] while over the past six months, the editor of a leading newspaper has called on the government no less than three times to bring Surinamese legislation in line with international human rights treaties relating to indigenous rights.[35]

For indigenous peoples and maroons, these promises and statements are still far from what is needed to achieve their desired result. Yet, human rights language and procedures provided them with an instrument that allowed their voices to be heard in the national debate on land rights and enabled them to oppose the views that have dominated the debate over the past 50 years. The West Suriname project, which has resurfaced recently and which threatens the livelihood of a number of indigenous communities, will be an important test case of the power of human rights to protect the rights of all Surinamese citizens.

Notes

1. Maroons are the descendants of African slaves who fled from slavery in the eighteenth and nineteenth centuries and established semiautonomous communities in the Interior of Suriname.
2. See *Report of the Special Rapporteur on the Situation of Human Rights and Fundamental Freedoms of Indigenous People*, Mr. Rodolfo Stavenhagen, Submitted Pursuant to Commission Resolution 2001/57, UN Doc E/CN.4/2002/97 and generally, Fergus MacKay, " 'Indigenous Peoples' Rights and Resource Exploitation," *Philippine Natural Resources Law Journal* 12, no. 1 (2004): 43–71.
3. See, e.g., Lynda Bell, Andrew Nathan, and Ilan Peleg (eds.), *Negotiating Culture and Human Rights* (New York: Colombia University Press, 2001).
4. Carol Smart, *Feminism and the Power of Law* (London and New York: Routledge, 1989). On the importance of rights discourse for racially marginalized groups, see Kimberlé Crenshaw et al. (eds.), *Critical Race Theory. The Key Writings That Informed the Movement* (New York: New Press, 1995).
5. This is a process that is occurring all over Latin America: A. Brysk, *From Tribal Village to Global Village. Indian Rights and International Relations in Latin America* (Stanford: Stanford University Press, 2000).
6. Peter Meel, "Not a Splendid Isolation. Suriname's Foreign Affairs," in R. Hoefte and P. Meel (eds.), *20th Century Suriname. Continuities and Discontinuities in a New World Society* (Kingston/Leiden: Ian Randle Publishers/KITLV Press, 2001), 148.
7. Although they share the same African ancestors, Creoles should not be mistaken for maroons who inhabit the interior.
8. Ad de Bruijne, "A City and a Nation: Demographic Trends and Socioeconomic Development in Urbanising Suriname," in Hoefte and Meel (eds.), *20th Century Suriname*, 38.
9. This includes people living in Paramaribo. There is no accurate data on indigenous and maroon people living in their tribal areas. Ellen-Rose Kambel, *Indigenous Peoples and Maroons in Suriname* (Washington, DC: Inter-American Development Bank, August 2006), 10–11.
10. Ellen-Rose Kambel, "Resource Conflicts, Gender and Indigenous Rights in Suriname. Local, National and Global Perspectives" (PhD thesis, University of Leiden, 2002), 30–32.
11. The 1629 Government Order (Ordre van Regieringe), a set of principles to guide Dutch colonial activities, which was valid in Suriname until 1869, explicitly stated that the property rights of the Spanish, Portuguese, and the

"Naturals" (indigenous peoples) shall be respected. Ellen-Rose Kambel and Fergus MacKay, *The Rights of Indigenous Peoples and Maroons in Suriname* (Copenhagen: IWGIA, 1999), 32.

12. Kambel and MacKay, *The Rights of Indigenous Peoples and Maroons in Suriname*, Annex, 202–205.

13. A. J. A. Quintus Bosz, "De Rechten van de Bosnegers op de Ontruimde Gronden in het Stuwmeergebied," in *Grepen uit de Surinaamse Rechtshistorie* (Paramaribo: Vaco Press [1965] 1993).

14. Robert Goodland, *Suriname Environmental and Social Reconnaissance. TheBakhuys Bauxite Mine Project*, VIDS/North South Institute, 2006, http://www.nsi-ins.ca/english/pdf/Robert_Goodland_Suriname_ESA_Report. pdf (accessed July 13, 2006).

15. Joop Vernooij, *Aktie Grondrechten Binnenland* (Paramaribo, 1988), 13.

16. Three legal sources were studied to determine the status of indigenous and maroon rights to land in Suriname: (1) international legal principles that were developed during the era of discovery; (2) English colonial constitutional law that was used to establish the legal basis of the claims made by the first European state (England) that succeeded in establishing a permanent settlement in Suriname; and (3) Dutch law and legal principles that applied during the early presence of the Dutch in Suriname. Kambel and MacKay, *The Rights of Indigenous Peoples and Maroons in Suriname*.

17. Kambel and MacKay, *The Rights of Indigenous Peoples and Maroons in Suriname*, 147.

18. Inter-American Development Bank (IDB), *Sector Study: Governance in Suriname* (Washington, DC: IDB, 2001), 4. See also H. Ramsoedh, "Playing Politics, Ethnicity, Clientelism and the Struggle for Power," in Hoefte and Meel (eds.), *20th Century Suriname*, 96.

19. P. Meel, "Towards a Typology of Suriname Nationalism," *New West Indian Guide* 72, nos. 3–4 (1998): 270.

20. Meel, "Towards a Typology of Suriname Nationalism."

21. W. Heilbron, "Staatsvorming en politieke cultuur in Suriname na de Tweede Wereldoorlog," *SWI Forum* 5, no. 2 (1988): 64.

22. J. Buddingh', *Geschiedenis van Suriname* (Zeist: Het Spectrum, 1995), 316.

23. See, e.g., the reaction of a minister after the Gran Krutu of 1995: "[P]owers have been active [in Asindon-opo] which have tried to stir up an atmosphere of incitement and resistance to the city. These powers must be suppressed quickly and forcibly because they constitute a threat to the national integrity." *Weekkrant Suriname*, August 31–September 6, 1995, "Establishment Highest Authority Interior A Fact."

24. See further Kambel, "Resource Conflicts, Gender and Indigenous Rights in Suriname," 121–126.

25. PARS/VIDS, *Report of the Gran Krutu at Galibi 20–22 November 1996* (Paramaribo, 1997), 13.

26. PARS/VIDS, *Report of the Gran Krutu at Galibi 20–22 November 1996*, 12.

27. See http://www.forestpeoples.org/documents/s_c_america/bases/suriname. shtml.

28. CERD (UN Committee on the Elimination of Racial Discrimination), *Prevention of Racial Discrimination, Including Early Warning Measures and Urgent Action Procedures Decision 1 (67) Suriname*, CERD/C/Dec/Sur/2, August 18, 2005, paras 3 and 4.

29. For a further discussion of the Saramaka case, see Fergus MacKay, "Indigenous and Tribal Peoples in Suriname: A Human Rights Perspective," in M. Forte (ed.), *Indigenous Resurgence in the Contemporary Caribbean. Amerindian Survival and Revival* (New York: Peter Lang, 2006), 155–173.

30. Judgment of the Inter-American Court of Human Rights in the Case of Moiwana Village v. Suriname Issued June 15, 2005, para 209.

31. Judgment of the Inter-American Court of Human Rights, para 131.

32. *De Ware Tijd*, November 29, 2005, "Suriname Bows for Moiwana Judgment Inter-American Court. Implementation within a Year."

33. *De Ware Tijd*, May 5, 2006, "Government Recognizes Land Rights Saramaka Tribe."

34. *Dagblad Suriname*, November 14, 2005, "Collective Ownership Rights Indigenous and Maroons."

35. *De Ware Tijd*, editorials, January 27, 2006 ("Rights of Indigenous People and Maroons"); March 24, 2006 ("Rights of Indigenous People and Maroons"); June 1, 2006 ("Free Domain and Land Rights").

Chapter 6

The Management of State Lands in Trinidad and Tobago

J. David Stanfield and A. A. Wijetunga

Introduction

Pressures for the conversion of state-owned land into private ownership have been sweeping the world in the past three decades. This conversion makes the private ownership of land compatible with the notions of market economies, where land markets should function to allocate land to various landholders, and not the administrative decisions of state agencies. In many countries of the Caribbean and around the world, however, the state remains an owner of significant areas of land. How the state manages that state-owned land is the subject of much discussion and debate, not only concerning the tenure forms for the allocation of state land to private use without transferring ownership but also concerning how effectively the state directly manages the land.[1]

This chapter describes and analyzes how state land has been managed in Trinidad and Tobago, based on studies[2] of a sample of state agencies.[3] These agencies perform management functions, such as identification of land through parcel surveys, determining the value of the land and evaluating its capability, conserving land for posterity, distributing land and determining tenure forms, and collecting rents. Two questions guided the data gathering: (1) Why have so many state land management agencies emerged in a small country in which a single entity was originally empowered to manage state-owned land? (2) How well are these various agencies of the state managing state-owned land?

State lands other than the officially identified forest area cover 52 percent of Trinidad and Tobago. The state is responsible for the management of this large land area, preservation where needed of lands for posterity, and promotion of development of land for various purposes, balancing the competing demands of the various sectors, be they agriculture, industry, commercial, housing, recreation, wildlife conservation, or tourism. In order to discharge these responsibilities, the state is expected to erect an institutional structure by virtue of which land resources are located, evaluated, conserved, and distributed for short-term economic growth balanced against the long-term health of the land and of the people. There is a recurring policy debate about land management, when policy objectives that focus on land as an economic resource collide with policy objectives based on land as a form of social empowerment and with policies for the sustainable use of natural resources.[4] What is clearly seen is that Trinidad and Tobago has so far failed to establish an adequate institutional structure for the management of a significant amount of state land.

Some Historical Notes on State
Land Management

The Crown Lands Ordinance of 1918, when Trinidad and Tobago was a British Crown Colony, provided that the administration and disposal of Crown Lands should be exclusively vested in and exercised by the Governor, who appointed a public officer named the "Sub-intendant" of Crown Lands whose duties were defined as the management of all lands of the Crown, prevention of squatting and encroachment, prevention of destruction of forest land, development of settlements, and allotment of Crown Lands including laying out of village lots.

In 1938, the post of Director of Surveys was created, responsible for the survey of all lands of the Crown. The Director of Surveys and the Sub-intendant worked very closely in the survey and management of the lands belonging to the Crown. Throughout subsequent decades the functions exercised by the Sub-intendant became so interwoven with those of the Director of Surveys that the two positions were filled by one person.

The apparent effectiveness of state land management at that time under that system was at least partly due to the ability of the Sub-intendant to delegate authority to local wardens for ensuring that land was properly managed. In 1959 during the reorganization of the Public Service, a decision was taken to separate the Lands function from the Survey function. The post of Commissioner of State Lands (CoSL) was created and classified but never filled and apart from a few structural changes within the Division, the old model continued to operate.

Following independence in 1962 the State Lands Act of 1980 (Chapter 57:01) replaced the Sub-intendant with a position of Commissioner of State Lands. However, the position of Commissioner of State Lands was never filled, and the Director of Surveys looked after the duties and functions of the Commissioner. It was filled only in 2005, as distinct from the Director of Surveys. Similar to the 1918 Act, under the State Lands Act, the Commissioner of State Lands has the responsibility for the management of all lands of the state, and all of the powers that were vested in the Sub-intendant under the earlier legislation. The Commissioner also has power to grant permits to use certain roads on state lands; to sign deeds and instruments as regards mining and licenses and other leases, surrenders, and grants of land; and to exercise rights over the foreshore or lands under territorial waters or for reclaiming lands from the sea. Most importantly, however, the Act provides a system for dealing with squatting and encroachment. The issues of squatting and encroachment upon state lands are given paramount importance under the State Lands Act, and the Commissioner exercises wide powers. The Commissioner institutes prosecutions for encroachment on state lands through the Director of Public Prosecutions at the Magistrates' Courts and ensures that the state's land reserves are preserved.

While the statutory responsibility for the management of all state lands was originally assigned to the Commissioner of State Lands, state land management functions are now scattered among several agencies with the creation of numerous other entities with special mandates for state land management for different constituencies. Some of these entities have been vested with the authority to manage state lands in place of the Commissioner, such as the Chaguaramas Development Authority. Other entities have been assigned some of the state land management functions of the Commissioner but not all of them, such as the Land Administration Division of the Ministry of Agriculture, which identifies the lessees but relies on the Commissioner to prepare and execute the leases and to take legal action when a lessee is in breach of the terms of the lease. Others have been created as corporate bodies with authority to manage state land, such as the National Housing Authority, while some others have been established as private stock companies where the state owns all or most of the stock, such as Caroni.

Perhaps this creation of other state land management forms was inevitable following independence as Trinidad and Tobago evolved into a more democratic state and developed a more diversified economy. Before World War II, the management of Crown Lands was relatively simple, with a small and relatively unified landholding class in tune with a colonial administration. After the war, and particularly after independence, the demands of the community at large for land increased in great measure, with the institutional arrangements not able to cater to such demand.

One factor has remained constant, however. Since 1941, the government policy has been to use long-term leases for the distribution of state-owned lands to private users, a policy deriving from the Land Grant Regulation of 1941. This regulation effectively precluded the granting of freehold interest in state land to holders and continues to be in effect to this day,[5] although the terms of leases can be for long periods (25 or 30 years renewable for another 25 or 30 years, with some extending to 199 years) and are negotiable thereby mimicking to a certain extent the legal security attached to freehold tenure. Another potential chink in the 1941 policy against conversion of state-owned land to private freehold ownership is the Land Adjudication Act of 2000 (and a bill for its amendment, 2005), as yet not in force, which grants an Adjudication Officer the authority to declare absolute titles to landholders who have openly and peacefully possessed state land for at least 30 years.

Policy Framework for State Land Management

State land management policy is based on a philosophy that must maximize this limited resource for development and the achievement of realistic social goals, while at the same time having due regard to environmental concerns. In recognition of existing land and resource tenure problems, the government in 1992 established a new land policy, with its goal to "maximize the benefits which the community derives from national land resources, while seeking a balance between current gains and sustainable development."[6] The policy also proposes goals of preventing prime agricultural land from being subjected to nonagricultural uses through the institution of land zoning; providing adequate security of tenure for tenants of state lands; discouraging land speculation and putting idle land into production; and promoting development that is economically, socially, and ecologically sustainable.

Pre-2001 Studies of State Land Management

Over the period 1985–2000, several studies have been done with respect to land management in general and the management of state lands in particular. In the early 1990s, a study culminated in the Land Rationalization and Development Program (LRDP) proposals.[7] A study of the Lands and Surveys Division management of state land[8] recommended major management improvements, with some limited implementation. In the late 1990s a study of the legal authority for state land management culminated in the preparation of a Cabinet note proposing the amalgamation of the Commissioner of State Lands, Valuation Division, and Property and Real Estate Services Division.

The studies produced a voluminous set of documents pertaining to the issues surrounding land policy and land management, including squatting and a comprehensive set of recommendations for reform of land management in Trinidad and Tobago. The analyses revealed a series of land management and tenure problems that constrained sustainable development of the country as well as the protection of areas not appropriate for agricultural or urban uses.

The indicators of weaknesses in state land management identified in these studies are numerous. The Commissioner had failed to collect land rents, resulting in a total arrears of about TT$15 million (US$2.5 million) for land leases managed by the Commissioner of State Lands and at least TT$8.4 million of quarry leases managed at least partially through the Commissioner of State Lands. The land parcels allocated to individuals were underutilized, and about one-third of state-owned agricultural parcels that have at some point been farmed by farm families today are entirely abandoned. The studies show that the bulk of the agricultural parcels are undocumented and carry insecure tenures, with only 11 percent of all state-owned agricultural parcels actually being farmed under a valid Standard Agricultural Lease. There is also the prevalence of extensive and uncontrolled squatting, with over 25,000 parcels of state land used for housing by squatters, and over 8,600 families are squatting on over 26,000 hectares of state-owned agricultural land. Degradation of the environment is evident with people building houses in environmentally sensitive areas and without provision for infrastructure investments. The studies also reveal that the Commissioner of State Lands does not adequately supervise quarry and mining leases. Finally, it appears that agricultural land is often exploited for short-term gain in unsustainable ways.

Case Studies of State Land Management Entities

In 2000, a series of studies were conducted of 11 state land management entities, which exercised some or all of the functions outlined above in reference to state-owned land. Out of these 11 agencies, more in-depth data gathering was done to document the financial situations (revenues and costs) and management constraints of seven agencies for which such information was available.

As noted above, over the years, the powers, duties, and functions of the Commissioner of State Lands have been taken away through numerous pieces of legislation. The Commissioner at present is left with the management of approximately 30,000 leases, the cancellation of expired leases, the issuance of new leases for isolated or abandoned pieces of state land found among already leased-out land, the acquisition of private land for public purposes, and certain land regulatory functions.[9]

Land Administration Division, Ministry of Agriculture, Land and Marine Resources

The statutory responsibility for the management of state agricultural lands not assigned to other entities is resident in the Commissioner of State Lands. However, the Land Administration Division (LAD) of the Ministry of Agriculture, Land and Marine Resources (MALMR) was created as a Division within the Ministry in 1994 by Cabinet Minute, and the estate management functions for those lands designated as "agricultural" have since rested with the Ministry.[10] An important exception is that the execution of lease agreements and dealing with squatters remains with the Commissioner of State Lands. The MALMR develops agricultural parcels for distribution, selects tenants and facilitates the leasing of these parcels to those selected.

There are approximately 17,000 parcels of state-owned agricultural land held presently or previously by farmers. Of these, only 11.5 percent are actually being farmed under a valid Standard Agricultural Lease (SAL). Nearly 6,000 parcels of state-owned agricultural lands, which have at some point been farmed by farm families, are today entirely abandoned. Only 50 percent of the people in possession of the land are listed in the Land Administration Division files as some type of documented tenant, while another 20 percent are "agents of the original tenants." Nearly 15 percent of the people in possession of state-owned agricultural land are squatters, without any documented right to the land. About 50 percent of these 17,000 parcels are less than 1 hectare in size, a group averaging only 0.5 hectares, and 45 percent of the parcels are between 1 and 5 hectares in size, averaging only 2.2 hectares.

National Housing Authority

The National Housing Authority's (NHA) traditional role has been the construction and allocation either by rental or mortgage of dwelling units with particular focus on the lower-income groups of society. It manages approximately 14,600 hectares of land for housing and approximately 24,000 rental and mortgage clients.[11] The chairman of the National Housing Authority has the power to sign all leases, mortgages, and licenses.

The agency's performance has been compromised by a perception that it is a social landlord. Many of its properties are in disrepair and the high cost of maintenance has prompted a policy switch to disposal by sale. Rents are artificially low. Counter to popular opinion, however, the rate of default on rental and mortgage payments at least in recent years is not high, according to reported statistics, particularly for rents. Just over 100 housing unit allocations occur annually, a mere fraction of the estimated demand for housing units. Even so, many of these are reallocations of existing units. Much of the land managed by the Authority has not been vested in it, which is a major problem for any divestment.

Sugar Industry Labor Welfare Committee

Established in 1952 as a statutory board under the Ministry of Housing and Settlements, the Sugar Industry Labor Welfare Committee (SILWC) is charged with the granting and monitoring of low-interest housing loans and the development of new settlements, in both cases for sugar workers and cane farmers. In these settlements, the SILWC has developed housing leases for the management of just 28 hectares of land.[12]

Caroni (1975) Limited (MALMR)

Caroni has been a private limited liability company with the government of Trinidad and Tobago holding all the issued share capital. At the time of the study, the company was run by a board of directors, which consisted of representatives from the trade unions, the cane farmers, and the private and public sectors. The company owned and controlled some 31,567 hectares of land, making it the largest single landholder in Trinidad and Tobago.[13] Caroni managed 4,800 hectares through leases to cane farmers and 1,824 hectares in other long-term leases—the rest was directly managed. Caroni also had 1,942 hectares occupied by agricultural and residential squatters, and another 909 acres of land leased to 4,700 household tenants.

Palo Seco Agricultural Enterprises Ltd.

The government of Trinidad and Tobago formed PETROTRIN, the national petroleum entity from the merger of TRINTOC and TRINTOPEC in 1993. Certain nonpetroleum-related assets of TRINTOC and TRINTOPEC (referred to as Residual Assets), including a significant quantity of land and property—approximately 10,118 hectares of land and approximately 2,500 units of housing—were vested in Palo Seco Agricultural Enterprises Ltd. (PSAEL) and used in traditional agricultural business, in new areas of agribusiness, and in real estate management. PSAEL manages about 6,880 hectares through residential and agricultural tenancies and manages the remaining 3,238 hectares directly.[14]

Chaguaramas Development Authority

The mandate of the Chaguaramas Development Authority (CDA) is to manage through leases to private individuals and companies the development of the Northwest Peninsula of Trinidad and Tobago. The goal is to maximize the returns from the 4,850 hectares of land under its control, comprising the entire Northwest Peninsula of Trinidad.[15] Forests and scrub vegetation make up more than 90 percent of the area. At present the CDA manages 104 commercial leases and only one agricultural land lease to the MALMR's Chaguaramas Agricultural Development Project.

The Property and Industrial Development Company of Trinidad and Tobago

The Property and Industrial Development Company of Trinidad and Tobago (PIDCOTT) was incorporated on January 1997 as a private company to manage 19 industrial estates located throughout the country, of which 18 are fully developed. The estates have a total land area of 340 hectares and over 500 tenants. Its primary function is to provide industrial accommodation for a wide range of industrial activities. In addition, it provides accommodation for office complex, shopping malls, resort properties, and beach facilities. Its range of property management services includes physical planning and development, estate agency and estate management, asset valuation, project management, auction sale, arbitration, collection of rents, and administration of costs.[16]

Comparison of Performances by State Land Management Agencies

The seven agencies selected for analysis are managing a total of 140,062 hectares[17] of state land as shown in table 6.1.

In both the quantity of land under tenancy arrangements and the number of tenancies, the Commissioner of State Lands is a larger manager of land than

Table 6.1   Hectares Managed by State Agencies

Agency	Hectares managed
CoSL-LAD	68,436
Caroni	31,567
NHA	14,600
PSAEL	10,118
CDA	4,856
PIDCOTT	371
SILWC	28
Subtotal	129,976
CoSL as agent for various agencies	10,086
Total	140,062

Source: Land Use and Administration Project (LUPAP), Ministry of Agriculture, Lands and Marine Resources of Trinidad and Tobago. (Mt. Horeb, WI: Terra Institute Ltd., 2000).

selected other agencies/companies. The Commissioner of State Lands is involved in the management of an estimated 30,000 tenancies (the exact number is unknown) on about 68,000 hectares of agricultural land in cooperation with the Land Administration Division and another approximately 10,086 hectares in a variety of other leases (housing, commercial, quarries, etc.).

Table 6.2 shows some statistics about the number of clients, costs of management, total revenues, and total amount of arrears (in lease payments).The cost estimates in table 6.2 are approximate. However, a comparison of the approximate cost of managing land on a per client basis (land management budget divided by number of clients) indicates the CoSL-LAD management costs are between those of Caroni and PETROTRIN. PIDCOTT's and NHA's costs are higher, but so are their revenues, and their estates are qualitatively different from those of the other agencies/companies under examination. This comparison suggests that the land management budget of the CoSL-LAD team is probably sufficient to fulfill its mandate, given that a comparable agency, Caroni (1975) Ltd., at the time of the study was spending slightly less per client and actually less per hectare to manage its leases.

Operational Efficiency and Effectiveness

What is of greater concern, however, is that for this expenditure, the efficiency of operation of the Commissioner of State Lands in association with the Land Administration Division does not compare favorably with the other agencies. On the basis of cost recovery, CoSL-LAD collects about 55 percent of its operating budget in lease revenue, while all the other agencies collect more than 100 percent. Although this indicator is contingent on the quality of lands in the agency's portfolio, recovering less than 100 percent means that the state is not recovering its own costs of managing its lands. This may make sense for protected

Table 6.2 Comparative Statistics of State Land Management

	Area managed (hectares)	Number of clients	Land management budget (TT$)	Land management budget/hectare (TT$)	Land management budget/client (TT$)	Total revenue from land management (TT$)	Annual amount in arrears (TT$)	Revenue as % of management budget
CoSL-LAD	78,572	30,000[a]	4,583,000	58	153	2,514,000	3,400,000	55
CDA	4,856	105	294,000	61	2,800	700,000	0	238
PIDCOTT	371	475	2,000,000	5,395	4,210	33,000,000	0	1,650
Caroni	31,566	10,200	1,300,000	41	127	2,500,000	N/A[d]	192
PSAEL	10,117	3,500	1,000,000	98	285	N/A	N/A	N/A
SILWC	28	300	200,000	7,059	666	400,000	100,000	200
NHA[b]	14,600	24,000	38,000,000	1,676	1,583	55,390,000	9%; 22%[c]	146

Notes: [a]CoSL has approximately 30,000 client files. The total land management budget of the CoSL is TT$3,595,000, to which should be added LAD's annual operational cost is approximately TT$988,000. Therefore, the total Cols-LAD annual management cost would be about TT$4,583,000. Other costs would include the services provided by the Chief State Solicitor, the Commissioner of Valuation, and the Survey Division, but these costs are not included in the table.
[b]NHA client agreements include rentals and mortgages. NHA management budget includes maintenance and construction funds.
[c]9% of rental payments, 22% of mortgage payments.
[d]N/A = Not available.
Source: LUPAP studies (Mt. Horeb, WI: Terra Institute Ltd., 2000).

Table 6.3 Time to Establish Leases

Agency	Months to establish a lease
CoSL	36
CDA	3
Caroni	4
PSAEL	6
PIDCOTT	4
SILWC	2
NHA	3

Source: LUPAP studies (Mt. Horeb, WI: Terra Institute Ltd., 2000).

areas and environmental reserves where the state's interest is long-term and valued in nonmonetary metrics, or for programs for economically vulnerable groups, but not for routine tenancy arrangements. The state is furthermore being inconsistent, achieving full cost recovery through some of its leases, but not others.

The measure of annual arrears also suggests that the Commissioner of State Lands is not performing as effectively as the decentralized agencies/companies in collecting revenue, with an estimated TT$3.4 million uncollected in 1999 (and cumulative arrears of approximately TT$14 million). The fact that the decentralized agencies/companies do not have as severe a problem with arrears indicates that the problem is not with the clients' willingness or ability to pay, but rather with the collection process of the Commissioner of State Lands.

Land Distribution

One of the driving forces behind the continual emergence of special agencies administering portions of state lands appears to be the need to make land available. All agencies can justify their existence on the basis of a structure designed to make a subset of state lands available for specific purposes, for example, NHA for housing, LAD for productive agriculture, and CDA for industrial and tourism purposes.

Table 6.3 indicates the amount of time required to establish a new lease. It suggests that 2–6 months is a feasible time period, as all of the decentralized agencies/companies fall into this range on the indicator. The CoSL's value of 36 months is therefore well outside the feasible time period for this type of transaction. Inordinate delays in establishing new leases frustrate the state's goal of making land available.

Conclusions

For most of the state land management agencies, their rental collections and lease preparation times are roughly acceptable, showing that state agencies in

Trinidad and Tobago can manage land. However, the main exception to this general conclusion is the Commissioner of State Lands, which has had serious land management problems.

The state management of land attempts to achieve goals of more equitable access to land and the stimulation of more investment in the land, by avoiding large land acquisition costs. However, the low performance level of the Commissioner of State Lands undermines these expectations for a significant area of land and number of clients.

While some agencies manage the state land under their control with reasonable effectiveness, several factors have led to ineffective management of state-owned lands by the Commissioner of State Lands.

The first and foremost factor that has contributed heavily to ineffective management is the shortcomings of the policy, legislative, and institutional framework. Proposals have been made for the adoption of a national land policy framework for Trinidad and Tobago. Legislative reform includes the proposed State Land Act to overcome the existing deficiencies in the legislation. Institutional reforms including the establishment of a State Land Management Authority have been proposed. However, very little has been achieved thus far in policy, legislative and institutional reforms.

The second is the fragmentation of management responsibilities for state land management and the inherent inefficiencies in existing public institutions. The management of leases for such agencies as the Land Administration Division (LAD) and the Commissioner of State Lands (CoSL) requires the action of several independent agencies.

The third factor is the inability/unwillingness of the state to take rigorous enforcement action against squatters and tenants in breach as and when required. The social and political pressures on government to satisfy the demands of the population for access to land have typically been made by recourse to "informal" allocations of state land. Squatting and encroachment cannot be addressed by legislation alone. The increase in squatting and encroachment may be taken as a symptom of land hunger and state ownership of a disproportionate share of the land in relation to the actual demand by the people. The inability of the government agencies to satisfy this demand needs to be addressed.

Fourth, the staff of the Commissioner of State Lands as well as those in the Land Administration Division are often shielded from the results of their work. Whether the management works well or poorly has little effect on the incentives that staff receive. This leads to low motivation to follow through, monitor, and where necessary improve management practices.

Finally, the nonavailability of market information on a transparent and accessible basis and failure to share information about land availability have resulted in the public not being aware of the location of state land for investment and their designated uses.

During the past decade, proposals have emerged to improve the efficiency and effectiveness in state land management.[18] However, implementation of these proposals has been very slow, at best.

The future for state land management in Trinidad and Tobago depends on the resolve of the government to determine the institutional framework for implementation of these policies, harmonizing legislation and modifying or repealing legislation that impact negatively on state land tenure.

It is quite clear from the above that constraints afflicting state land management in Trinidad and Tobago can only be overcome through a concerted effort in implementing policy, legal, and institutional reform. It is also clear from the major restructuring of Caroni lands, which began in 2005, that state land management in Trinidad and Tobago would continue to be an important government policy. The Trinidad and Tobago model of land management with a substantial state role remains in significant contrast to the model of predominant private ownership of land and the operation of unfettered land markets.

Notes

This chapter is based on studies done by A. A. Wijetunga, Allan Williams, Robin Rajack, Kelvin Ramkisoon, Jacob Opadeyi, Malcolm Childress, Christendath Harry, Jacqui Ganteaume-Farrell, Steve Ventura, and Shivanti Balkaransingh, under the general guidance of Thackwray Driver, Programme Coordinator, Agriculture Sector Reform Programme, and Asad Mohammed, Chairman of the Land Use Policy and Administration Project (LUPAP) Steering Committee. The views expressed do not necessarily reflect those of any of these individuals.

1. Steven C. Bourassa and Yu-Hung Hong (eds.), *Leasing Public Land: Policy Debates and International Experiences* (Cambridge, MA: Lincoln Institute of Land Policy, 2003); Allan N. Williams (ed.), *Land in the Caribbean: Proceedings of a Workshop on Land Policy, Administration and Management in the English-Speaking Caribbean* (Wisconsin: Land Tenure Center, University of Wisconsin, 2003).

2. The studies were part of a Land Use Policy and Administration Project (LUPAP), which had as one objective the development of a conceptual framework and an implementation plan for the establishment of an entity responsible for state land management. Copies of reports from this project can be obtained from Terra Institute (www.terrainstitute.org) or from Allan Williams, lupap@tstt.net.tt.

3. The agencies selected were those with identifiable costs linked with the management of state-owned land, either through leases or through direct management.

4. For a summary of this debate in the Caribbean context, see J. David Stanfield, Kevin Barthel, and Allan N. Williams, "Framework Paper for Land Policy, Administration and Management in the English-speaking Caribbean," in Williams (ed.), *Land in the Caribbean*.

5. Kelvin Ramkisoon, *Legislative Enactments Relating to Land Management and Land Administration in Trinidad and Tobago, 1994–1999*. LUPAP Report (Port of Spain, Trinidad and Tobago: LUPAP, 1999). See also Kelvin Ramkisoon, *An Analysis of the Legal Framework for State Land Management in Trinidad & Tobago* LUPAP Report (Port of Spain, Trinidad and Tobago: 2000).

6. Ministry of Planning and Development of the Government of the Republic of Trinidad and Tobago, *A New Administration and Distribution Policy for Land* (Port of Spain, Trinidad and Tobago: Ministry of Planning and Development of the Government of the Republic of Trinidad and Tobago, 1992).

7. Land Tenure Center, *Land Rationalization and Development Programme, Final Report* (Wisconsin: University of Wisconsin, 1992).

8. R. A. Baldwin and F. Reyes, *Land Records Management Project—Final Report* (Port of Spain: Government of the Republic of Trinidad and Tobago, 1996).

9. A. A. Wijetunga, *Assessment of the Commissioner of State Lands.* LUPAP Report (Port of Spain, Trinidad and Tobago: Terra Institute Ltd., Mt. Horeb, Wisconsin, 2000).

10. Jacqui Ganteaume-Farrell, *Land Administration Division, Ministry of Agriculture, Lands and Marine Resources.* LUPAP Report (Port of Spain, Trinidad and Tobago: Terra Institute Ltd., Mt. Horeb, Wisconsin, 2000).

11. Robin Rajack, *National Housing Authority.* LUPAP Report (Port of Spain, Trinidad and Tobago: Terra Institute Ltd., Mt. Horeb, Wisconsin, 2000).

12. Christendath Harry, *Sugar Industry Labour Welfare Committee.* LUPAP Report (Port of Spain, Trinidad and Tobago: Terra Institute Ltd., Mt. Horeb, Wisconsin, 2000).

13. Malcolm Childress, *Caroni (1975) Ltd: Land Management Functions.* LUPAP Report (Port of Spain, Trinidad and Tobago: Terra Institute Ltd., Mt. Horeb, Wisconsin, 2000).

14. Malcolm Childress, *Petrotrin/Palo Seco Agricultural Enterprises, Ltd.: Land and Property Management by a State-Owned Natural Resource Producer.* LUPAP Report (Port of Spain, Trinidad and Tobago: Terra Institute Ltd., Mt. Horeb, Wisconsin, 2000).

15. Terra Institute Ltd./Centre for GeoSpatial Studies, University of the West Indies, *Chagaramas Development Authority,* LUPAP Report (Port of Spain, Trinidad and Tobago: Terra Institute Ltd., Mt. Horeb, Wisconsin, 2000).

16. Jacob Opadeyi, *Property and Industrial Development Company of Trinidad and Tobago.* LUPAP Report (Port of Spain, Trinidad and Tobago: Terra Institute Ltd., Mt. Horeb, Wisconsin, 2000).

17. An estimate of 140,062 hectares is arrived at by taking the total land area of the country, 512,600 hectares, multiplying by 0.52 (the widely cited figure for the percentage of state ownership of land) and subtracting the 126,490 hectares of forest land, i.e., 512,600X0.52=266,552–126,490=140,062.

18. See these LUPAP reports: A. A. Wijetunga, *Policy for Management of State Land.* LUPAP Report (Port of Spain, Trinidad and Tobago, 2000); A. A. Wijetunga, *Manual of Procedures for State Land Management—Commissioner of State Land.* LUPAP Report (Port of Spain, Trinidad and Tobago, 2000); A. A. Wijetunga, *Project for the Creation of a New Lease Management System for the Commissioner of State Lands.* LUPAP Report (Port of Spain, Trinidad and Tobago, 2000); A. A. Wijetunga, *Concepts and Language to Assist Preparation of Legislation to Establish the State Land Management Authority.* LUPAP Report (Port of Spain, Trinidad and Tobago, 2001); Allan Williams and A. A. Wijetunga, *The State Land Management Authority: Business Plan.* LUPAP Report (Port of Spain, Trinidad and Tobago, 2001).

Chapter 7

The Participation Paradox: Stories from St. Lucia

Jonathan Pugh

Introduction

Like in other Caribbean countries, tourism is now being used as the engine of growth for St. Lucia. So far, the outcome of this process has been, generally, positive, in that the country has been able to generate the much needed revenue, develop its infrastructure and provide employment, without causing serious sociocultural problems.

Boxill, Taylor, and Maerk (eds.), *Tourism and Change in the Caribbean and Latin America*, 99

There are countless Jalousies [an all-inclusive hotel in Soufrière St. Lucia] in the Caribbean. As such, it raises questions about sovereignty (when beaches and valleys become foreign fields). It also presents dilemmas about the environment, and about social and cultural relations between visitors and hosts . . . Like St Lucia [other Caribbean governments] . . . have thrown out alternative proposals which offered longer-term solutions based on sustainable development.

Pattullo, *Last Resorts*, 4

Such quotes show that the relationship between tourism and land and development divides people who comment on the Caribbean. Tourism is certainly one of the most explicitly *political* issues across the region. And so how the Caribbean goes about reconciling such political divisions tells us a lot about the relationship between politics, land, and development more generally in the region. But before we get into this relationship in this chapter, warning bells may already be sounding in some reader's minds. Did not the first edition of *Land and Development in the Caribbean* by Besson and Momsen[1] point out that *context is central* in the Caribbean, that ways of development are not *intrinsically* good or bad but rather they are dependent upon how and why they are implemented, in different settings, through different *practices?*

This more generic point about the nondeterministic nature of development programs has also more recently been highlighted in the edited case study text *Environmental Planning in the Caribbean.*[2] That text also emphasizes how context is crucial when it comes to the *implementation* of a given environmental planning discourse. And so, while Pattullo encourages a political campaign against all-inclusive tourism across the Caribbean, it is clearly not difficult to imagine situations where that form of tourism is positive for land and development, in other contexts being negative. Moreover, given that it is "contextual practices" and not "words" that have the impact on land and development, it could be that programs signified under the label of "sustainable development" or "participatory planning" or "empowerment" can also sometimes have negative consequences when it comes to *practices.* It depends who gets behind such programs, why, and how. And could it not also be that people can even change their minds about the impact of such projects and programs over time, also depending upon what place they are looking at them from?

One example of this point will be seen in this chapter. Many fisherpeople from Soufrière, St. Lucia, are now in more conflict with ecotourism, sustainable development, and participatory planning initiatives than they are with the hotel that sits on the Jalousie plantation estate (the plantation discussed in the above quote by Pattullo). And so, some fisherpeople campaign against the negative impacts of sustainable development, participatory planning, and empowerment programs upon their livelihoods, while supporting all-inclusive hotels. Other fisherpeople do not. Time and space and individual perception change the impact of a development on land. As Besson and Momsen pointed out in their first edition of this text, context really does count when it comes to land and development in this region of constant change and differences.

And taking this lead, drawing upon research conducted over the past seven years, I examine the contextual effects of a particular mode of participatory planning in St. Lucia for sustainable development. Initiated in 1994, the Soufrière Marine Management Area (SMMA) is one of the most prestigious examples of what has become known as "communicative planning" to have taken place in the Caribbean, if not the wider Southern Hemisphere. Reflecting this, in 1997 the SMMA won the first British Airways Tourism for Tomorrow / World Conservation Union Special Award for National Parks and Protected Areas for its ability to shape a local consensus between the different conflicting interest groups, empowering these groups in the process. The emphasis was particularly between reducing conflict between fishing and tourism "groups," as they became known through the process of participatory planning. Before turning to this case study, I shall provide some general information on St. Lucia and the town of Soufrière in particular.

St. Lucia is 616 square kilometers in size with a population of 168,458.[3] It is a mountainous, largely forested country, which is part of a volcanic island chain in the Eastern Caribbean. The official language is English, but most people speak French Patois, particularly in the town of Soufrière, which is the focus of this chapter—a reflection of the fact that the country changed rule between the English and the French over 14 times before it was finally

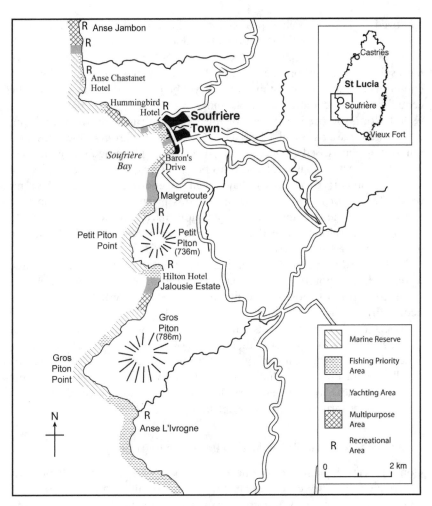

Map 7.1 The Soufrière Marine Management Area in 2003

Source: Author.

ceded to the English in 1814. Slavery was abolished in 1838, and St. Lucia became independent from England in 1979. Eight thousand people live in the town of Soufrière (see map 7.1). With regard to the years that will be discussed in this chapter, total tourist stay-over arrivals to St. Lucia increased from 138,427 in 1990 to 253,463 in 2002.[4] With this increase in tourism to Soufrière, there has been a commensurate increase in divers in Soufrièrian waters, from approximately 1,250 dive permits being issued in 1995 to around 4,000 in 2000.[5] And the SMMA was designed to reduce the conflict between these different interests.

The SMMA can be seen as part of a wider trend in planning for such developing world countries as St. Lucia, which is rewarded by donor agencies in particular. For example, on December 13, 2002 the Caribbean Development Bank approved a US$3.36 million project for the St. Lucia Tourism Development Programme. The size of this donation was undoubtedly influenced by St. Lucia's image as being at the forefront of programs that are framed around the ideas of local solutions to local problems, empowerment, interest group inclusion, and consensus-building activities: in short, as will be explained in this chapter, the central themes of communicative planning.

Reflecting the rise in support for this style of planning in the Caribbean, the United Nations Small Island Developing States Programme of Action reinforces an increased emphasis upon participatory planning more generally.[6] The 1994 meeting that resulted in this program was, at the time, the largest intergovernmental conference to have taken place since the Rio Earth Summit of 1992. One of the major outcomes of this program is that participatory approaches to the building of local institutions have become the number one priority for development in the region, being placed even higher than the generic category of "poverty alleviation."[7]

With regard to the fieldwork presented in the following pages, I continue to research in Soufrière on an ongoing basis. Over the past seven years I have obtained copies of most of the literature associated with the history and geography of the town, interviewing more than 500 people throughout St. Lucia and beyond with this purpose. Research was undertaken in 1998, 1999, 2000 and 2003, amounting to a total of 17 months in the field. Unless otherwise indicated, all interviews that are noted below were conducted by me. Before turning to the empirical example of the SMMA, I shall explain my main theoretical concerns and problems with communicative planning (as the dominant form of participatory planning) more generally.

The Participation Paradox: In Theory

Communicative planning, as one specific approach to liberal democratic governance, involves encouraging different presignified interest groups to come together. These interest groups (such as "women," "fisherpeople," and "tourist operators") then communicatively "feel their way" toward a consensus. The results of the discussion that takes place between the different groups are usually presented in the form of a plan.[8] The reader will note that those who participate in participatory planning initiatives in the Caribbean and elsewhere[9] are generally signified as part of an "interest group," in order to take part in a participatory process of "empowerment," to produce a "consensus" between these groups. However, as will be seen from the rest of this chapter, I have many concerns about this approach.

First, from the above, we can see that communicative planning aims to produce a "postpolitical" consensus. Its implementation illustrates how progress is no longer seen to be achieved through competing visions of, say, Left and Right, but by forming a consensus for all concerned—that is, taking the political out of life.[10] As the story of Soufrière illustrates, this raises many questions. What do we do with those who are excluded from consensus?[11] What do we do about the fact that, as the St. Lucian Nobel Prize-winning poet Derek Walcott[12] points out, St. Lucians do not fit neatly into identity boxes? And therefore what do we do about the fact that if you *force* people into an "interest group," then this can build stereotypes, increasing, rather than reducing conflict?

A note on what an "interest group" means is therefore appropriate. It is really only at times of *common* purpose, social solidarity, and aspiration that an "interest group" actually emerges. The suffragettes, the workers movements of the early 1900s, or the antislavery movements fall under this categorization.[13] In a sense, it is the extent of our *attachment* and sense of being bound to these movements that produces our identity—a common sense of aspiration temporarily fixes the identity of those involved behind a wider shared purpose. But to try and *force* this common bond and identity through a set of procedures and labeling, to try and install and force *one* identity over a person, causes many problems ("fisherperson" versus "hotelier" will be the example used in this chapter). The following stories from St. Lucia show what happens when elites attempt to install "interest groups" and a "consensus" in a specific locality through processes of "empowerment."

Stereotypes and Individuality

One of the main coastal communities of Soufrière is located at Baron's Drive, which is inhabited by 380 people (see map 7.1). Fishing is a particularly important industry for those living at Baron's Drive, where the majority of fisherpeople in Soufrière (100, compared to 170 in the town as a whole) are to be found. Someone who is signified as a "fisherperson" in Soufrière (and in many countries across the Caribbean more generally for that matter, see http://www.planningcaribbean.org.uk) is prescribed an often marginal position in social and physical space. As the following few interviews conducted during the field research over the past seven years illustrate, fisherpeople are often considered by others, and themselves, as contributing less effectively to development than tourism.

For example, those living at Baron's Drive are spatially signified by some leading tourist interests from Anse Chastanet Hotel as "the quaint fishing village . . . but in need of help" (interview undertaken in 2003). The owner of the Hummingbird Hotel says that "the key to helping those guy's [the fisherpeople] is progress, structure and order. . . . They [the fisherpeople] want to go back in time, not forward" (interviewed in 2003). Another member of staff from the Hummingbird Hotel signifies fisherpeople as "long ago people" (interviewed in 2000). As a fisherperson from Soufrière stated, fishing is increasingly considered "not a useful thing to do in Soufrière" (interviewed in 2000). This creates a particular space-time imaginary—fishing spaces are seen as places of the past.

However, while this dominant space-time imaginary exists at one level, at other levels it is not so evident. This illustrates the point that we do not neatly fall into certain categories (such as "fisherperson"). The chair of the Soufrière Fisherman's Co-operative, for example, is not simply "a fisherman."

He is also related by family to a key member of the Soufrière Regional Development Foundation. This member of the Foundation (the leading business organization in Soufrière) is a close friend of the manager of Anse Chastanet Hotel. That hotel was the most politically influential hotel in the mid-1980s—the formative stages of the SMMA—and involved in the appointment of the SMMA manager, for example. Thus, while the chair of the Fisherman's Co-operative is subjected by the hegemonic relations of power that place fishing in a *general* space-time imaginary (because he is a "fisherperson"), due to his specific connections, his identity is more complex than the stereotype "fisherman" would suggest. He is clearly not just "a fisherperson," stigmatized *only* with that stereotype. His connections with leading people from the town have meant that he is able to fish in the area he chooses: specifically outside of the Hummingbird Hotel (see map 7.1).

Another example of how individuals do not fit neatly into one category and stereotype—such as "hotel owner"—is the owner of that Hummingbird Hotel (see map 7.1). As in the case discussed above, she further illustrates that a person's identity is determined by the complex power relations that they are engaged in. For example, the manager of the Hummingbird Hotel has a close friendship with the Prime Minister of St. Lucia. He has assisted her in stopping fishing, at certain times, outside of her hotel (despite the efforts of the chair of the Fisherman's Cooperative and some of his supporters). Yet, the Prime Minister, physically located in Castries (see map 7.1), does not command total power in Soufrière. Soufrière is a physically isolated town, well known for its "own way of doing things" (Cabinet Minister interview in 1999). This means that the Prime Minister's power to prevent the chair of the Fisherman's Co-operative from fishing outside of the Hummingbird Hotel is limited. And so, while the hotel owner of the Hummingbird has some power—due to her connections with the Prime Minister and position in tourism—this power is limited for many reasons. In turn, the simple point is that not all hoteliers and fisherpeople in St. Lucia have the same power to influence planning decisions as others in their stereotyped "interest group."

This section of the chapter has therefore shown that individuals have multiple identities when it comes to daily life. And while stereotypes, such as "fisherperson" or "all-inclusive hotel" are important, they do not *determine* us. All "academics" and "women" do not fit into homogeneous groups with the same interests or access to power relations. This begs one important question for development planning in the Caribbean: why does the dominant form of participatory planning that is implemented in the region—which will now be discussed—treat people as if they do?

The Soufrière Marine Management Area

In order to prevent the conflicts that were taking place in Soufrière between different individuals, the SMMA local communicative planning initiative was initiated and supported by a wide range of people in 1991. People from across the town initially appreciated the emphasis upon local solutions to local problems, feeling that the developed world and the capital city of St. Lucia had too often interfered with their development processes. The SMMA was supported by over 100 people from Soufrière who were concerned about a range of conflicts over fishing grounds, pollution, and diving activities in particular. It was particularly dominated by the Soufrière Regional Development Foundation and its close links with Anse Chastanet—the leading dive resort in Soufrière.

Specifically following communicative approaches to planning, individuals were signified as being part of "interest groups" (fisherpeople, hotel, diving, yachting, and others). Despite there being clear differences in the power of the different individuals in Soufrière (some examples being discussed in the previous section), these people were therefore *stereotyped*. The purpose of this was to produce a consensus between the "signified" groups. After a continuous period of consultation and participation between 1991 and 1994 involving these *installed* "groups," a consensus was produced in June 1994. This is represented by the SMMA zoning map (see map 7.1).

As can be seen from map 7.1, the local SMMA consensus—represented in the SMMA zoning map—results in exclusion. The SMMA zoning map delineates what actions are permitted in Soufrière Bay. This map is a way of visualizing a field to be governed: what is to be surveyed, what knowledge is to be sought, what is to be improved, what is to be abnormalized and what is to be normalized. As can be seen from map 7.1, the SMMA signifies and places bodies in particular positions in space, partitions, isolates, and distributes them, while defining the instrumental modes of intervention that they are to be subjected to. Actions are to be corrected according to the communicative consensus that has been reached and under which interest group they are signified as being part of.

Turning first to the impact of the zoning map upon the interest group that are signified as "fisherpeople," according to the scientific evidence there are good reasons for designating the marine reserves to prevent fishing, as they have resulted in an increase in fish in the SMMA.[14] There has been a tripling of commercially important fish stocks since the SMMA was established.[15] But what is noticeable about the SMMA management plan is that there are no formal measures for controlling the number of divers in the areas that they are permitted and no significant procedures for controlling hotel pollution (supported by personal conversations with St. Lucian government agencies in 2004). This is despite the fact that scientific evidence, although much less publicized, suggests that there is a need to control the impact that coastal development has upon sedimentation rates.[16] Furthermore, a report produced by the Caribbean Natural Resources Institute—one nongovernmental organization which was central to the initiation of the SMMA—in the first year of the consultation exercise stated, "[I]t is strongly suspected that an increase in recreational diving is correlated with an increase in physical damage to reefs."[17] One hotel in particular, Anse Chastanet, is a leading diving resort in Soufrière.

In short, working through the power relations connected to specific individuals, it would therefore appear that certain space-time imaginaries have been fixed through the SMMA communicative planning initiative. Put simply, up until 1997, fishing was to be largely excluded on social and scientific grounds, whereas tourism was not. The significant exception being that the chair of the Fisherman's Cooperative (and other fisherpeople) could fish outside of the Hummingbird Hotel, a local-owned hotel.[18]

Communicative Planning as a Process of Empowerment

This process of stereotyping to create exclusion of certain fisherpeople is further illustrated by the way in which the SMMA empowered those involved in communicative planning. Acting as the facilitator between the signified interest groups, the publicly unelected manager of the SMMA has attempted to get these groups to reach common ground on the different conflicts that exist in Soufrière. This facilitator is thus the expert that has been central in empowering the different groups; yet, in line with mainstream empowerment and communicative planning theory, he is not considered as the authority, but more the *therapist* who can be questioned by those involved as he assists them in "feeling their way" toward consensus. Words such as "therapist" signify apparent neutrality to an individual who, as the following explains, is central to giving meaning to the identities of different signified interest groups. That is, the SMMA manager plays an important part in creating stereotypes.

For example, an important element of the 1995 Communications Plan produced for the SMMA was the need to create an understanding of the benefits of marine reserves.[19] However, because marine reserves had been preconstituted as a means of reducing fishing, and *not* diving activities or hotel pollution, a discussion of their benefits is clearly biased in a certain direction. This illustrates that the publicly unelected SMMA manager is clearly not neutral. He has played a central part in bringing different people's identities into being, through supporting the way in which they have been signified as one interest group—"fisherpeople"—via spatial strategies of exclusion. The SMMA manager therefore brought fisherpeople into a process, which while enabling them to influence discussions, also has the effect of allowing them to be acted upon (through their exclusion from large areas of Soufrièrian waters). In this regard, it is important to say that the author of the Communications Plan also notes, "During this process, a number of problems, which cannot necessarily be solved by improved communication and information flow, were raised."[20]

The Consequences of This Approach to Planning in St. Lucia

The fixation of particular "interest groups" in the way discussed above was largely maintained between 1994 and 1997 in Soufrière. Most people seemed to want to give the SMMA a chance. However, in 1997 things changed. In 1997 a change in geographies of power enacted contradictory struggles within many involved in the SMMA. There were changes in the global tourist market in 1996 and the development that was there before the Hilton was closed. As a result, unemployment in Soufrière increased from 16.5 percent in 1996 to 29.7 percent in 1997.[21] This meant that many people turned from working in the hotel to fishing as a source of income. And as a result the marine reserves began to be disregarded by fisherpeople more than before.

At this time, old conflicts also resurfaced between "locals" and "environmentalists," becoming rearticulated in new ways through the SMMA. Conflicts between these two groups had been at the heart of the development of the area between the Pitons more generally, where the Hilton is now located (see map 7.1). In the early 1990s, both environmentalists and fisherpeople had received jobs during the development of that area into all-inclusive resort facilities (the former through writing plans about how it should be saved from development, the latter from being employed as builders in developing it). As the following shows, both groups have "moved" and reformed, through the SMMA.

This became particularly apparent at the time of the 1997 general election in St. Lucia. In 1997 Soufrièrians knew that candidates would make promises in return for their votes. One fisherperson stated that the "opportunity" of the 1997 general election made fisherpeople "think about the SMMA and how it stop us doing what we want" (interviewed in 1999). The momentum for a direct challenge to the SMMA gathered apace as fisherpeople began to articulate particular space-time imaginaries against the tourist industry, such as "Slavery is in the soil" (fisherperson interviewed in 1998). The successful District Representative noted how he had campaigned during this election under the premise that "[t]he Soufrière Marine Management Area is a political organization that has acted undemocratically, and as such needs to be challenged" (interviewed in 1999).

Soufrière was partially resymbolized as being taken over by large hotel owners, pitting "black tradition" against "white tourism, dominated by white environmentalists" (as many interviewees described the situation in 1999 and 2000). In response to the stereotyping of the identities of "space" and "time" and "people" through the SMMA, relations between fisherpeople and hoteliers became constituted as friend/enemy. At one point in the mid-1990s, the manager of the SMMA was taken by those signified as fisherpeople to a nearby cliff, and, threatening to push him over the edge, he was told by the fisherpeople that they should be given more respect and money than they had previously received from the SMMA.

Conclusion

This chapter suggests that we should not see such terms as "interest group," "consensus," or "empowerment" as *preexisting* moral justifications for governance. To fix and stereotype the identities of individuals, space, and time by operating through these apparently neutral terms can have significant consequences. It can create and then pit "group" against "group," rather than breakdown the idea that groups are only formed momentarily, through a common and shared cause.[22]

Having said this, the events that have taken place in Soufrière indicate that social engagement with the institutions that articulate such postpolitical definitions of morality is essential if they are to be challenged. As shown in the last section of the chapter in particular, the actions of "fisherpeople" from Soufrière show how oppressive space-time imaginaries cannot be transformed through bypassing such "representative" institutions as the Soufrière Marine Management Area, as if doing so would make them go away.

In this regard, it is heartening to note that during my last discussion with the manager of the SMMA in 2003, he acknowledged that in recent years the SMMA had shifted to dealing more with *unequal* power relations. He stated that he does not assume that everyone from the same "interest group" has the same access to the same power relationships. This at least appears to be a different approach from the earlier years of the SMMA. My hope is that this acts to challenge the power relations of certain hoteliers over access to land and water in particular.[23]

Notes

I am grateful to the Economic and Social Research Council for supporting my PhD (Ref: R00429834850) and my three-year Research Fellowship (Ref: R000271204).

1. J. Momsen and J. Besson (eds.), *Land and Development in the Caribbean* (London: Macmillan Caribbean, 1987).

2. J. Pugh and J. H. Momsen (eds.), *Environmental Planning in the Caribbean* (Aldershot: Ashgate, 2006).

3. July 2006 estimate, from CIA factbook, http://www.cia.gov/cia/publications/factbook/geos/st.html.

4. Government of St. Lucia, *Government Statistics*, Government of St. Lucia, St. Lucia, 2003, http://www.stats.gov.lc/ (accessed March 2, 2003).

5. Soufrière Marine Management Area Web site, 2003, http://www.smma.org.lc/.

6. United Nations Economic Commission for Latin America and the Caribbean, *National Implementation of the Small Islands Developing States Programme of Action: A Caribbean Perspective* (Trinidad: United Nations Economic Commission for Latin America and the Caribbean, 1998).

7. United Nations Economic Commission for Latin America and the Caribbean, *National Implementation of the Small Islands Developing States Programme of Action.*

8. P. Healey, *Collaborative Planning: Shaping Places in Fragmented Societies* (Basingstoke and London: Macmillan Press, 1997).

9. G. Mohan, "Beyond Participation: Strategies for Deeper Empowerment," in U. Kothari and B. Cooke (eds.), *Participation: The New Tyranny* (London: Zed Books, 2001), 153–167.

10. R. M. Nettleford, *Mirror, Mirror: Identity, Race and Protest in Jamaica* (Singapore: LMH Publishing Ltd., 1998).

11. J. Pugh, "The Axis of Western-Style Democracy," *Jamaican Observer*, Sunday, February 2, 2003, 10; J. Pugh, "Participatory Planning in the Caribbean: An Argument for Radical Democracy," in J. Pugh and R. B. Potter (eds.), *Participatory Planning in the Caribbean: Lessons from Practice* (Aldershot: Ashgate, 2003); J. Pugh, E. Hinds, C. Ifill, and A. Watson, *Developing Institutional Capital in the Fisherfolk Communities of the Caribbean: The Case of St Lucia*. A report produced under the program Developing Institutional Capital in the Fisherfolk Communities of the Caribbean, Funded by the United Kingdom Foreign and Commonwealth Office, 2004.

12. Derek Walcott, *Collected Poems 1948–1984* (London and Boston: Faber and Faber, 1986).

13. E. Laclau and C. Mouffe, *Hegemony and Socialist Strategy: Towards a Radical Democratic Politics* (London and New York: Verso, 1985).

14. Gell (2002) Report on sedimentation rates in Soufrière, http://www.smma. org.lc/ (accessed April 2, 2004).

15. Roberts (2002) Report on sedimentation rates in Soufrière, http:// www. smma.org.lc/ (accessed in April 2, 2004).

16. M. Nugues, C. Schelten, and C. Roberts (2002) Report on sedimentation rates in Soufrière, http://www.smma.org.lc/ (accessed in 2002); Schelten (2002) Report on sedimentation rates in Soufrière, http://www.smma. org.lc/ (accessed April 2, 2004).

17. A. H. Smith and T. van't Hof, *Coral Reef Monitoring for Management of Marine Parks: Cases from the Insular Caribbean* (IDRC Workshop on Common Property Resources, Winnipeg, Canada, 1991), 2.

18. J. Pugh, "The Disciplinary Effects of Communicative Planning in Soufrière, St Lucia: The Relative Roles of Governmentality, Hegemony and Space-Time-Politics," *Transactions: Institute of British Geographers/Royal Geographical Society* 30, no. 3 (2005): 307–322.

19. N. A. Brown, *Soufrière Marine Management Area (SMMA) Communication Plan prepared for the Soufrière Regional Development Foundation*. Caribbean Natural Resources Institute (CANARI) Technical Report No. 230 (St. Lucia: Caribbean Natural Resources Institute [CANARI], 1995).

20. Brown, *Soufrière Marine Management Area (SMMA) Communication Plan*, 2.

21. Government of St. Lucia, *Government Statistics*.

22. Pugh, "The Disciplinary Effects of Communicative Planning in Soufrière, St Lucia."

23. While there are multiple sites of spatiopolitical and economic engagement for the tourist sector to be assisted through, fisherpeople do not have the same opportunities. With this in mind, the present author has begun to engage with fisherpeople from across seven countries in the Eastern Caribbean. We are bearing in mind that the first regional union for fisherfolk that could emerge from these negotiations can only be considered a serious "interest group" if there are common concerns between fisherpeople (see http://www.planningcaribbean.org.uk). That is, this interest group has to emerge from common bonds. It cannot be installed.

Chapter 8

Land Disputes and Development Activity in the Dominican Republic

Donald Macleod

This chapter will focus on the southeast region of the Dominican Republic, particularly the coastal village of Bayahibe, a fishing community increasingly influenced by tourism, situated next to the Del Este National Park. The central themes will be the land disputes that have arisen, the variety of development initiatives in progress, and the importance of understanding these events in the light of the community's history, which in turn reflects the distribution of power. These issues, while concentrating on a localized region, have a strong resonance throughout the Dominican Republic (DR) and other Caribbean countries.

The conclusion offers an analysis and model of power and its relevance to understanding the complex relationship between land and development. A brief historical outline will serve to introduce the more pertinent events and give a perspective from a villager who is a key actor in development and land issues.

Bayahibe and History

The following version of the history of Bayahibe is based on the personal interpretation given by Eduardo Brito, a native and resident of Bayahibe. Eduardo is a qualified architect and has returned to live in Bayahibe, "to fight for the village" in his words. Part of this fight relates to the Britos's dispute over land ownership: the family, composed of some 200 descendants in 2002, claim that they are the rightful owners of the coastal area. The Britos contest ownership with the regional Council of Yuma and a large company, Central Romana, which bought the local interests from Gulf and Western in 1985 (approximately 450 square miles of land, sugar refinery, and hotels). The following summary of his view of events will clarify these issues:

> In 1798 Juan P. Brito arrived in Bayahibe from the island of Puerto Rico. He began fishing and farming, married and fathered four children. His youngest

was Juan Brito, born in 1837, who inherited land worked by his father. Juan Brito decided to buy the land in 1875, marked it out and purchased it from the state, some 20,000 tareas (629 square metres = 1 tarea). At this time there were around 12 other homes in the area. The region was able to support farmers, fishermen and lumbermen, although most of the wood eventually disappeared. There was regular maritime traffic along the coast to Santo Domingo and goods were exchanged. By the 1890s there were more farmers than fishermen living in the area and five big boats powered by wind and steam regularly visited the port. Juan Brito married a woman from Santo Domingo and they had nine children, each of whom would be entitled to inherit a share of the land.

A road was built from Bayahibe to the large town of Higuey in 1914 and there were plans to make Bayahibe a municipality, but the project faltered and boats eventually went to the nearby port of Boca de Yuma (on the other side of the national park). Bayahibe was effectively abandoned. Following the US troop occupation in 1916 more infrastructural improvements were made and the area remained agricultural, but the economy declined during the war, becoming purely subsistence. After 1924 production and commercial exchange picked up, and the nearby port and sugar town, La Romana, grew considerably. During the period of Trujillo's dictatorship between 1933 and 1961 Bayahibe suffered many hardships, men were taken away for the navy, my father had problems and my uncle was killed with three others. The villagers concentrated on fishing as the primary industry during this period.

After the end of the dictatorship internal tourism began in the region with local Dominican visitors, and by 1969 international tourism reached La Romana with the opening of the La Romana Hotel owned by the U.S. company Gulf and Western (G&W). G&W had bought the U.S.-owned South Puerto Rico Company and in 1967 was a vast landowner, predominantly of sugar plantations. It also claimed ownership of land occupied by Bayahibe and in 1973 moved the entire village along the coast, some half a mile, to a new site supplied with new accommodation, with the intention of building a hotel on the old site. This deal was overseen and agreed by President Balaguer. A letter sent to the President of the DR (Fernandez) in 1998 by Eduardo Brito and his colleague mentions how, during this time, the residents of Bayahibe were "treated like animals."

G&W sold their Dominican interests in 1985, and Central Romana bought the contested land and built a hotel, "Casa del Mar." The consequent increase in tourism helped to spur in-migration to Bayahibe, and its population grew steadily at around 5 percent per annum. A village committee granted land to the needy (referred to as "immigrants" by Eduardo, as opposed to resident "natives"). More hotels were built in the region during the late 1970s, although Bayahibe remained composed of only 35 houses strung along the main road "Calle Juan Brito." By 1982 the villagers had begun to build tourist cabins. It was in this year that the residents found someone to represent their interests nationally in the form of Alberto Giraldi, a native of France and a PRD (Dominican Revolutionary Party) politician, elected as senator for La Romana province. He was a "nationalist," worried about foreign business interests and defended the villagers in their legal struggle for rights to what they believed was their land. These sentiments may be seen in the context of a national movement in politics, literature, and folklore, as a search for freedom against foreign interference and control.[1]

Senator Giraldi, who defended Bayahibe, is celebrated as the "Father of the liberation of Bayahibe." His portrait, together with that of Juan Brito, the "Founder of the village," is mounted prominently on a tree in the village square. The villagers have created a modest place of historical import to the community, a public recognition of local community heroes. Eduardo places himself in this historical tradition of people who have fought for the rights of the village.

Land Disputes

The major dispute in Bayahibe (population 1,800 in 2002) centers on the fact that the regional Council of Yuma claims that Juan Brito gave them his land, whereas the Brito family claim that this is untrue and that he did not even sign the document of donation. Within the past few years a land tribunal has found in favor of the Britos and the latest move of the Yuma council has been a request to be co-owners of the land. A further complication involves the supposed sale of the land by Yuma to G&W, on which the hotel "Casa del mar" was eventually built. The Yuma council insists that they did not sell the land but rented it to G&W. One result of this is that the Britos are now claiming the sale price and interest from the Council of Yuma and also rental income for the period from the hotel's current owners. Villagers were aware of this and quoted the figure of "250 million pesos" (US$16,700,000)[2] when asked about the claim. Many knew the "lot number" of the land parcels under scrutiny.

In 1997 the newspaper *El Nacional* commented on G&W's purchase of land (including Bayahibe) for a bargain basement price in 1973 (a deal overseen by President Balaguer) and criticized it as being unjust. Because of this long-running dispute and the vagaries of the justice system—with possible appeals to higher courts—there were no absolutely clear answers to land entitlement in Bayahibe by 2002. Villagers involved in the legal negotiations, namely Eduardo and his colleagues at the "Foundation for the Development of Bayahibe," believed that residents could be secure in their property and need not fear enforced evacuation. Nevertheless, the following examples highlight the general sense of insecurity about land ownership and its basis in experience, locally and nationally.

Land Ownership and Insecurity—Examples

1. A rumor had circulated in Bayahibe during 1996 that the village and its land was to be sold for the development of a hotel on the plot, just as had happened previously in 1973. Such was the persistence and credibility of the rumor that village representatives petitioned government ministers and alerted the media including a letter sent to Senator Giraldi published in the

daily newspaper "Hoy" on October 11, 1996. The villagers' worries proved to be unfounded, but the incident illustrates the lack of confidence in their collective security.

2. During the construction of the Casa del Mar hotel, around 1997, the owners blocked off the entire beach on which Bayahibe once stood and sealed off public access to the villagers, many of whom had once fished and moored their boats by the beach. They also closed off an access road to the beach. This infuriated the villagers, and they protested vigorously, closing off the main highway between Santo Domingo, La Romana, and the eastern hotels by occupying it from the early hours of the morning. They won back the use of the road and were given access to half the beach, some 400 meters.

3. A national park was created on land donated by G&W in 1975 with the proviso that it be preserved for conservation purposes. The park, known as Del Este, borders Bayahibe and includes land that was at one time used for livestock grazing, subsistence agriculture, wood collection, and hunting. Access was thereafter halted. In addition, the government appropriated land owned by small farmers to increase the park's area, and in some instances the owners have still not been compensated.[3] Villagers say that "the new owners of the park have taken the best land for themselves." They are acutely aware of the high value of the coastal land in this area.

4. A 62-year-old man, his two sons, and their neighbors (two Haitian families) were forcibly ejected from their homes that were demolished in front of them in November 1999. The man was a carpenter who had built many of the impressive gaff-rigged fishing yachts and smaller *Yola* fishing boats, of which Bayahibe is so proud: the yachts feature in postcards and advertising hoardings. He had built his breeze-block home seven years earlier on land at the periphery of the village and also built the two adjoining wooden homes *Bohios* in which the Haitian families dwelt. He was from Samana, in the north of the island, and was descended from American slaves who escaped to the DR and freedom. His family and his Haitian neighbors were evacuated by the "landowner" who claimed that the carpenter did not pay for his property, which the carpenter disputes. The landowner took the carpenter to court and won, after which the police carried out the swift demolition job.

5. Around the same time in 1999 a story appeared in the national press of a "squatter" camp of 800 families demolished by the police, leaving them homeless—they had occupied part of the green belt surrounding the capital city, Santo Domingo. There are commonly held beliefs that people have a right to claim ownership of land on which they reside if they are not challenged after a period of five years. This instills a curious mix of desperation and hope amongst poor Dominicans, and an entire community has arisen on land that is continually contested—Padre Nuestro—a satellite community to Bayahibe, about 1 mile inland from the coast. According to one report commissioned by the Parks in Peril program[4] its population in the mid-1990s was 30, whereas by 1999 it contained around 1,000 people (Bayahibe Foundation census).[5]

The examples outlined above serve to impart the general sense of insecurity about land rights and ownership that people have in and around Bayahibe. Historically in the DR land has not been a desperately scarce resource; often people squatted on land and through various means established control over it. Changing political regimes have occasionally led to gifts of land to squatters, or alternatively, to state appropriation of land.[6] The land surrounding Bayahibe, including the satellite community Padre Nuestro, is not well suited to agriculture. Work is increasingly inhibited by the lack of soil and clean freshwater, the local subterranean water supply having become contaminated by both human waste and salt water through inadequate sewage facilities, overextraction of reserves and changing water levels.

A contrast with attitudes toward land in Jamaica as recorded in Besson and Momsen's *Land and Development in the Caribbean* is enlightening, where the symbolic value of family land is high and denotes an "infinite" resource for future generations. Some of this sentiment is related to the memory of slavery and the need for independence.[7] In contrast, the memory of slavery in the DR is generally repressed, influenced by an official focus on the Spanish and indigenous Indian (Taino) roots, the relatively low proportion of slaves in the founding population, and the early eradication of slavery following Haitian intervention.[8]

There is no real sense of hunger for workable land in and around Bayahibe, although there is a strong desire for a secure plot for a house. Land is more likely to be regarded as a commodity, with only a few descendants of peasant farmers continuing to work hard on growing produce in their backyards or in a nearby allotment. Bayahibe's recent dependence on fishing as a mode of livelihood also directly affects the general attitude, where the focus of attention has been on maintaining boats and equipment.

Development Activities

The specific experience of Bayahibe and the general history of the DR have shaped the community's needs and desires to a large degree. By examining them we are able to gain a deeper understanding of the background to development activities and problems faced in this country.

Gardner and Lewis organize the notion of the anthropology of development around three themes: (1) the social and cultural effects of economic change; (2) the social and cultural effects of development projects (and why they fail); and (3) the internal workings and discourses of the "aid industry."[9] These themes are all relevant to the activities experienced in the DR under scrutiny and form a useful guide with which to approach them, focusing on the effects of economic change and the self-conscious, planned "development" projects.

In Bayahibe, following its mixed agricultural and fishing peasant economy, fishing grew to dominance in the twentieth century, but has recently been spectacularly usurped by tourism as the primary source of income, a trend throughout coastal areas in the DR.[10] This development has not been officially planned and is very much a response by indigenous inhabitants to opportunities around them. For example, in Bayahibe the majority of male workers are involved in taking tourists by boat to the nearby island of Saona in the national park, a 30-minute journey. The tourists arrive in the morning by coach from all over DR and depart in the afternoon without entering the village; they travel in motor boats ("launches") that are owned by local men or foreign business consortiums. This activity began around 1985 and has mushroomed to the point where more than 100 men in the village are directly involved in the transportation, and only 15 remain as professional fishermen. In contrast, Boca de Yuma, a village on the other side of the national park, has very little tourism and has experienced a rapid growth in men fishing professionally, with over 250 working full-time at sea.

Very few foreign tourists stay in Bayahibe village—on average fewer than 10 stayed per day from July 1999 to March 2000, but at Christmas and New Year there were up to 100 per day. Visiting construction and hotel workers also use rented village accommodation throughout the year.

The income from the boats is the main source that flows to other service industries locally as indirect expenditure, especially the general store, smaller outlets, cafes, and restaurants. In addition, the building and operation of luxury hotels along the coast have led to opportunities of employment in construction work (mostly undertaken by Haitians) and employment in the hotels at service levels: gardening, cooking, and security. It is said that almost all of the households in Padre Nuestro are dependent on work at the hotels. The level of pay is relatively low, between US$135 and US$200 per month, and the turnover of staff is high; however, the increasing expansion and construction of new hotels ensure a regular demand for cheap labor.

One interesting planned development has been the establishment by local men of a "Syndicate" for launch captains based in Bayahibe. It was formed in 1998 to create an equitable way of dealing with work and payment from boat trips. Previously there was open competition for tourists who were simply approached on arrival by boat captains offering varying prices. The majority of captains are satisfied with the imposed rota system arrangement, being able to ensure a regular income, with a fixed high price in a captive market. However, some dissenters criticize the fact that they will be restricted in their earnings.

Despite the drawbacks for some entrepreneurial boat owner-captains, the Syndicate is a good example of the villagers' determination to see economic fairness and hence social support in Bayahibe. It represents an important grassroots confrontation with the general economic ethos pervading the country, fostered by the IMF and international business interests, that is creating a neoliberal drive toward low wages, competition, and profit without social support. Witness the relentless tourism industry, industrial free zones, and paltry social services.[11]

Another local initiative, the most important planned "development" organization in Bayahibe, is "The Foundation for the Development of Bayahibe." This is a group whose membership is drawn from householders in the village and is overseen by the unpaid elected President and the Secretary, helped by a waged assistant. The President Ernesto Brito, an ex-fisherman in his early sixties who is employed by the National Park Service, says the idea for a foundation was first mooted by a resident Frenchman. The village had no official council and needed a body to champion its interests. Eduardo Brito is the secretary and the intellectual motor behind the activities. In 1998, together with Ernesto, he sent a letter to the President of the DR criticizing the government for neglecting Bayahibe, particularly in respect to infrastructural development. Further, he suggested the government build a marina for the hundreds of launches and catamarans that now clog up the bay inhibiting swimmers and others. Eduardo has helped to orchestrate the legal proceedings defending the Britos's land claim and continues to oversee the activity.

In his own words, Eduardo wants "an improvement in the culture of the people" in the sense of education, technical schools, a library, and a theater: he wants to "help the formation of the people." Additionally he pointed out that the basic infrastructure needed attention: the lack of a potable water supply, inadequate telephone network, unplanned sewage system, unmetalled roads, and lack of a recreational park. Also, the village needed a promenade by the coast, something for the tourists—a gift shop, a center where people could pay for public utilities, a post office, a local council with offices, and conditions for improving the natural environment.

The Foundation has been the focal point for village environmental activities including a reforestation program backed by the National Botanical Gardens and the Dominican nongovernmental organization (NGO) "Ecoparque." But it is the national park Del Este that is the common denominator and primary magnet for many groups in the region. It is listed as a "Park in Peril" by The Nature Conservancy (TNC) of the United States and as such attracts substantial funding from U.S. organizations. USAID is a major donor and money is channeled via "ProNatura," a Dominican group, through to active NGOs. Ecoparque operates in the national park, Bayahibe, Boca de Yuma, and the island of Saona where up to 350 people still live. MAMMA, a marine conservation NGO, has worked in the park and receives funding for projects including surveys of marine life, constructing acceptable mooring points and promoting knowledge about marine conservation. It is run by a marine biologist from a Dominican university.

In the year 2000 Ecoparque was headed by an agronomist helped by a Dominican graduate in environmental science from an American university, a graduate in social sciences from a Dominican university, and an administrator. It had also requested the help of a U.S. Peace Corps Volunteer (PCV) experienced in environmental matters and ecotourism: this person was based in Bayahibe and worked at the local school helping to teach about environmental issues such as refuse and pollution.

The fee income of Del Este, gained from entrance payments of US$1.50 per visitor was larger than the total combined income of all the other 15 parks in the country due to the volume visiting the beaches of Saona via Bayahibe. This sum goes to the Dominican National Park Directorate (DNP) headquarters from where it is distributed throughout the organization. The theft of some fees by a DNP employee at Bayahibe increased the local residents' suspicion of the organization: they already regard it as having taken the best land without compensating the people and as having neglected to plough the profits from the park back into Bayahibe. Furthermore, the soft punishment of the thief served to enforce the belief that corruption is rife in the DNP.

Conclusion: Land, Development, and Power

American aid, business interests, and media coverage illustrate relationships in which the United States enjoys economic superiority and has a proven power to influence activities in the DR through a vast network. Such activities have been touched on in our examination of development work: the USAID and TNC involvement with the Park in Peril program, the consultants, and the PCVs, all of whom increase American influence, including an intellectual element in the sense of values, behavior, attitudes, and education. It was a U.S. company, G&W, that created the park in the first place. And U.S. money helped create the huge sugar plantation economy on which La Romana, the largest town in the region, was founded.

Throughout history powerful groups of people have fought one another to gain control over resources in the Dominican Republic. European countries eventually gave way to the resident population's desire to separate from their colonial masters. But due to financial problems, its strategic position, and the geopolitical maneuvers of the two superpowers, USA and Russia, the DR was occupied by a foreign army twice in the twentieth century. Currently, international economic interests largely determine the fate of the DR in terms of income, employment, and, increasingly, social support.[12] Tourism, industrial free zones, the commodities market, and remittances from the United States are at the mercy of overseas powers and global economic trends. This fact has an immediate impact on development in all its forms and impinges on land disputes.

Power is also a component of everyday face-to-face interaction and local events. There are numerous examples of the grassroots reality of social organization in which residents are able to exercise aspects of power in their daily lives that counter the macrolevel: the institutional and the state machine. These include the Brito family as a unit fighting the local council and business consortiums, individual Britos imposing their opinions and desires upon the community, and the boat captains organizing a syndicate to defend themselves as a community. There are also the naval officials who take "tips" from fishermen, allowing them to hunt without restriction, and local policemen who demand money from stallholders to keep operating: they are all exercising a form of personal power. This is an abuse of their official status, but a way of supplementing a meager income and maximizing their opportunity in a job that they may lose for other reasons. Stories circulate that these representatives of the state are pressurized by their superiors to extract wealth from the public and pass it up the chain of command; indeed, the commonplace nature of such bribery and extortion, together with its openness, suggests it is widely tolerated by all levels of society. It is possible to interpret this as a form of direct taxation.

Power has been defined as follows:

> The ability of a person or social unit to influence the conduct and decision making of another through the control over energetic forms in the latter's environment.[13]

An examination of power by Macleod expands on this definition and introduces a model, analyzing the actual exercise of power that is composed of three interlinked levels of control: (1) primary, relating to a socially recognized understanding or contract; (2) secondary, relating to the physical manifestation of the primary understanding, through control over all types of resources; and (3) tertiary, relating to the intellectual manifestation of the primary understanding, through control over communication and publicly advanced ideas.[14]

This model can be applied to almost any social situation but is particularly relevant to the issues we have dealt with in this chapter. For example, the United States' relationship with the DR, based as it is on economic superiority that underpins the primary level, a socially recognized understanding, often supported by a legally based "contract." This is manifest at the secondary level by actual purchasing and selling power, and development funding. At the tertiary level it is manifest by the concepts of conservation, development, and, more broadly, neoliberalism.

Similarly, when examining the interaction of fishermen and policing authorities we see at the primary level the generally accepted social recognition of state authority. In addition to this, we see the locally specific understanding that a "tip" is necessary in order for the individual representatives of state authority to "turn a blind eye"—or simply to allow the lawful activity to take place. At the secondary level of control the physical exchange of goods for access to maritime resources takes place in the form of extortion. The tertiary level is usually manifest in a limitation on discussing these activities, as well as the general acceptance of this behavior as the status quo.

Such relationships of control appear throughout social activities in the DR, as witnessed with land disputes. If we consider the case of the carpenter who lost his home (as did his Haitian neighbors), we can see that power, manifest by the police demolishing his property, rested on a legal contract—symbolized in material form by the title deeds belonging to the landowner. Despite the general public feeling that the eviction was undeserved, and the carpenter's protestations that he had paid the landlord, the fear of physical power behind the law prevailed. Lawyers are popularly believed to be corrupt—people spoke of them taking bribes from rich men—which means that in practice the final say goes to those with physical force backed by money.

An interesting comparison is revealed when we recall the problems arising after Juan Brito purchased the land around Bayahibe: the Council of Yuma later claimed that he donated it to them and they sold this land to an

American company. Again, actions were backed by force supported by wealth. Similarly, the American invasions of the DR, which ostensibly brought stability to the country, also protected American national security and financial interests. Political interests often boil down to economic interests, which in turn may be linked to kinship. The carpenter in the above example was from another part of the island, and his neighbors were Haitians, facts that muted any real protest in the community in which they had minimal family connections.

The economic development of the region, fueled by international exports and tourism, has led to the rapid inflation of land values and a harsher delineation between the powerful (those with control over their environment) and the powerless. By considering the situation of land ownership through the lens of power relationships we can better understand the pattern of development and the conflicts that arise, as well as the fundamental problems that frame development activity in a particular place. In the case of Bayahibe, we should be able to compare its experience with other case studies for a deeper understanding of the process of development.

Notes

1. See G. Pope Atkins and Larman Wilson, *The Dominican Republic and the United States: From Imperialism to Transnationalism* (Athens, GA: University of Georgia Press, 1998).
2. U.S. dollars will be used throughout at the exchange rate of 15 Dominican pesos for 1 U.S. dollar.
3. See K. Guerrero and D. A. Rose, "Dominican Republic: Del Este National Park," in Katrina Brandon, Kent Redford, and Steven Sanderson (eds.), *Parks in Peril: People, Politics and Protected Areas* (Washington, DC: Island Press, 1998), 193–216; Donald V. L. Macleod, "Parks or People? National Parks and the Case of Del Este, Dominican Republic," *Progress in Development Studies* 1, no.3 (2001): 221–235.
4. Guerrero and Rose, "Dominican Republic."
5. The entire community of Padre Nuestro had been relocated by 2006 and the homes demolished in preparation for sale of the land.
6. See Eugenia Georges, *The Making of a Transnational Community: Migration, Development and Cultural Change in the Dominican Republic* (New York: Columbia University Press, 1990).
7. Jean Besson, "A Paradox in Caribbean Attitudes to Land," in Jean Besson and Janet Momsen (eds.), *Land and Development in the Caribbean* (London: Macmillan Caribbean, 1987), 13–45.
8. See Bernardo Vega (ed.), *Ensayos Sobre Cultura Dominicana* (Santo Domingo: Museo del Hombre Dominicano, 1997).
9. Katy Gardner and D. Lewis, *Anthropology, Development and the Post-Modern Challenge* (London: Pluto Press, 1996).
10. Cf. Carel Roessingh and Hannek Duijnhoven, "Small Entrepreneurs and Shifting Identities: The Case of Tourism in Puerto Plata (Northern Dominican Republic)," *Journal of Tourism and Cultural Change* 2, no. 3 (2004): 185–201.

11. See Thomas Klak (ed.), *Globalization and Neoliberalism: The Caribbean Context* (Oxford: Rowman and Littlefield Publishers, 1998).

12. Cf. Atkins and Wilson, *The Dominican Republic and the United States*; James Carrier and Donald V. L. Macleod, "Bursting the Bubble: The Socio-Cultural Context of Ecotourism," *Journal of the Royal Anthropological Institute*, n.s. 11 (2005): 315–334; David Howard, *Dominican Republic: A Guide to the People, Politics and Culture* (New York: Interlink Books, 1999); Klak (ed.), *Globalization and Neoliberalism*.

13. Raymond D. Fogelson and Richard N. Adams (eds.), *The Anthropology of Power* (New York: Academic Press, 1977).

14. Donald V. L. Macleod, "Office Politics: Power in the London Salesroom," *Journal of the Anthropological Society of Oxford* XXVIIII, no. 3 (1998): 213–219.

Chapter 9

Land Policy in Jamaica in the Decade after Agenda 21

Learie A. Miller and David Barker

Introduction

Historically the natural environment has always been exploited to fulfill human needs but during this century the scale of these demands has grown so rapidly and large that the ecosystems upon which our health and livelihoods depend have been immensely degraded. The reality of a growing population, of increased ecological fragility, the close interdependence of the economy and the environment, and a vulnerability to natural hazards makes it imperative that a small island developing state like Jamaica pays keen attention to how it manages the resource base on which its populace depends.

The need to strive for the ideal of integrating environment and development was the major theme at the 1992 UN Conference on Environment and Development (UNCED) in Rio, where a strategy on sustainable development was advocated and generally accepted in the form of Agenda 21.[1] In effect, Agenda 21 was a blueprint for the global and local actions to affect the transition to sustainable development, defining the rights and responsibilities of states and including a set of principles to support the sustainable management of forests, to protect biodiversity and prevent global climate change, among other things.

Specific to land management, Agenda 21 adopted a broader integrative view and included natural resources such as soils, minerals, water, and biota. These resources are organized in ecosystems to provide a variety of environmental services essential to the maintenance of the integrity of life-support systems and the productive capacity of the environment. Land is a finite resource, while the natural resources it supports can vary over time and according to management conditions and uses.

A critical aspect of Agenda 21 was the identification of small island developing states (SIDS) as a "special case" for environment and development. Jamaica is one of 23 SIDS located in the Caribbean.[2] SIDS confront a different range of environmental and developmental problems compared to larger, developing countries and have weaker capacities for solving them.[3] Their land policy frameworks need to address specific problems that arise from the interaction of economic, political, and environmental processes at the local, national, regional, and global scales. SIDS have significant geographical and other characteristics that impinge on and constrain land policy and resource management, including

- small population and geographical area;
- narrow range of natural resources;
- vulnerability to natural disasters;
- vulnerability to globalization;
- small domestic markets and tax base;
- high costs of public administration and infrastructure; and
- high levels of biodiversity and endemism.

The sustainable development challenges facing SIDS are acute because economic, social, environmental, and political processes are closely related.[4] National population may be relatively small, but population density tends to be high, and its geographical distribution may create spatially variable population pressure on land resources in environmentally sensitive regions of a country. The result may be overexploitation of natural renewable resources such as forests and fisheries and, as a result, overall environmental degradation.

Coastal zone management and watershed management are key aspects of land policy. Environmental conservation and the drive toward tourism development intersect in the coastal zone that, for most Caribbean islands, is generally more densely populated than the interior. Yet, coastal ecosystems are physically connected to terrestrial ecosystems: rivers transport sediment from eroded hillsides and agricultural pollutants into the coastal zone. Thus, poor land use from upland interior watersheds can affect offshore coral reef systems and inshore fisheries.[5] Managing the coastal zone poses challenges because of its vulnerability to the impact of global warming and sea level rise and the prospect of increasing strength and frequency of tropical storms and hurricanes. These, in turn, impact negatively on social and economic development and the environment.

Moreover, the Caribbean region is one of five "hot spots" for global biodiversity with a high biological diversity per unit of land area.[6] Islands such as Jamaica have high levels of endemism among flora and fauna but exhibit high extinction rates too. Conservation of endangered island species, especially endemics, is critical to maintaining global biodiversity as well as preserving a country's environmental heritage.

In Jamaica, prior to 1990 there were policy deficiencies to effectively address issues such as biodiversity conservation or squatting. In other areas, such as forestry, policies were outdated and woefully inadequate. This chapter evaluates the changing policy landscape with respect to land and natural resources management. First, we highlight relevant environmental and economic features of the country as a small island developing state that need to be accommodated in formulating land policy. Second, we identify and discuss three policy areas, national land policy, parks and protected areas, and forestry, and how they have been influenced by Agenda 21's blueprint for action.

Land, Environment, and Economy

Jamaica has a land area of approximately 10,900 square kilometers but is an archipelagic state with legal jurisdiction over marine space that is approximately 24 times larger than the total land area. It has an exclusive economic zone (EEZ) of 235,000 square kilometers.[7] The rugged interior includes mountain ranges and highly karstic plateaus and hills, surrounded by flat/gentle coastal plains. More than half of the island is above 305 meters and half the island has slopes of over 20 percent. The highest peaks, in the Blue Mountains, reach a maximum height of 2,256 meters. The coastal plain is narrow along the north coast with most areas being less than 3.2 kilometers wide. The southern coastal plain tends to be much wider and more extensive especially along the eastern and western ends of the country as well as the southern plains of St. Catherine and Clarendon. These southern coastal plains along with a few interior valleys constitute the country's prime agricultural lands. However, there are constraints to the use of the coastal plains for agriculture as they include important wetlands such as the Black River Morass. Agriculture including fisheries, forestry, and pastures, occupies more than half of the country's land area.

The coastline is irregular and exhibits a diversity of natural ecosystems. It is approximately 885 kilometers in length and includes sandy beaches, rocky shores, estuaries, wetlands, sea grass beds, and coral reefs. Vast stretches of white sand beaches are found along the north coast. These white sand beaches originate from the offshore coral reefs from various processes including the erosion of offshore coral and accumulation from calcareous algae. In contrast, many of the south coast beaches are nourished by river sediment (offshore coral reefs are not as extensive) and are typically dark in color.

The island has been deforested since the earliest European contact. In the early plantation period, lowland areas were cleared for sugar and cattle and upland areas for coffee. After emancipation, inland watersheds were put under environmental pressure by land-hungry small farmers.[8] In recent times, the FAO (Food and Agriculture Organization of the United Nations) claimed Jamaica had a deforestation rate of 6.7 percent,[9] one of the highest in the world, but research by the Forestry Department estimates an annual rate of deforestation between 1989 and 1998 of 0.1 percent.[10] Nevertheless, many of Jamaica's watersheds remain badly degraded.

Jamaica has been an island for more than 12 million years. Its mosaic of landscapes, ecosystems, and high level of biodiversity is reflected in numerous endemic plants and animals. However, habitat destruction and the introduction of invasive species have led to the extinction of a number of species, and many other species are endangered.[11]

The economy is dependent on export agriculture (sugar and bananas), mineral exploitation (bauxite), and tourism, but as is typical of SIDS, there is a close interdependence between economic development and the natural environment. Geographically, plantation-type agriculture is located mainly in areas with flat to gentle sloping lands having fertile soils, while tourism development is concentrated along the coast at locations with white sand beaches. Population was estimated at 2.6 million in 2001 of which 55 percent live in urban areas. Kingston's population is around 716,000, and 9 other parish capitals are also located along the coast with the concomitant pressures associated with coastal developments.[12]

Policy makers have found it challenging and problematic to effectively integrate Jamaica's environment and development considerations while addressing pressing social and economic issues. There is increasing pressures on scarce land resources that often result in intense competition and conflicts and suboptimal use of both land and land resources. However, a persistent problem for the development and implementation of policies on land resources is the country's modest economic performance.

Following economic downturn in the 1970s, Jamaica came under the strictures of an IMF/World Bank Structural Adjustment Program (1981–1985). Thereafter, successive governments embraced market liberalization, but within 10 years the financial services sector was in meltdown due to the rapid expansion of unregulated and poorly managed financial institutions.[13] This prompted drastic government intervention, and FINSAC (Financial Sector Adjustment Company) was created in 1996 to rehabilitate the financial sector and to create a more responsible regulatory system. It was achieved at a colossal cost of J$150 billion to the Jamaican taxpayer,[14] and this huge debt hung like a millstone around the country's neck for a further 10 years, severely constraining central government's ability to adequately finance its programs, including policy initiatives.

Jamaica's Response to Agenda 21

One strategy the government has successfully pursued since Agenda 21 has been to improve the availability of information for making policy decisions and evaluating future changes on land-use and natural resources management. Data and information have been compiled and disseminated through a Jamaica National Environment Action Plan (JANEAP), and three State of the Environment Reports (SOE) for the years 1995, 1997, and 2001.[15] Another response is that the country has become a signatory to a number of environmental treaties and protocols as a further sign of its global responsibility and commitment to sustainable development (table 9.1).

Moreover, a series of new policies pertaining to land and its management have been introduced in the decade after the Rio Summit in 1992. The aim was to correct existing policy deficiencies or to introduce new policies where there was a policy vacuum. They were formulated in the context of the reform of public sector agencies and a neoliberalized market economy. Table 9.2 shows three land-related policies and the years they were promulgated: a National Land Policy, a Policy for a System of Parks and Protected Areas, and a Forest

Table 9.1 Selected Treaties and Protocols to which Jamaica is Signatory

Name of treaty	Date of accession
Convention for Protection of Ozone Layer	1993
Montreal Protocol on Substances that deplete the Ozone Layer	1993
UN Framework Convention on Climate Change	1995
Kyoto Protocol to UN Framework Convention on Climate Change	1999
Convention on Biological Diversity	1995
Convention on International Trade in Endangered Species of Wild Flora and Fauna (CITES)	1997
Convention on Wetlands of International Importance Especially as Waterfowl Habitats (Ramsar)	1997
UN Convention to Combat Desertification	1997

Source: *Jamaica National Assessment Report of Barbados Program of Action* (Kingston, Jamaica: Ministry of Land and Environment, 2003).

Table 9.2 Selected Policy Development after Agenda 21

Year	Policy
1996	National Land Policy
1997	Policy for a System of Parks and Protected Areas
2001	Forest Policy

Source: *Jamaica National Report to the World Summit on Sustainable Development 2002* (Kingston, Jamaica: Ministry of Land and Environment, June 2002).

Policy. Associated with these new policies were other long-term programs, strategies, and action plans, for example, programs associated with watershed management and coastal management, some of which were funded by international donors such as USAID, CIDA, the World Bank, and the IADB.

All these policies were the subject of extensive public consultation, the likes of which had not been undertaken previously in the country. Partnerships with civil society and public participation in policy discussion were an important feature of Agenda 21's recipe for local action, and these partnerships have brokered new ground in participatory planning and consultation for the country.

However, effective implementation of land policy in its various forms remains an elusive goal for a variety of reasons, the principal being the severe budgetary constraints on government expenditure resulting from the collapse of the financial sector in the mid-1990s.

National Land Policy

National Land Policy has identified many critical land issues and associated causes. Land problems have resulted from various causes including degradation of forests and watersheds, scattered and linear development, unplanned urban development, squatting, illegal development activities, occupation of hazard-prone and other unsuitable areas, increased living costs, and environmental pollution.[16] National Land Policy has sought to be comprehensive and has many facets, including

- geographic information systems;
- land resources and land use;
- land titling, tenure, and access;
- acquisition, pricing, and divestment of government-owned lands;
- taxation;
- incentives for property development;
- environment, conservation, and disaster preparedness;
- management of lands with specific reference to government-owned lands; and
- legislation, institutional framework, and reform.

The formulation of a national land policy triggered a number of important initiatives, including the development of a National Networked Geographic Information System, the strengthening of the role of the Land Information Council of Jamaica (LICJ), the establishment of a modern national geodetic infrastructure comprising geodetic control points and other geodetic facilities compatible with Global Positioning Systems (GPS). A significant effort was made to provide land titles especially to persons who were beneficiaries of former land settlement programs. A land divestment program was prompted by the land policy as the government being the largest owner of land (many parcels were underutilized and not properly managed) sought to divest these lands in a fair and transparent manner.

The policy also highlighted the approximately 45 percent of parcels not on the Register Book of Titles, and attempts were made to regularize some of these. One notable project was the Land Administration and Management Project (LAMP), which was jointly supported by the Inter-American Development Bank (IADB) and the government of Jamaica. LAMP involved a pilot program to prepare a cadastral map of 30,000 parcels of land in the parish of St. Catherine and to undertake tenure clarification and regularization of these parcels.[17]

Although the land policy identified squatting as a major problem, the years since the policy was promulgated have seen a major increase in the incidence of squatting despite several attempts by regulatory agencies to curtail the practice. Squatting occurs in close proximity to towns and cities and other areas of potential employment, for example, around the major tourist resort areas. As a consequence, people seeking somewhere to live have illegally occupied areas considered marginal or environmentally fragile.

As in other areas of policy, constraints with respect to financial, technical, and human resources to review and update existing plans and prepare new plans for the country have been identified. They are considered a hindrance to achieving the objectives of the national land policy to ensure the sustainable, productive, and equitable development, use, and management of the country's natural resources including land.[18]

Policy for a System of Parks and Protected Areas

Jamaica has an extraordinary diversity of flora and fauna, land and water habitats, and landscapes. The development of a system of protected areas is a key part of national development strategy. Policies for the management and conservation of Jamaica's diversity of natural resources and landscapes are set out in two Green Papers:

1. *Policy for Jamaica's System of Protected Areas*;[19] and
2. *Towards a National Strategy and Action Plan on Biological Diversity in Jamaica.*[20]

The IUCN's (International Union for the Conservation of Nature and Natural Resources) classification of parks and protected areas was used to design a National Protected Areas System and an associated Policy Framework.[21] By linking the national system to an internationally recognized system for parks and protected areas, access can be gained to technical and financial support from the global community.[22]

Parks and protected areas have multiple purposes:

- conservation (protection of natural ecosystems and cultural heritage);
- sustainable use of renewable natural resources (forests, wetlands, inshore fisheries);
- tourism and recreation; and
- education and research.

Limited land space and fragile ecosystems, and conflict and competition over the use of parks and protected areas, make land management difficult. The global community tries to mitigate these problems by advocating a national *system* of parks and protected areas, whereby each country establishes its own categories for different users. Table 9.3 shows Jamaica's classification.

The NRCA has identified more than 150 geographical areas in need of some type of protection, amounting to 83 percent of the island's land area.[23] Table 9.4 identifies the declared protected areas and their management bodies. Map 9.1 shows the location of these protected areas, which include marine parks in the main tourist resorts. Note too that the Negril Environmental Protected Area includes the entire Negril watershed and adjacent marine ecosystems. This reflects an important contemporary concept in land management, defining project area boundaries inclusive of terrestrial and coastal

Table 9.3 Categories of Protected Areas in Jamaica

Jamaica's designation for parks and protected areas	Equivalent IUCN category
National nature reserve/wilderness area	I
National park, marine park	II
Natural landmark/National monument	III
Habitat/species management area	IV
National protected landscape or seascape	V
Managed resource protected area	VI

Source: Natural Resources Conservation Authority Policy for Jamaica's System of Protected Areas, Kingston, Jamaica, 1997.

Table 9.4 Jamaica's Protected Areas

Protected area	Date declared	Management body (NGO)
Montego Bay Marine Park	1992	Montego Bay Marine Park Trust
Blue and John Crow Mountains National Park	1993	Jamaica Conservation Development Trust
Negril Environmental Protection Area	1997	Negril Area Environmental Protection Trust
Negril Marine Park	1998	Negril Coral Reef Preservation Society
Palisadoes/Port Royal Protected Area	1998	
Coral Spring–Mountain Spring Protected Area	1998	
Portland Bight Protected Area	1999	Caribbean Coastal Area Management Foundation [C-CAM] and the Urban Development Corporation
Ocho Rios Marine Park	1999	Friends of the Sea
Mason River Protected Area	2002	Institute of Jamaica

Source: NEPA 2006 (*excludes 20 areas designated as game reserves*).

ecosystems. The idea is to create integrated land management units, and Jamaica has applied this principle for both protected area management and watershed management projects such as Ridge to Reef.[24]

While progress in designating new protected areas has been slow, introducing effective systems of management for those already declared has been even more problematic. Management functions have been delegated under several arrangements.[25] The Portland Bight Protected Area is an example of comanagement between the Caribbean Coastal Area Management (C-CAM) Foundation and local stakeholders/communities.[26] The boundary includes the regionally significant, dry limestone forest of the Hellshire Hills where the once thought extinct Jamaican iguana (*Cyclura collie*) was rediscovered in 1990, as well as Jamaica's main coastal fishery. The area has multiple resource

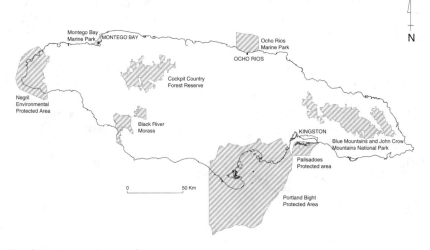

Map 9.1 Jamaica: Protected Areas
Source: Authors' Research.

management problems including overfishing, charcoal burning, pollution of the freshwater and marine ecosystems, and sedimentation from deforestation of inland watersheds.

Management efforts have met with varying degrees of success.[27] Although the NGOs have generated a fair amount of public education and interest for their protected areas, sustainable funding remains a major concern for them and the government and for the proper management of the areas.

The slow progress in designating protected areas is well illustrated by the case of the Cockpit Country. This region's unique conical karstic landscape combines a tropical wet limestone broadleaf rainforest with high biodiversity and endemism. Species diversity among its plants and animals is exceptional, and the area is a refuge for endangered endemic parrots and the Giant Swallowtail butterfly. While the core area is still relatively intact, there was 16 percent reduction in contiguous forests between 1981 and 1987.[28] The southern borders are particularly vulnerable to deforestation and encroachment from small farmers.[29] The forests are major sources of yam sticks, charcoal, and commercial hardwood timber.[30] Sections of the Cockpit Country have significant bauxite deposits, casting the specter of further environmental damage from bauxite mining.

The Cockpit Country is managed as a forest reserve and is worthy of World Heritage status.[31] The area's unique landforms and ecology have historical and cultural significance because the Leeward Maroons fought the British army here to a stalemate in military campaigns during the eighteenth century.[32] Despite active lobbying by groups such as South Trelawny Environmental Association (STEA) and the Windsor Research Centre, the Cockpit Country does not yet have national park status, nor has much progress been made on

managing land pressure around its sensitive border regions.[33] The Nature
Conservancy (TNC), through its Parks in Peril (PiP) program is working in
conjunction with the Forest Department and the local community in a number
of projects, including biodiversity and sustainable livelihoods.[34]

Generally speaking, the sustainability of the system of protected areas
seems to be in doubt and the momentum gained from the promulgation of
the policy in the early years after Agenda 21 has been lost. Since the mid-
1990s, less and less funding has been forthcoming from central government
to support existing declared protected areas, much less to designate others of
critical importance such as the Cockpit Country.[35] In terms of international
recognition three wetlands have been declared as Ramsar sites but the country has no world heritage site or biosphere reserve.

Forest Policy

The Forest Policy sought to establish goals and priorities pertaining to the
conservation and protection of forests and the sustainable management of
forested lands and watersheds.[36] Goals and priorities included the following:

- Forest lands have to be conserved to protect and enhance native and
  endemic flora and fauna.
- Mangrove forests must be conserved to protect coastal diversity and near-
  shore marine environments.
- Forest management is to support development of the National Park and
  Protected Areas System.
- Forests have to be protected from all threats including damage from fires,
  illegal cutting, theft of trees, illegal hunting, and soil erosion.
- There should be no net loss of forest cover permitted on lands owned by
  government. Where forest stands are wholly or partially cut or otherwise
  damaged, they should be promptly reforested with the same or other suitable species.
- Forested watershed should be conserved and managed to minimize flooding on communities, farms, roads, and bridges; minimize soil erosion,
  siltation of rivers, and sedimentation of near-shore marine environments to
  protect coral reefs and sea grass bed. Forest wastershed should also be
  managed to ensure an adequate supply of quality water for domestic consumption and other purposes.
- Soils and environmentally sensitive areas should be protected. Uses of forest land, including the removal of tree cover, should be limited according
  to slope, soil depth, and proximity to watercourses. Protective buffers of
  forest cover are to be maintained adjacent to waterways, streams, rivers,
  and wetlands.
- Degraded watersheds are to be rehabilitated and tree cover restored.

The strategies and tools for implementation included community participation, public awareness and environmental education, forest research, cooperative

management agreements, regulation of forest industries and forest land use, promotion of investment in forestry, forestry sector training and human resource development and planning and monitoring. Importantly because organizations such as the National Environment and Planning Agency (NEPA) and the Commissioner of Lands could have overlapping responsibilities in forest management, this policy also sets out explicitly the role that each agency is expected to play with respect to forestry.

The government of Jamaica and the Canadian International Development Agency (CIDA) through its Trees for Tomorrow project have provided substantial support over the past decade. Greater community participation was achieved through a pilot project in the Buff Bay/Pencar watersheds in eastern Jamaica. It resulted in the establishment of a Local Forestry Management Committee (LFMC) by residents who through their meetings expressed an interest in obtaining harvesting licenses for timber in the forest reserves, participating in reforestation and serving as honorary forest wardens.[37] Lessons learned in attempts to build community participation include the need for resources (human and financial) to initiate the process, the need to build trust among the community and for the government agency to act as a catalyst, and the need to temper the community expectations that often exceed the initial intentions of the process. Further success with this approach will be very much dependent on resources available to the Forestry Department.[38]

Conclusion

In the post-Agenda 21 era, Jamaica has addressed land and natural resources management in a variety of comprehensive ways, including promulgation of new policies where previous policies were lacking or in need of revision. This chapter has highlighted three policy areas: land policy, parks and protected areas, and forest policy. Each was formulated through an extensive consultative process of public discussions and meetings held across the country. The meetings benefited from substantial input from members of the public who attended. For example, it was through these meetings that many candidate sites for inclusion in the Policy for a System of Parks and Protected Areas were identified. The success the Forest Department has achieved with private landowners with regard to tree planting was also directly related to information provided at such public meetings.

While three major policy initiatives have been the focus of this chapter, several others are still the subject of deliberation either within organizations, in the public domain, or at the level of Cabinet. These include the following:

• Policy for Use of Foreshore and Floor of the Sea (Draft);
• Coral Reef Protection and Preservation Policy and Regulation (Draft);
• Wetlands Policy (Draft);
• Watershed Management Policy (Draft); and
• National Hazard and Mitigation Policy (Draft).

Successful conclusion of these and other initiatives would further contribute to improving management of the country's resources.[39]

The policy landscape in recent years has been dynamic, adaptive, and has evolved as different issues emerge. There is a well-established system to generate new policies with the appropriate public participatory component. While there will always be the need for new policy initiatives (e.g., currently no policies govern the protection of rivers, caves and offshore cays), those already in place have attempted to address many critical development issues. It is clear that others in draft form need to be quickly finalized.

Critically, however, the successful implementation of many of these innovative land management policies introduced since Agenda 21 have been stymied by inadequate funding from central government to provide essential support for human and physical resources. The country's persistent economic problems, most recently, the crisis brought about by the overzealous liberalization of the financial sector in the early 1990s, continue to adversely affect all areas of central government policy.

Notes

1. United Nations Division on Sustainable Development (UNDSD), *Agenda 21* (New York: UN Department of Economic and Social Affairs, 2004), http://www.un.org/ esa/sustdev/documents/agenda21/english.
2. SIDSNET   (http://sidsnet.org/docshare/other/20040219161354_sids_statistic.pdf).
3. C. H. Douglas, "Development Typologies, Strategies and Priorities for Small Island States," *Caribbean Geography* 13, no. 2 (2005): 110–113.
4. D. F. M. McGregor and D. Barker, "A Geographical Focus for Environment and Development in the Caribbean," in D. Barker and D. F. M. McGregor (eds.), *Environment and Development in the Caribbean: Geographical Perspectives* (Kingston, Jamaica: UWI Press, 1995), 3–17.
5. R. B. Potter, D. Barker, D. Conway, and T. Klak, *The Contemporary Caribbean* (Harlow, UK: Pearson/Prentice Hall, 2004), 36–37.
6. *Caribbean Environmental Outlook* (Nairobi, Kenya: UNEP/CARICOM, 2005).
7. L. A. Miller, *Integrated Environmental Management and Planning* (Handbook prepared for Management Institute for National Development [MIND] Project of the Environmental Action Programme [ENACT], Kingston, Jamaica, 2001).
8. D. Barker, "A Periphery in Genesis and Exodus: Reflections on Rural-Urban Relations in Jamaica," in Robert B. Potter and T. Unwin (eds.), *The Geography of Urban-Rural Interaction in Developing Countries* (London: Routledge, 1989), 294–322.
9. FAO (Food and Agriculture Organization of the United Nations), *Latin America and the Caribbean National Forest Programmes* (Santiago, Chile: FAO Regional Office, 1998).
10. O. B. Evelyn and R. Camirand, "Forest Cover and Deforestation in Jamaica: An Analysis of Forest Cover Estimates over Time," *International Forestry Review* 5, no. 4 (2003): 354–362.
11. http://www.earthtrends.wri.org.

12. Planning Institute Of Jamaica (PIOJ), *Economic and Social Survey of Jamaica* (Kingston, Jamaica: PIOJ, 2001).

13. V. L. Kerr, "Corporate Governance in the context of Globalization," in Madhav Mehra (ed.), *Corporate Governance Challenges in a Disparate World: Driving Globalization without Its Discontents*, World Council for Corporate Governance, April 25, 2004, 17–25, http://www.wcfcg.net/ICCG%205.pdf (last accessed, February 19, 2007).

14. Wilberne Persaud, *Jamaican Meltdown: Indigenous Financial Sector Crash 1996* (Lincoln, Nebraska: Iuniverse Publishers, 2006).

15. Jamaica National Environmental Action Plan (JANEAP), *Natural Resources Conservation Authority with Planning Institute of Jamaica* and *Jamaica: State of the Environment*. Reports, 1995, 1997, and 2001 (Kingston, Jamaica: NRCA, Government of Jamaica, 2002).

16. J. daCosta, *Land Policy, Administration and Management Case Study Jamaica* (Workshop on Land Policy, Administration and Management in the English-Speaking Caribbean, Trinidad and Tobago, March 19–21, 2003), http://www.basis.wisc.edu/event_Caribbean.html.

17. daCosta, *Land Policy, Administration and Management Case Study Jamaica*.

18. daCosta, *Land Policy, Administration and Management Case Study Jamaica*.

19. NRCA Green Paper, *Policy for Jamaica's System of Protected Areas* (Kingston, Jamaica: Government of Jamaica, 1997).

20. NRCA/NEPA Green Paper No. 3/01, *Towards a National Strategy and Action Plan on Biological Diversity in Jamaica* (Kingston, Jamaica: Government of Jamaica, 2001).

21. http://www.iucn.org/themes/wcpa.

22. A. Phillips and J. Harrison, "The Framework for International Standards in Establishing National Parks and Protected Areas," in S. Stolton and N. Dudley (eds.), *Partnerships for Protection: New Strategies for Planning and Management for Protected Areas* (London: Earthscan, 1999), 13–17.

23. NRCA Green Paper, *Policy for Jamaica's System of Protected Areas*.

24. Ridge to Reef Project, Government of Jamaica, NEPA/USAID, 2000–2005.

25. M. Figueroa, "Co-Management and Valuation of Caribbean Coral Reefs: A Jamaican NGO Perspective," Worldfish Center, http://www.worldfishcenter.org/Pubs/coral_reef/pdf/section3-5.pdf (last accessed February 19, 2007).

26. CCAM Foundation, *Portland Bight Protected Area Management Plan, 1999–2004* (Clarendon, Jamaica: CCAM [Caribbean Coastal Area Management] Foundation Publishers, 1999).

27. Figueroa, "Co-Management and Valuation of Caribbean Coral Reefs."

28. L. A. Eyre, "The Slow Death of a Tropical Rainforest: The Cockpit Country of Jamaica, West Indies," in M. Luria, Y. Steinberger, and E. Spanier (eds.), *Environmental Quality and Ecosystem Stability* (Jerusalem: Environmental Quality, ISEQS Pub., 1989), IV-A: 599–606.

29. D. Barker, "Yam Farmers on the Edge of Cockpit Country: Aspects of Resource Use and Sustainability," in D. F. M. McGregor, D. Barker, and S. Lloyd Evans (eds.), *Resource Sustainability and Caribbean Development* (Kingston, Jamaica: UWI Press, 1998), 357–372.

30. D. Barker and C. Beckford, "Yam Production and the Yam Stick Trade in Jamaica: Integrated Problems for Planning and Resource Management," in D. Barker and D. F. M. McGregor (eds.) *Resources, Planning and*

Environmental Management in a Changing Caribbean (Kingston, Jamaica: UWI Press, 2003), 57–74.

31. L. A. Eyre, "The Cockpit Country: A World Heritage Site?" in Barker and McGregor (eds.), *Environment and Development in the Caribbean*, 259–270.
32. L. A. Eyre, "The Maroon Wars in Jamaica—A Geographical Appraisal," *Jamaica Historical Review* 12 (1980): 80–102.
33. http://www.cockpitcountry.com.
34. The Nature Conservancy, Parks in Peril, 2005, http://parksinperil.org/wherewework/Caribbean/Jamaica/protectedarea/cockpit.html (last accessed, February 19, 2007).
35. L. A. Miller, "Perspectives on the Sustainability of Protected Areas in Jamaica," *Caribbean Geography* 10, no. 1 (1999): 52–62.
36. Forest Department, *Forest Policy* (Kingston, Jamaica: Government of Jamaica, 2001).
37. T. Geoghegan and N. Bennett, *Risking Change: Experimenting with Local Forest Management Committees in Jamaica.* CANARI Technical Report No. 308 (Laventille, Trinidad and Tobago: Caribbean Natural Resources Institute [CANARI], 2002).
38. M. Headley, "Participatory Forest Management: The Jamaica Forestry Department Experience," *Unasylva* 54, no. 214/215 (2003): 44–49.
39. L. Davis-Mattis, "Jamaica's Commitment to the Conservation and Management of Natural Resources" (National Environment Planning Agency Discussion Paper, 2002).

Part III

Land for the Peasantry?

Chapter 10

"Squatting" as a Strategy for Land Settlement and Sustainable Development

Jean Besson

Introduction

Informal occupation or "squatting" is an escalating phenomenon in the postcolonial world. As Robert Home and Hilary Lim observed in 2004, "The millions of people in the world who lack access to land where they can find secure shelter present a great global challenge to law, governance and civil society. About half of the world's population (three billion people) now live in urban areas, and nearly a billion are estimated to be living in informal, illegal settlements, mostly in the urban and peri-urban areas of less developed countries."[1] At the turn of the millennium, Hernando de Soto argued that such poverty can only be reduced by replacing customary land tenure with legal property rights,[2] and (as Home and Lim summarize) that such property rights "are the hidden infrastructure that can help achieve sustainable development goals."[3]

These global issues of land and development are reflected in the Caribbean region, the world's oldest colonial/postcolonial sphere, where land tenure and use have been controversial in relation to plantations, peasants, and towns since the European conquest of 1492.[4] Here too, as elsewhere in the developing world, rapid urbanization has been a major process of social change since the mid-twentieth century.[5] David Satterthwaite noted in 2002 that "[m]ore than two-thirds of the world's urban population is now in Africa, Asia, Latin America and the Caribbean. . . . Africa now has a larger urban population than Northern America; so too does Latin America and the Caribbean—which also has close to three-quarters of its population living in urban centres."[6] Informal occupation or squatting is a significant theme in this increasing urbanization in the Caribbean region, as studies including Trinidad, Jamaica, Puerto Rico, Martinique, and Barbados show.[7]

Moreover, urbanization took place in the Caribbean long before the mid-twentieth century—as the region was "urbanized" by pronounced plantation systems with "factories in the field," even during slavery and by the development of rural proletariats after emancipation.[8] In addition, Caribbean "squatter peasantries" emerged soon after the conquest in opposition to the plantations, especially in the mountainous interiors of the Greater Antilles. These early squatter peasants were wiped out by the escalating plantation system and replaced by postindentured "early yeomen," "protopeasant" plantation slaves, "runaway peasantries" (escaped slaves or maroons), and postslavery peasants in free villages and in posttreaty maroon polities.[9] However, squatter peasants reemerged in the Caribbean region, for example, in Jamaica, Trinidad, and the Eastern Caribbean including Barbuda.[10]

Within these contexts, a conference on land policy, administration, and management in the Caribbean in 2003 highlighted that international donor agencies and Caribbean nation-states have embarked on intensive land registration and land titling in the region.[11] This approach is consistent with de Soto's recommendations and with colonial/postcolonial critiques of Caribbean peasants and their customary tenures as obstacles to development.[12] However, at that conference I argued that, in the drive to expand land markets, a secure place needs to be found for Creole tenures rooted in Caribbean history, culture, and land.[13]

In that paper and other works, I focused on "family land" and "common land" embedded in kinship and community.[14] This chapter takes those perspectives further, highlighting the importance of informal occupation or "squatting" on "captured land" as a strategy for land settlement and sustainable development. Against the global and Caribbean regional backgrounds, I focus on informal occupation as a creative mode of land and development in western Jamaica, at the Caribbean core, where I have undertaken fieldwork in three parishes (Trelawny, St. Elizabeth, and St. James) from 1968 to 2007.[15] This part of Jamaica was the heart of plantation slavery in the island and is characterized by postcolonial land monopolization through persisting plantations, bauxite mining, and tourism. This area also has a history of pronounced peasantization. Here, runaway slaves "captured" Crown Land and established an enduring maroon polity and former "protopeasant" slaves founded persisting free villages, through squatting and land purchase. Here also, some of the descendants of plantation slaves are creating vibrant squatter settlements in overlapping contexts of peasantization and urbanization.[16]

From "Squatting" to an Enduring Maroon Polity

My research in western Jamaica included fieldwork in Accompong Town (formerly Accompong's Town and also known as Accompong) in St. Elizabeth, in the southern area of the precipitous Cockpit Country that straddles the interior of the adjoining parishes of Trelawny, St. Elizabeth, and St. James. Accompong is the only surviving village of the historic Jamaican Leeward Maroon polity and is the oldest persisting corporate maroon society in African-America.[17] Its history is rooted in seventeenth- and eighteenth-century marronage, when enslaved Africans and Creoles escaped from the lowland plantations into the Cockpits and squatted on Crown Land. Such informal occupation of colonial state land provided a base for successful guerrilla warfare against the British colonists in the First Maroon War of 1725–1738 under the leadership of Colonel Cudjoe.

This captured land also became the basis for the establishment of two Leeward Maroon villages: the primary settlement of Cudjoe's Town in St. James and the secondary community of Accompong's Town in St. Elizabeth (led by Captain Accompong, Cudjoe's "brother"). After Colonel Cudjoe forced the British colonists to sue for peace, a colonial treaty was signed in March 1739 between Cudjoe and Edward Trelawny, the British Governor of Jamaica, which granted the maroons their freedom and 1,500 acres of legal freehold land. This land grant consolidated the captured land of Cudjoe's Town, renamed Trelawny Town after the treaty. However, Accompong's Town continued to informally occupy Crown Land until the land grant to the Leeward Maroons was increased to 2,559 acres around 1758.[18]

In 1795–1796 the Second Maroon War was fought between the Trelawny Town Maroons and the British colonists. The war was triggered by an incident involving the whipping of two maroons by the colonial authorities for the theft of two pigs in Montego Bay but was fueled by a deeper discontent regarding access to land.[19] Following this war, the Trelawny Maroons were betrayed by the colonists and deported to Nova Scotia, and their lands were confiscated by the colonial state.[20] It was in the aftermath of these events that Accompong Town became the sole surviving village of the Leeward polity.

Today Accompong Town's common treaty land, which evolved from captured land, sustains a voting population of around 3,300 adults who claim descent from Cudjoe. The maroon-peasant economy is based on the cultivation of food-forests in house yards and provision grounds, cash cropping, rearing livestock, and utilizing the forest for medicines and timber. Production is for household use and sale to peasant markets on the plains, and bananas, sugarcane, and yams are sometimes sold for export. Since the rocky road to Accompong was built in the 1940s, the maroon economy has included labor migration, and some maroons reside elsewhere in the island or in England and the United States. Such migrants retain inalienable rights to the commons and often return to live or visit.[21]

The common treaty land is, however, not only the basis of a transnational peasant economy. This land has also been transformed into a sacred landscape (with symbolic groves and graves reinforced by Myal ritual),[22] which is the anchor of maroon culture, society, and identity; a symbol of Jamaican nationhood; and the springboard of a developing heritage-tourism industry.[23] The land captured by their ancestors has therefore sustained the Accompong Maroons into the twenty-first century. This sustainable development has included standing fast in the face of recent external attempts to "develop" the commons through individualization of the treaty land in the contexts of the international tourist and bauxite-mining industries. Such attempts, which would enable land subdivision, titling, sale, and taxation, are part of a global trend to expand land markets into the new millennium.[24]

Squatting and Postslavery Peasantization

In contrast to Accompong, where squatting laid the foundation of an enduring maroon polity based on treaty land, the lands of Cudjoe's Town/Trelawny Town in St. James evolved from captured land to treaty land to confiscated land (after the deportation of the Trelawny Maroons in 1796). However, my research in Maroon Town (a community established on the site of Trelawny Town and renamed in memory of the deported maroons) reveals that the Trelawny Town lands were subsequently purchased and transformed into family lands by the descendants of slaves, planters, and maroons within the context of Jamaican postslavery peasantization. Squatting again played a part in this development. My research indicates that by the 1840s, a few years after Emancipation in 1838, squatters from Me-No-Sen-You-No-Com (a nontreaty foraging squatter settlement of mulatto maroons who captured Crown Land in the Cockpits of Trelawny Parish a few miles from Trelawny Town, from the time of the Second Maroon War until 1823) purchased the confiscated land, developed a postslavery village, and created family lands. On these lands (augmented by more recently purchased and rented lands) Maroon Town has developed as a banana-farming and migrant labor community, which is anchored by the family lands and kin-based cemeteries of its Old Families and is also developing a heritage-tourism industry.[25]

More direct continuity between captured land, purchased land, and family land can be identified in the free villages of Aberdeen in St. Elizabeth and Martha Brae in Trelawny. Evidence from archives, fieldwork, and oral tradition indicates that Aberdeen was established in the southeastern foothills of the Cockpit Country in the 1840s, a few years after Emancipation, by ex-slaves from Aberdeen Estate bordering the maroon commons (augmented by some maroons who "came out" from Accompong) who squatted on plantation mountains south of Aberdeen estate nearer to the plains.[26] Narratives recount that such captured land was then surveyed and subdivided for sale, enabling the squatters to purchase land and the colonial government to impose taxation. This oral tradition is consistent with historical accounts of government land retrieval, registration, land sale, and taxation that took place in Jamaica, especially in the 1860s and 1870s under Crown Colony government in the aftermath of the Morant Bay Rebellion of 1865—and at around this time Aberdeen became a Moravian free village.[27]

Many landholdings in Aberdeen today are family lands transmitted from such squatters and land purchasers. These family lands, which interrelate with more recently purchased land and rented land, sustain the community by providing the basis for cultivating food crops and cash cropping in bananas, sugarcane, and yams. With their burial grounds, these family lands also provide sites of identity for transnational cognatic lineages whose members include migrants in North America and Britain.

Martha Brae was established around 1762 as the first town in the eastern part of old St. James. Laid out on the edge of Holland Estate, on the Martha Brae River about 2 miles inland from the coast, it was founded to import enslaved Africans for the surrounding plantations and to export plantation products to England. When the new parish of Trelawny was created out of the eastern part of old St. James in 1771, Martha Brae became Trelawny's first capital. However, by around 1800, Martha Brae was eclipsed by the new slave-trading seaport of Falmouth, which became the parish capital. By the 1840s, the former colonial planter town of Martha Brae was appropriated by ex-slaves, from the adjoining plantations of Holland and Irving Tower, and transformed into a free village in association with the Baptist Church at the vanguard of the flight from the Caribbean estates. Informal occupation or squatting by emancipated slaves between 1838 and 1840 played a central role in this transformation. After the planter-controlled parish Vestry, who owned the captured lots, retrieved the land for sale, titling, and taxation, the freed slaves purchased the lots from the Vestry, created family lands, and developed their kin groups, economy, and community which have sustained their descendants into the twenty-first century.[28]

By 2006, Martha Brae had been impacted by the Jamaican transisland highway (Highway 2000) that passes immediately along the northern boundary of the village, which is once again taking on the appearance of a town with the escalating replacement of wooden cottages by concrete houses financed with migrant earnings and remittances. This highway is welcomed by some people in Martha Brae, as providing easier access to the cities of Montego Bay and Kingston. However, it has had a more controversial impact on Martha Brae's satellite squatter settlement of Zion established at the Holland plantation during the period of my fieldwork (1968–2006) and on Zion's adjoining squatter swamp at Lyon's Morass, as discussed below.

Squatter Peasants and Urban Development

When I began my fieldwork in the free village of Martha Brae in 1968, there were no houses on that part of the Holland plantation (bordering Martha Brae) owned by the Trelawny Parish Council (which succeeded the Parochial Board, successor to the Vestry) now known as "Zion." But an immigrant from St. James who had bought a house yard in Martha Brae (and who became a leading Revival-Zionist there), had just captured land at Holland for a provision ground.[29] By the end of 1968, one chattel cottage had been established on captured land at Holland and two others followed in 1971. All three households were headed by established immigrants in Martha Brae, who had been tenants on the land of other villagers.

A few more chattel houses were moved to Zion in 1972, "cotched"[30] defiantly behind the Parish Council's "No Squatting" sign, and by 1979 the area contained around 30 households many of whom were Revival-Zionists and Rastafarians—who have made their "Zion" on this captured land in "Babylon." By 1995 Zion had become a vibrant squatter settlement of some 70 house yards (including a Revival tabernacle, Revival balm yards, and a Rastafarian "Uprising Club"), consolidated on about 30 acres of captured land, and the Parish Council was surveying and subdividing the land with a view to retrieval, sales, titling, and taxation. Water and electricity had been installed and metered, though not all households could afford these services. At the turn of the millennium, although no land sales had been made these were anticipated and Zion (which by then had several small grocery shops and rocky roads) was being referred to as a "town."[31] This was still the situation in 2006.

The capturing of land at Zion provides a vivid illustration of the process of informal occupation that has been a recurring theme of land and development in the Caribbean region, including western Jamaica, since the European Conquest. As this "squatting" occurred at Zion throughout the period of my fieldwork, this also provided a unique opportunity to understand the entire process of this strategy of land settlement.

Tom and Mary Grant were the founders of Zion, having "captured" land there in 1968—soon after I first met them in Martha Brae, where they had settled as landless "Strangers" in the 1950s. Until 1968, they lived as tenants in three different yards belonging to Old Families in Martha Brae: first in little rented houses on family land and then in a wooden chattel cottage of their own on a house spot leased on family land—where I had first met them. Shortly after, they decided to acquire land of their own on the Holland plantation. In 1995, when I interviewed them again (and when Mary explained that "[o]nly little piece [of land] we capture here now fe weself"), they had been together for nearly 50 years. Tom was by then retired, from cutting sugarcane on Holland and Hampden Estates and harvesting cane in the United States. Mary used to help him cut cane at Hampden and Holland but now worked in their own house yard, though she still did an occasional day's wage labor washing clothes. By then, in addition to her seven children, she had a "whole heap" of grandchildren, great grandchildren, and great, great grandchildren and had become a Revivalist (besides being a member of the Falmouth Baptist Church).

Mary described how she and her family had moved to Zion. They first moved their chattel house by truck to the "bottom road" (the south side of the Carib Road, which now forms the northern boundary of Zion), but they had been evicted from that spot by the police, the Parish Council, and a court case. However, a partially successful legal defense had resulted in a compromise whereby they were able to relocate (from an area where building had initially been planned) to their present house spot that is now the heart of Zion (called "Top Zion" by 2006). There was neither water nor electricity when they first captured the land; now both facilities were available in the squatter settlement. They themselves had water in the yard but could not afford electricity.

Tom and Mary created a house yard on the captured land. They erected a fence, planted ackee and breadfruit trees, cultivated pumpkins and bananas, and kept chickens in a coop. When they brought the cottage from Martha Brae it was just a two-roomed board house on pillars, but at Zion they added a third wooden room and a concrete verandah. They also built three outhouses: a kitchen, a shower, and a pit-latrine. Tom and Mary appreciated that the

Parish Council had now "run out" (surveyed and subdivided) the land at Zion and intended to sell "lots" but felt that their future was uncertain and unclear and were worried about raising the cash for the potential purchase. If they were able to buy the land, they intended to leave it for those of their children who are landless, thereby creating family land to sustain those in need. However, when Tom died in 1998 (at which time Revival wakes were held in his house yard at Zion and he was buried in the Martha Brae cemetery), he was still a squatter peasant.[32]

In 2006 Mary was still at Zion, where some of her adult children have now established their own house yards. One of Mary's daughters also has a shop there. Another daughter, a Revivalist who lives at Zion, is a dry-goods higgler at Falmouth's Ben' Down Market, the largest transnational rural market in Jamaica.[33]

The second house yard at Zion was established by Cynthia and Owen Rogers in 1971. I first interviewed Cynthia in 1968, when they were living in a chattel cottage on a house spot that they had leased in the yard of long-established Strangers who had purchased land in Martha Brae, and they later moved this cottage on a truck to Zion. I interviewed Cynthia again in the 1990s there, where they had extended their cottage which by then had running water and electricity. They had made a yard around the house, planting bananas and breadfruit, avocado, mango, citrus, and ackee trees. Cynthia was not sure of the size of her yard (which is only a few square chains) but thought it might be two "lots" in terms of the Parish Council's subdivision: "Dem decide to sell us [the land] now. Dem seh dem 'lot' it out, but dem don't tell me is one lot me getting, or two lots, or whatever. But they are looking at it." Cynthia, who like the Grants lived at the heart of Zion (now Top Zion), described the establishment and growth of the squatter settlement:

> Mary Grant was living at the bottom. But after a while dem move her and tell her to come up here, 'cause the Mayor [of the Parish Council] never want any houses down on the bottom road. But after a while the people them were *flowing* on the land and they [the Council] never want it like that, because them did want the land to sell. So them tell her to move come up here. And then after now, the people them *still* disobey and them go down there [to the bottom road]. . . . [P]eople still pass [disregard] them order and go on the land and *live*.[34]

Owen died in 1994, but Cynthia was still at Zion in 2006.

Discussion with the Parish Council and its land surveyor in 1995 provided a legal viewpoint on the squatter settlement. Since the 1950s the Parish Council has owned the part of Holland plantation now informally occupied as Zion. They estimated the captured land as 30 acres and confirmed that there were around 70 households that had settled there. Zion had been surveyed and subdivided into 146 lots. Any house yard considered too large had been subdivided into two or three lots, ranging from around one-seventh to one-quarter of an acre and the land is likely to be sold by the square meter (being just

2 miles inland from the world-famous tourist North Coast). From a confrontational situation between 1968 and 1979, the Council had now adopted a placatory position. Its aim is to resolve the "potentially explosive situation" by imposing a legal freehold land settlement (with reduced land-holdings) on the squatter camp, in order to register the squatters as legal titled occupiers on the Land Tax Roll—even though they did not apply to buy the land. Metered services had also been introduced or improved.[35]

In 2006, however, this formalization of Zion was still pending. Meanwhile, the Holland plantation had been further urbanized by the sale of land adjoining Zion to the Catholic Church, which has established the Holland High School. The Revivalist-Rastafarian squatter settlement is therefore now bordered by this school on one side and the Baptist Church's William Knibb High School on the other.

The imminent formalization of Zion, established on the southern side of the Carib Road at Holland, both compares and contrasts with the situation of those "squatters" who captured land on the north side of the Carib Road. That land is on Cave Island Pen or Lyon's Morass,[36] an area of protected swamp that was owned by the Agricultural Development Corporation of the Jamaican government's Lands Commission. By 2001 these squatters had been given notice of eviction on the ecological grounds that, with no organized amenities, effluence is seeping into the swamp and is in danger of destroying the nutrients that feed the fish life in the sea by Falmouth and that cutting of the mangrove for building and charcoal burning is having a similar effect.[37]

However, in 2006 these squatters were still there, the captured swamp was now controlled by the government's Urban Development Corporation, and the squatters' situation had worsened due to the construction of the transisland highway. Since 2005, a section of the highway has been completed to pass immediately behind and above the squatter swamp (bypassing Falmouth and along the northern boundary of Martha Brae). This highway has blocked the "gully course" or drainage from further inland, causing flooding of the squatters' houses when it rains. The government has promised to install larger drainage culverts, and there is an ongoing discourse regarding the relocation of the squatters to the government land settlement at Hague, on the eastern side of Martha Brae.

Meanwhile, government development plans are moving forward, in the context of heritage tourism, for the architectural restoration of colonial Georgian Falmouth which is now a World Heritage Site. To facilitate this tourist development (in time for the Cricket World Cup in 2007), which includes restoring slave masters' town houses and establishing a slavery museum, squatters descended from plantation slaves have been relocated within the former slave-trading planter town.[38]

Conclusion

This chapter has examined, in global and Caribbean regional contexts, the role of informal occupation or "squatting" in the overlapping processes of peasantization and urbanization in western Jamaica, highlighting examples where captured land has laid the foundations of a maroon polity, postslavery villages, a plantation town, and a squatter swamp. These examples show that (with the possible exception of the squatter swamp) squatting can provide a basis for viable land settlement and sustainable development, including transformation to legal property rights such as treaty land and purchased land. These examples further show that such legal property rights may then become transformed again into Creole tenures (e.g., family land and sacred land) that reflect Caribbean culture building in the face of colonial/postcolonial land monopoly.[39] This conclusion is reinforced by Home and Lim's critique of de Soto (that draws on my work on Caribbean family land and related studies in Trinidad and Africa), which highlights "the role of colonial and postcolonial governments in constructing exclusion and illegality"[40] and recommends that "[w]ithout more participatory local strategies, the management of land, that most basic resource of the modern territorial nation-State, will not meet the needs of 'the poor.'"[41] My analysis likewise advances a wider social science approach that situates ethnography and "indigenous knowledge" at the heart of sustainable development.[42] This chapter underlines the significance of this ethnographic approach by highlighting the role of the local Creole wisdom of squatters at the heart of the Caribbean, a region that has been Eurocentrically described as the Third World's third world but that is more accurately explored as the First World's first annex.[43]

Notes

1. Robert Home and Hilary Lim, "Introduction: Demystifying 'The Mystery of Capital,' " in Robert Home and Hilary Lim (eds.), *Demystifying the Mystery of Capital: Land Tenure and Poverty in Africa and the Caribbean* (London: Cavendish, 2004), 1. Informal occupation is also found in the so-called First World; e.g., in 2005 a London Borough Council evicted squatters (including a Rastafarian) after a 30-year dispute over the informal occupation of council housing (BBC TV News, November 29, 2005). Likewise, in 2006, a court ruling evicted Irish "travelers" or gypsies from council property in Yorkshire, England (BBC TV News, March 8, 2006).
2. Hernando de Soto, *The Mystery of Capital: Why Capitalism Triumphs in the West and Fails Everywhere Else* (London: Black Swan, 2000).
3. Home and Lim, *Demystifying the Mystery of Capital*, 149.
4. Sidney W. Mintz, "Enduring Substances, Trying Theories: The Caribbean Region as *Oikoumenê*," *Journal of the Royal Anthropological Institute* 2, no. 2 (1996): 289–311.
5. Vandana Desai and Robert B. Potter (eds.), *The Companion to Development Studies* (London: Arnold, 2002), 241.
6. David Satterthwaite, "Urbanization in Developing Countries," in Desai and Potter (eds.), *The Companion to Development Studies*, 243.
7. Charisse Griffith-Charles, "Trinidad: 'We Are Not Squatters, We Are Settlers,'" in Home and Lim (eds.), *Demystifying the Mystery of Capital*, 99–119; Jimmy Tindigarukayo, "The Squatter Problem in Jamaica," *Social and Economic Studies* 51, no. 4 (2002): 95–125; Helen I. Safa, *The Urban Poor of Puerto Rico*

(New York: Holt, Rinehart and Winston, 1974); Michel S. Laguerre, *Urban Poverty in the Caribbean* (New York: St. Martin's Press, 1990); Robert B. Potter, *The Urban Caribbean in an Era of Global Change* (Aldershot: Ashgate, 2000); M. Watson and R. Potter, *Low-Cost Housing in Barbados* (Barbados: University of the West Indies Press, 2001).

8. Sidney W. Mintz, "The Caribbean as a Socio-Cultural Area," in Michael M. Horowitz (ed.), *Peoples and Cultures of the Caribbean* (Garden City: Natural History Press, 1971), 38.

9. Sidney W. Mintz, *Caribbean Transformations* (New York: Columbia University Press, 1989), 146–179; Richard Price (ed.), *Maroon Societies: Rebel Slave Communities in the Americas.* 3rd ed. (Baltimore: Johns Hopkins University Press, 1996); Jean Besson, *Martha Brae's Two Histories: European Expansion and Caribbean Culture-Building in Jamaica* (Chapel Hill: University of North Carolina Press, 2002); Jean Besson, "Sacred Sites, Shifting Histories: Narratives of Belonging, Land and Globalisation in the Cockpit Country, Jamaica," in Jean Besson and Karen Fog Olwig (eds.), *Caribbean Narratives of Belonging: Fields of Relations, Sites of Identity* (Oxford: Macmillan), 17–43.

10. Jean Besson, "Religion as Resistance in Jamaican Peasant Life," in Barry Chevannes (ed.), *Rastafari and Other African-Caribbean Worldviews*, Institute of Social Studies (The Hague and London: Macmillan, 1995), 43–76; Besson, *Martha Brae's Two Histories*; Thackwray (Dax) Driver, "Watershed Management, Private Property and Squatters in the Northern Range, Trinidad," *IDS Bulletin* 33, no. 1 (2002): 84–93; David Lowenthal and Colin Clarke, chapter 11, this volume.

11. Allan N. Williams (ed.), *Land in the Caribbean: Proceedings of a Workshop on Land Policy, Administration and Management in the English-Speaking Caribbean* (Port of Spain, Trinidad and Tobago: Land Tenure Center, University of Wisconsin-Madison, March 19–21, 2003).

12. de Soto, *The Mystery of Capital*; Mintz, *Caribbean Transformations*, 146–147; Driver, "Watershed Management"; Besson, *Martha Brae's Two Histories*, 195.

13. Jean Besson, "History, Culture and Land in the English-Speaking Caribbean," Feature Address in Williams (ed.), *Land in the Caribbean*, 31–60.

14. For example, Jean Besson, "Caribbean Common Tenures and Capitalism: The Accompong Maroons of Jamaica," *Plantation Society in the Americas* IV, nos. 2 and 3 (1997): 201–232; Jean Besson, "The Appropriation of Lands of Law by Lands of Myth in the Caribbean Region," in Allen Abramson and Dimitris Theodossopoulos (eds.), *Land, Law and Environment: Mythical Land, Legal Boundaries* (London: Pluto Press, 2000), 116–135; Besson, *Martha Brae's Two Histories*; Besson, "Sacred Sites, Shifting Histories."

15. I undertook fieldwork in the free villages of Martha Brae, The Alps, Refuge, Kettering and Granville, the town of Falmouth, and the squatter settlements of Zion and Lyon's Morass in Trelawny (1968–2006); Accompong and Aberdeen in St. Elizabeth (1979–2007); and Maroon Town, St. James (1999–2007). I am grateful to the British Academy, the Carnegie Trust, the Nuffield Foundation, the Social Science Research Council, the University of Aberdeen, and Goldsmiths College, University of London, for financial support.

16. Besson, "Caribbean Common Tenures and Capitalism"; Besson, *Martha Brae's Two Histories*; Besson, "Sacred Sites, Shifting Histories"; and Jean Besson,

Transformations of Freedom in the Land of the Maroons (Kingston, Jamaica: Ian Randle, forthcoming).

17. Besson, "Caribbean Common Tenures and Capitalism."
18. Mavis C. Campbell, *The Maroons of Jamaica 1655–1796: A History of Resistance, Collaboration and Betrayal* (Trenton: Africa World Press, 1990), 127, 181–183.
19. The whipping of the maroons was carried out by a runaway slave in the presence of slaves, which exacerbated the humiliation of the maroons. Carey Robinson, *The Fighting Maroons of Jamaica* (Kingston, Jamaica: Collins and Sangster, 1969), 82.
20. Campbell, *The Maroons of Jamaica*, 243.
21. David Barker and Balfour Spence, "Afro-Caribbean Agriculture: A Jamaican Maroon Community in Transition," *Geographical Journal* 154, no. 2 (1988): 198–208; Besson, "Caribbean Common Tenures and Capitalism."
22. Myal ritual in Accompong focuses on the ancestral spirits of the First-Time Maroons.
23. Besson, "Caribbean Common Tenures and Capitalism"; Besson, "Sacred Sites, Shifting Histories"; Besson, *Transformations of Freedom.*
24. Besson, "Caribbean Common Tenures and Capitalism"; Besson, *Transformations of Freedom.*
25. Besson, "Sacred Sites, Shifting Histories"; Besson, *Transformations of Freedom.*
26. Besson, "Caribbean Common Tenures and Capitalism"; Besson, "The Appropriation of Lands of Law."
27. Claus Stolberg and Swithin Wilmot (eds.), *Plantation Economy, Land Reform and the Peasantry in a Historical Perspective: Jamaica 1838–1980* (Kingston, Jamaica: Friedrich Ebert Siftung, 1992); Besson, "The Appropriation of Lands of Law"; Besson, *Transformations of Freedom.*
28. Besson, *Martha Brae's Two Histories.*
29. Besson, *Martha Brae's Two Histories*, 248.
30. In Jamaican Creole, "cotched" indicates temporary and precarious settlement.
31. Besson, *Martha Brae's Two Histories*, 151.
32. Besson, *Martha Brae's Two Histories*, 151–153.
33. See Besson, *Martha Brae's Two Histories*, 203–208.
34. Besson, *Martha Brae's Two Histories*, 153–154. As another resident at Zion said in 2006: "We all capture the land and just tek a chance!"
35. Besson, *Martha Brae's Two Histories*, 156.
36. Holland was at one time owned by the English Lyon planter family, see Besson, *Martha Brae's Two Histories*, 331 (n. 37).
37. Besson, *Martha Brae's Two Histories*, 156, 335 (n. 30).
38. Hon. Kingsley C. Thomas, OJ, "New Developments for the Restoration of Falmouth, Jamaica" (presentation to The Friends of the Georgian Society of Jamaica, London, February 21, 2006).
39. And therefore transformations among various types of peasant formations.
40. Home and Lim, *Demystifying the Mystery of Capital*, 149.
41. Home and Lim, *Demystifying the Mystery of Capital*, 155.
42. Jean Besson and Janet Momsen (eds.), *Land and Development in the Caribbean* (London: Macmillan, 1987); Trevor W. Purcell, "Indigenous Knowledge and Applied Anthropology: Questions of Definition and Direction," *Human Organization* 57, no. 3 (1998): 258–272; Paul Sillitoe, Alan Bicker, and Johan Pottier (eds.), *Participating in Development: Approaches to Indigenous*

Knowledge (London: Routledge, 2002). In the case of the Caribbean, "indigenous knowledge" refers to the local Creole wisdom of the peasantry, see Besson and Momsen (eds.), *Land and Development in the Caribbean*; Purcell, "Indigenous Knowledge and Applied Anthropology."

43. Sidney W. Mintz, "On the Concept of a Third World," *Dialectical Anthropology* 1 (1976): 377–382.

Chapter 11

The Triumph of the Commons: Barbuda Belongs to All Barbudans Together

David Lowenthal and Colin Clarke

A distinctive community has long occupied Barbuda, one of the most thinly inhabited Caribbean islands. Barbuda's 1,200 people manifest a sense of identity and an attachment to locality that stem from traditions reaching back over two centuries. Close-knit yet by no means claustrophobic, parsimonious but not miserly, conservative but not reactionary, Barbudans' approach to using and stewarding their resources reflects long legacies of isolation, ecological constraint, family closeness, and social interdependence.

Barbudans both at home and abroad remain profoundly attached to their island, in large measure because they have long controlled it in common. How did a tiny community of freed African slaves and their descendants on this ill-favored, scantily productive margin of the Caribbean plantation realm achieve this extraordinary feat? How did these part-time peasant cultivators, livestock hunters, fishermen, and wreckage salvagers establish collective rights to their island and its resources?

Barbuda's arid climate and infertile sandy soils precluded development for agricultural export commodities and confined its proprietors instead to subsidiary extractive uses. Without a plantation regimen, slaves on Barbuda were largely left to shift for themselves. After emancipation, Barbudans accustomed to managing their own affairs engaged in running conflict with absentee lessees and, later, with the Crown for access to and control over island resources. Three threads dominated Barbudan peasant history: common land tenure; communal land use for shifting cultivation and open-range livestock; and emigration as a safety valve for the island's limited resources and a source of remittances and other benefits.[1]

Environment

Barbuda, 30 miles north of Antigua in the Leeward Islands, comprises 62 square miles. A small karstic plateau rises to 50–125 feet above the low limestone plain. "Barbuda is one of the flattest islands I have ever had the pleasure of landing on," remarked a colonial doctor weary of the Lesser Antilles' steep volcanic slopes.[2] Most soils are shallow and infertile. Precipitation averages below 40 inches annually; seasonal aridity is common, droughts are frequent. Rains often fail for several successive years. Sandy beaches alternate with submerged rocky shoals, lethal to ships, whose foundered hulks and cargoes were long a local mainstay.

Most of Barbuda is a scrub wilderness roamed by deer, pigs, and feral stock, descendants of animals imported by early European traders and settlers. Remnants of a presettlement evergreen woodland—white cedar, loblolly, turpentine, and whitewood—survive among columnar cactus, thorny shrubs, and grassy glades, xerophytic species suited to soils degraded by intermittent clearance for provision grounds, grazing, and charcoal burning.[3] Although many Barbudans engage in shifting cultivation, none are full-time farmers. The countryside is uninhabited, the law once requiring, and custom still persuading, all Barbudans to live in or near the island's one village, Codrington. Tourism is confined to self-contained resorts on the island's opposite shore.

Barbudans versus Lessees

For more than 200 years from the late seventeenth century, Barbuda was leased by the Crown to one family, the Codringtons. The original lessee, Christopher Codrington, was governor of the Leeward Islands, but his heirs lived in England, rarely visiting the island. Barbuda supplied lucrative Codrington sugar estates on Antigua with timber, ground provisions, fish, livestock, and draft animals. Barbuda was also a rich source of salvage from ships wrecked on its coral reefs. As late as the 1850s the Codringtons netted £4,000 a year from Barbudan stock and £300 from salvage operations.[4]

Initially worked by a few indentured whites, then by slaves from Africa, Barbuda remained little inhabited for a century. By the late eighteenth century, however, relatively benign circumstances had greatly increased the slave population. Housed and well fed through their own efforts, spared the rigors and torments of a plantation regimen, Barbudans were free in almost all but name. While slave numbers elsewhere in the Caribbean dwindled, between 1800 and 1832 Barbuda's population rose from 300 to 500; Christopher Bethell Codrington protested he could not feed so many small children.[5] In the light of his earlier expressed hope that given its healthfulness and fecundity the island might become "a Nursery for Negroes" to work his Antiguan estates,[6] this increase spawned the belief that Barbuda had been used to breed slaves—a belief we elsewhere show groundless, though to this day ineradicable.[7]

Under slavery Barbudans built a cohesive Creole community whose solidarity thwarted absentee proprietors and hapless local overseers. Attempts to induce Barbudans to labor on Antiguan estates met with scant success. No manager left virtually on his own could coerce a community several hundred strong.[8] As emancipation loomed Codrington himself lauded their steadfast attachment. Almost all Creoles, locally born rather than African, they were "one united family so attached to Barbuda that force alone or extreme drought . . . can alone take them from that island!"[9]

Emancipation in 1834 scarcely altered Barbudan life. Transition from slaves to freemen was less abrupt and less consequential than elsewhere. They did not become landowners: Barbuda in its entirety was still assigned to Crown lessees, with peasant tenancies and livelihoods at the mercy of absentee proprietors. An 1835 agreement secured Barbudans' employment on Codrington enterprises at specified rates of pay.[10] But the contract soon lapsed, and lessee–islander relations reverted to coercion overlain by patronage. Wages were often arbitrarily withheld, "recalcitrant" Barbudans transported to Antiguan jail or plantations.

Emancipation left the Barbudan economy, like its society, substantially unchanged. "The only exports from the Island," noted an 1850 observer, were "cattle, principally for the Antigua estates of Sir William Codrington, sheep and firewood—the people are principally engaged in the cultivation of provisions, Yams, Potatoes, Indian Corn &.,—and receive in money wages, and the proceeds of their own farm industry, enough to supply them with clothing, and the simple necessities."[11]

Barbudans continued their diverse occupations—hunting and fishing, tending provision grounds, cutting wood and burning charcoal, salvaging wrecks—sometimes employed by proprietors or government, more often in disregard of these authorities, frequently in open defiance. Agents and officials continually complained about Barbudan poaching, periodically issuing such admonitory fiats as "ordering all Guns belonging to negroes to be sent off the Island."[12]

While proprietors and government officials condemned Barbudan encroachments, Barbudans demanded redress against interference with their livelihood. An 1869 Barbudan petition against the gun fiat protested that

> We are deprived of the use of our fire arms whereby most of us live in shooting any large fish, turtle or wild birds . . . We are told to take out licences yet if we are seen with a gun (not even shooting) we are taken before the Magistrate of "Antigua" and severely punished . . . Our little gardens are gone to waste and if such as are still in a little cultivation was to be injured by weather . . . and we by sickness are not able to have the fences repaired directly it is taken and burned saying our intention is only to catch the wild beasts of Mr. Codrington's.[13]

Relinquishing their lease in 1870, the Codringtons took all horses and cattle off the island, leaving only the deer and sheep, largely because it proved impossible to round them up.

Subsequent lessees did even less well than the Codringtons. Barbuda's value "had rested primarily on its direct association with the large Antiguan sugar-estates and in the profits of salvage. The latter had been limited by the occurrence of fewer wrecks and by regulations [introduced in 1855]. The former was lost when the Codringtons surrendered their lease."[14] Finding

Barbuda unprofitable, each lessee in turn gutted its resources and neglected its inhabitants. William and Robert Dougall's Barbuda Island Company never invested the annual £1,500 required by their lease. Only £700 rather than their promised £6,000 worth of stock were introduced, with barely a score of Barbudans employed as graziers. Despite alleged attempts to plant India-rubber seeds (*Ficus elastica*), sisal, coffee, kola, and cacao, the Dougalls' plantings proved negligible.

In 1898 a derelict Barbuda was forfeited to the Crown for the nonpayment of rent. A visiting official found the deer almost exterminated, satinwood and logwood depleted, cattle famished, fences in disrepair. There were only four men to round up about 100 horses, 80 cattle, 4 milch cows. The two paddocks "had long since become filthy and variously overgrown not only with bush, but dense thickets." The cattle had "bad bullets in them, probably put there by Dr. Dougall's gunners . . . sent out for deer by moonlight, . . . the effects of stray bullets or mistaken shots."[15]

"The Island and the people have been starved and degraded by the Dougalls," concluded the Colonial Office. Little wonder "the villagers have taken one or two [cattle], whether live or dead."[16] Indigent islanders complained the lessees had taken their stock, closed provision grounds, threatened to evict them, intending "to cast out our old mothers, the helpless and the infirm, and everything that is near and dear to us upon the wide elements, to suffer and die."[17] Only traditional hunting, farming, and pilfering enabled Barbudans to survive. If sympathetic to their plight, however, the government proved little more helpful than the leaseholders.

Barbudans versus the Crown

Lease termination left Barbuda to the Leeward Islands colonial government in Antigua. To provide employment and offset costs of administration and rudimentary social services, a government stock farm was established in 1901, trial cotton plots in 1903. Annual grants of £500 paid for fencing, cutting wood for sale, cotton experiments, cattle purchases, and mule breeding.[18] Barbudans turned government grazing lands to their own purposes, enclosing government stock "in an exhausted and insufficient 'meadow,' while the whole of the rich pasture outside the enclosure was left free for horses, cattle and donkeys belonging to the villagers."[19] Nevertheless, the stock farm flourished, with 161 horses, 108 cattle, and 5 mules by 1905; there was a good market for Barbudan beef and draft animals. By 1909 government-owned beasts were valued at £3,000.[20]

Most profitable was cotton—a crop that had briefly flourished there during and after slavery. Fifty-five acres were planted in 1905. A year later 38 bales were shipped, with cotton in hand valued at £1,000, and 150 acres under cultivation, employing 80 Barbudans. "Until recently a drag on Antigua," wrote the manager,[21] Barbuda's progress warranted constructing a cotton ginnery in 1909.[22] Profits soared to £1,145 on the eve of World War I; 130 more acres were planted. The stock farm throve, mule breeding succeeded,

60 acres of coconuts were planted. Barbuda's 1,000 "prosperous and contented" inhabitants were, enthused Governor Hesketh Bell, "a pattern to the rest of the islanders."[23] The cotton boom enabled many Barbudans to buy passage overseas.

The outflow, coupled with raised living standards among those who remained, caused an unprecedented labor shortage. Government projects were left uncared for during World War I. Never before had Barbuda lacked labor to work its limited arable acreage, noted Agricultural Inspector Tempany. "The present difficulties are . . . due to the increasing prosperity and independence of the people on the one side and of the attempt to expand Government enterprise on the other."[24]

Following a shipwreck off the island in 1915, the labor shortage escalated into open conflict. When the island manager arrived to oversee salvage, he disturbed Barbudans pilfering the vessel; in retaliation, persons undiscoverable burned his boat and wagon. To punish Barbudans for this outrage, the Governor of Antigua imposed previously unenforced rents on cultivated plots—5 shillings per acre per annum—and doubled animal head taxes.[25] Imposing ground rents had a purpose beyond punishment. The government thereby sought to force Barbudans to work on its cotton plantation. Laborers "show a disinclination . . . for cotton picking; in the . . . cultivation of land and planting of crops the deficiency has been most severely felt."[26]

Ultimately the islanders, who petitioned the Crown against this semi-indentured servitude, won their case thanks to drought. Drought ruined the maize crop in 1916; low market prices more than halved estimated cotton profits. Postwar droughts doomed both cotton and cattle ventures, and in 1922 Barbuda was hit by a hurricane "without precedent within the memory of the oldest inhabitants."[27]

Subsequent government developments—a new cotton plantation, stock improvement, vegetable growing—were all frustrated by periodic crippling droughts, notably one lasting 20 years until 1973. Cotton was again the major casualty. Reestablished on peasant plots in 1947, cotton throve until 1952, when 15,300 pounds were exported. But output then plummeted, and by 1971 cotton vanished.

Episodically induced to labor in lessees' and government projects, Barbudans clung in the main to customary modes of subsistence. When overoptimistic developments failed, they habitually reverted to their swidden plots, livestock, and fishing grounds. Barbudans have had good reason to prefer being their own masters: 250 years of experience showed time and again how unreliable and exploitative are alternative modes of resource use sponsored by bosses and non-natives. Above all, they learned that only ownership in common guaranteed access to scanty precious resources.

Common Ownership

Barbuda's residents seem always to have believed themselves its owners. Even as slaves, Barbudans asserted a possessiveness possible only in an island almost utterly beyond control by outside masters, whether slaveholders or colonial officials. And the island's small size, homogeneity, and meager soils, together with the familism of the slaves and their descendants, made Barbuda a possession not to be parceled out to individuals but jointly held in common. Unlike other inherited family land in the Caribbean,[28] Barbudan communal ownership rests on their "cherished delusion that they are Squatters in No Man's Land."[29]

An unceasing barrage of petitions made Barbudans' insistence on traditional common rights proverbial at the Colonial Office. Their forefathers, Barbudans kept claiming, had had use of land throughout the island, access to provision grounds everywhere, permission to hunt deer and wild pig, to impound cattle, to keep goats and sheep, to cut firewood, to burn charcoal, to fish, and so on.[30] No documents but usage over many generations attested these collective "rights." All Barbudans belonged to the few score families long established there; all insisted, with one voice, that Barbuda was theirs alone. No outsiders, whether proprietors, government officials, or other West Indians (above all Antiguans) could abrogate exclusive Barbudan entitlement. Continuity of family, of community, of persistently claimed rights helped maintain traditional modes of livelihood, prudently restricted environmental exploitation, and generally sustainable resource use.[31]

These customary rights stemmed from the time of slavery. Although Barbudan slaves legally owned nothing, they regularly took forest products for their own use; from their allotted provision grounds they fed themselves and sold produce to Antigua. A postemancipation agreement with Codrington's manager reaffirmed all Barbudans' customary rights to provision grounds.[32] Excluded areas reserved for the proprietor's hunting were never demarcated.

Barbudan provision grounds engendered conflict throughout the nineteenth century. Leaseholders sought to confine residents' cultivations to near the village; Barbudans insisted on scattering them throughout the island, in locations hidden from proprietorial view. Lessees' managers charged that travel to provision grounds far from the village served as a cloak to poach deer and livestock; villagers complained that proprietors' animals menaced their growing crops.[33] Barbudans' provision grounds were censured as seedbeds of insubordination: "They wish to be allowed to cut land in the bush just when they please and abandon it again and cutting out a fresh lot when and where it suits them . . . they object to be located in one place where they can't do this."[34] In the end, proprietors proved powerless to prevent Barbudans from cultivating more or less wherever they chose.

When in 1898 the Colonial Office took over Barbuda from the last lessee, Barbudans became, as they wished, Crown tenants in common. A 1904 Ordinance, still in force, confirmed possession of individual house sites in Codrington village and of most of the rest of the island as tenants in common.[35] Government efforts to exact even a nominal rent for provision grounds came to naught against Barbudan insistence that free possession was traditional. Barbudans were only tenants at will, to be sure; theoretically, the Crown could turn them out at any time.[36] But the Colonial Office recognized that law was not social reality: everyday practicality if not simple justice entitled Barbudans to "their" island. Wrote Agricultural Inspector Tempany in 1915:

> In the mind of the peasantry a fixed and rooted idea exists in relation to certain supposed rights which they possess in the island. In point of fact these rights have many times been shown to have little or no real existence: on the other hand the feeling exists and in any legislation or action in relation to the villagers . . . due consideration must be paid to this feeling which constitutes a factor capable of causing considerable difficulties.[37]

Only from specific government project sites—cotton plots, livestock pens, a coconut plantation—were Barbudan cultivators then excluded. A barbed wire fence, episodically renewed and often moved, divided Barbuda roughly into two halves, for grazing livestock and for provision grounds. But this fence, easily and frequently breached, never totally debarred any area from cultivation. The wire itself has long since disappeared, cannibalized to reinforce the fencing around shifting provision grounds.

By 1920 Barbudans had legal entitlement to roughly half the island; by 1983, with final decolonization, they controlled virtually all its resources de facto. Barbudans' exclusive right to their land was a key issue when in 1981 Barbuda was propelled, against its will, into independence from Britain in partnership with larger and more powerful Antigua. Land ownership has been contested with Antigua ever since, Barbudans insisting that "they leave this little precious rock for Barbuda and Barbudans alone."[38] Against Antigua, the Barbudan Council maintains that no land in Barbuda can be sold or developed without its sanction.[39]

From the eighteenth century to the present, usage has progressively confirmed persistent Barbudan claims to the entire island and its resources. And nonalienable land underpins the enduring basis of the islanders' community.

Communal Land Use

Common control facilitates two distinctive and useful Barbudan modes of land use—shifting cultivation for provision grounds and open-range pasturage for livestock. Shifting cultivation is well suited to Barbuda's impoverished soils. Cultivators typically demarcate a "ground" of between half an acre and 2 or 3 acres, enclose it against feral animals, cut and burn the brush, and plant a variety of catch crops: sweet potatoes, yams, maize, beans, pigeon peas, squash, peanuts. One or two years' planting exhausts the soil; the fencing is removed to a new ground, while the abandoned area gradually regenerates. Some plots are planted on a longer-term basis with rotational fallowing, but here too tenure is temporary, cultivation conferring no permanent rights.

Common tenure and communal use reflected the community's solidarity and respected Barbuda's resource limitations. And common rights, along with swidden cultivation (viewed as interlinked evils by colonial officials), safeguarded Barbudans against both external tyranny and economic exigency.

No wonder government advisors condemned shifting cultivation as primitive and wasteful and sought to mandate permanent cropping. They coupled a misguided faith in Barbudan soil fertility with wrath against a feckless peasantry that saw no bounds to its land rights and labor freedom. Typical was Tempany's 1916 diatribe (compare chapter 2):

> The standard of cultivation in the peoples' grounds in Barbuda is of the lowest description. This is largely the result of [allowing] the peasantry . . . to cultivate as much land as they wish without let or hindrance. As a result a false feeling of proprietorship has grown up amongst the people combined with the idea that the soil is of very little value . . . It is absurd to suppose that a system whereby people are allowed to work land ad libitum for a few years, without any outside market for produce, and then, when fertility has become reduced owing to bad methods, move on to fresh plots, can be productive of benefit. The only result can be the evolution of a thriftless and unproductive community, this has indeed happened in Barbuda.[40]

Permanent settlement on individually leased plots would stimulate Barbudan enterprise, encourage manuring and other beneficial practices, increase productivity, and ultimately enable a much larger population (of other West Indians) to develop the island. "Some restrictions on the tenure of the land are likely to be in best interest of the people themselves and of the Government, as in addition to other advantages it would tend to induce the people to value the privilege of working land more highly."[41]

Barbudans rejected these adjurations as threats to their corporate autonomy and individual freedom of action, including whether or not to cultivate from year to year, depending on the availability of other resources. And contrary to government views on soil depletion, episodic swiddening left most of Barbuda under permanent cover, maintaining an ecological balance that permanent cultivation would have severely deranged.

Like slash-and-burn cultivation, management of open-range livestock at modest levels of exploitation suits Barbuda's soils and climate. Cattle, horses, sheep, and goats are owned, earmarked, and branded by individuals who eventually round them up for sale and slaughter, but meanwhile all animals roam together unrestricted throughout the bush. Feral cattle can withstand Barbuda's droughts, to which tamed and penned animals, lacking adequate fodder and unable to forage, would soon succumb.[42] "Banking on the hoof" enables Barbudans to cope with drought-induced fluctuations of income from other sources.[43]

Open-range husbandry has helped sustain Barbudan unity. "More than any other cash or subsistence pursuit," notes an anthropologist, "cattle keeping provides a way for Barbudans to adjust to environmental change, to strengthen social bonds and community solidarity, to create a prestigious social and economic place for men in a society with scanty resources, and finally to extend economic involvement with the world beyond Barbuda."[44] It made good sense, therefore, for Barbudans to sabotage cattle management and enclosure schemes imposed by proprietors and later by government.

Emigration

Migration complements Barbuda's distinctive communal modes of sustenance. As population outgrew resources, many young Barbudans have had to leave or starve. But emigrants and their descendants continue to share in the communal ownership and use of Barbudan land (compare chapters 17 and 18). And remittances and periodic returns play a major role in furbishing the island with modern goods and ideas, notably in housing, health care, and education.

During slavery, owner and slave alike regarded expatriation as a punishment, and many Barbudans resisted leaving to labor on Codrington sugar plantations in Antigua. Those transported there caused more trouble than they were felt to be worth.[45] After emancipation, however, there was not enough work for all. The two years following the end of slavery saw the departure of more than a hundred Barbudans, one-fifth of the island's population.[46]

Proprietorial repression was seen as a major cause of emigration. In 1869 the lessee's manager burned the provision grounds, and islanders grieved that "We Barbudans are worse than wandering birds migrating from land to land the home we love so dearly has to be abandoned through hunger. We have to leave our old parents sick and tattered with age."[47] Without proprietors' wages Barbudans might well have starved. Moreover, expatriation was still used as punishment, while Barbudans who had left voluntarily were sometimes prevented from returning. The outflow was frequently substantial; at the leasehold termination in 1898 "few young men [were] to be found living there."[48]

Emigration became an institutionalized response to Barbudan population–resource balance. The constant removal of young adults reduced the birth rate, so that the community grew slowly enough not to endanger the island's fragile resources. The present-day resident population of 1,200 is little more than twice what it was a century ago.

Barbudan émigrés today inhabit three principal communities. Many reside in St. John's, Antigua; many more are in New York City, whose Barbudan roots stem from the late nineteenth century; in Britain Leicester has been the major center for Barbudans since the West Indian exodus of the late 1950s. Barbudans overseas retain their Barbudan identity by adjacent residence, continual homeland contacts, visits back and forth even by remote relatives, and the return of retired émigrés to the island.

Barbudans are in constant touch with the outside world. News, ideas, and money flow back to the parent community. The meager harvest of Barbudan resources formerly went to enrich proprietors in Antigua and England; today largesse from Barbudan sons and daughters scattered throughout the world supplements the resources of those who remain in the island.

Conclusion

Communal ties and familial solidarity enabled descendants of slaves on post-emancipation Barbuda to cope with a harsh environment and a succession of aloof, misinformed, and often actively hostile absentee proprietors, managers, and administrators. A unified people keenly conscious of the importance of traditional resource ownership and land tenure made the best of their constricted milieu and fragile ecology. And collective ownership and communal management on Barbuda have been supplemented by long habits of locally supportive emigration and return.

Only private ownership could protect a community from resource depletion, famously reasoned Garrett Hardin; otherwise, "as population grows and greed runs rampant, the commons collapses." But thanks to regular emigration Barbuda's population has not burgeoned, nor have its meager resources declined. Barbudans have turned their commons into a triumph, in exceptional contradistinction to the widely assumed "tragedy of the commons."[49]

Notes

1. We addressed some of these issues in David Lowenthal and Colin Clarke, "Common Lands, Common Aims: The Distinctive Barbudan Community," in Malcolm Cross and Arnaud Marks (eds.), *Peasants, Plantations and Rural Communities in the Caribbean* (Leiden, Neth: Royal Institute of Linguistics & Anthropology; Guildford, UK: University of Surrey Dept. of Sociology, 1979), 142–159.

2. George E. Pierez, "Report of the Senior Medical Officer on Barbuda," May 8, 1897, in Leeward Islands Governor George Melville to Secretary of State for the Colonies (hereafter S/S Cols) Joseph Chamberlain, C.O. 152/300, the National Archives, Public Record Office, London (hereafter TNA, PRO).

3. David R. Harris, *Plants, Animals and Man in the Outer Leeward Islands: An Ecological Study of Antigua, Barbuda and Anguilla*, University of California Publications in Geography, vol. 18 (Berkeley: University of California Press, 1965), 19–23, 35–41.

4. Douglas Hall, *Five of the Leewards, 1834–1870: The Major Problems of the Post-Emancipation Period in Antigua, Barbuda, Montserrat, Nevis and St. Kitts* (Barbados: Caribbean Universities Press, 1971), 77.

5. Christopher Bethell Codrington to Lord Bathurst, April 1, 1826, Codrington Mss. (hereafter Cod. Mss.), D1610, T9, C33. These manuscripts, previously in Gloucestershire County Record Office, were sold at auction in London in 1980; their current whereabouts are unknown to us. Most extracts cited here are in David Lowenthal and Colin G. Clarke, "Slave-Breeding in Barbuda: The Past of a Negro Myth," *Annals of the New York Academy of Sciences* 292 (1977): 510–535.

6. C. B. Codrington to William Codrington, June 17, 1790, Cod. Mss., D1610, T9, C29.

7. Lowenthal and Clarke, "Slave-Breeding in Barbuda."

8. R. Jarrett to Christopher Codrington, December 8, 1829, Cod. Mss., D1610, T9, C29, also in Codrington to Sir George Murray, March 16, 1830, C.O. 7/30 (Individuals), TNA, PRO.

9. Codrington to E. G. Stanley, June 1, 1834 (Draft) and Memorial [1833], Cod. Mss., E.36.

10. Agreement between John Winter and the People of Barbuda, May 4, 1835, Enclosure 6 in E. Murray Macgregor to Lord Aberdeen, May 16, 1835, C.O. 7/41, TNA, PRO.

11. James Sheriff to James Higginson, January 8, 1850, in Higginson to S/S Cols, January 22, 1850, C.O. 7/95, TNA, PRO.

12. W. Cowley to Sir William Codrington, May 10, 1863, Cod. Mss. C.50.

13. Petition of Barbudans to the Crown, December 23, 1869, Enclosure 1 in Benjamin Pine to S/S Cols, December 23, 1869, C.O. 7/138, TNA, PRO.

14. Hall, *Five of the Leewards*, 66–69.

15. J. F. Smyth to Melville, in Fleming to S/S Cols, October 11, 1898, C.O. 152/237A, TNA, PRO.

16. Colonial Office Minute, Lucas, 1898, C.O. 152/235, TNA, PRO.

17. Petition of Barbudans to Her Majesty's Commission of Enquiry into the Depressed Condition of the Islands, in Fleming to Chamberlain, April 24, 1897, C.O. 152/218, TNA, PRO.

18. Strickland to Chamberlain, February 9, 1903, C.O. 152/277, TNA, PRO.

19. Sands, Curator, Antigua Botanic Garden, in Strickland to Chamberlain, April 1, 1903, C.O. 152/278, TNA, PRO.

20. E. St. John Branch, Manager, October 7, 1909, C.O. 152/312, TNA, PRO.

21. St. John Branch, 1906, in Beckham Sweet-Escott to Elgin, C.O. 152/289, TNA, PRO.

22. St. John Branch, October 7, 1909, C.O. 152/312, TNA, PRO.

23. Bell to Chamberlain, March 13, 1914, C.O. 152/340, No. 106, TNA, PRO.

24. H. A. Tempany, Report on the Labour Conditions in Barbuda, April 29, 1915, Enclosure 6a in Bell to S/S Cols, April 7, 1916, C.O. 152/350, No. 127, TNA, PRO.

25. Acting Governor Best to S/S Cols, August 1, 1916, C.O. 152/351, TNA, PRO.

26. H. A. Tempany, Report on the Labour Conditions in Barbuda, April 29, 1915, Enclosure 6a in Bell to S/S Cols, April 7, 1916, C.O. 152/350, No. 127, TNA, PRO.

27. Geoffrey Downing, Manager, to Colonial Secretary, September 19, 1922, C.O. 152/386, TNA, PRO.

28. Riva Berleant-Schiller, "Ecology and Politics in Barbudan Land Tenure," in Jean Besson and Janet Momsen (eds.), *Land and Development in the Caribbean* (London: Macmillan, 1987), 116–131.

29. Letter to Secretary of State for the Colonies from Acting Governor Best, accompanying the Petition, April 7, 1916, C.O. 152/350, No. 127, TNA, PRO.

30. For example, Petition of Barbudans to Joseph Chamberlain, June 24, 1901, and Oliver Nugent to Colonial Secretary, in Fleming to Chamberlain, August 26, 1901, C.O. 152/264, No. 488, TNA, PRO.

31. For example, John F. Smyth, October 16, 1897, in Fleming to S/S Cols, January 5, 1898, C.O. 152/288, No. 8, TNA, PRO.

32. Agreement between John Winter and the People of Barbuda, May 4, 1835, Enclosure 6 in E. Murray Macgregor to Lord Aberdeen, May 16, 1835, C.O. 7/41, TNA, PRO.

33. G. Holborow to William Codrington, February 2, 1860 (?), Cod. Mss. C 52; Inhabitants' Petition against Messrs. Cowley and Hopkins, September 10, 1867, C.O. 7/130, No. 102, TNA, PRO.

34. Arthur W. Holmes à Court, Surveyor of Public Works, in Fleming to Chamberlain, April 24, 1897, C.O. 152/218, TNA, PRO.

35. Antigua Ordinance No. 2 of 1904, C.O. 354/19, TNA, PRO.

36. Berleant-Schiller, "Ecology and Politics in Barbudan Land Tenure."

37. H. A. Tempany, Report on the Labour Conditions in Barbuda, April 29, 1915, Enclosure 6a in Bell to S/S Cols, April 7, 1916, C.O. 152/350, No. 127, TNA, PRO.

38. Arthur Nibbs, "Independence for Antigua and Barbuda," *Barbuda Voice* 9, no. 1 (March 1979): 3. For Barbudan plaints against Antiguan land stealers, see David Lowenthal and Colin G. Clarke, "Island Orphans: Barbuda and the Rest," *Journal of Commonwealth & Comparative Politics* 18 (1980): 293–307, at 298–301.

39. Riva Berleant-Schiller, "Statehood, the Commons, and the Landscape in Barbuda," *Caribbean Geography* 3, no. 1 (1991): 43–52.

40. H. A. Tempany, Copy of Minute by Superintendent of Agriculture, March 31, 1916, Enclosure 7 in Bell to Chamberlain, April 7, 1916, C.O. 152/350, No. 127, TNA, PRO.

41. H. A. Tempany, Report on the Labour Conditions in Barbuda, Enclosure 6a in Bell to S/S Cols, April 7, 1916, C.O. 152/350, No. 127, TNA, PRO.

42. Denis Reynolds to Sir William Codrington, December 29, 1783, Codrington Correspondence, University of Texas Microfilm, D99.

43. K. V. Flannery, "Origins and Ecological Effects of Early Domestication in Iran and the Near East," in Peter J. Ucko and G. W. Dimbleby (eds.), *The Domestication and Exploitation of Plants and Animals* (London: Duckworth, 1969), 73–100, at 74.

44. Riva Berleant-Schiller, "The Social and Economic Role of Cattle in Barbuda," *Geographical Review* 67 (1977): 299–309, at 309.

45. Lowenthal and Clarke, "Slave-Breeding in Barbuda," 521–527.

46. Henry Loving to E. Murray MacGregor, May 15, 1835, Enclosure 5 in MacGregor to Lord Aberdeen, May 16, 1835, C.O. 7/41, No. 100, TNA, PRO.

47. Petition of Certain Inhabitants of Barbuda to the Governor of Antigua, January 12, 1869, Enclosure 1 in Benjamin Pine to the S/S Cols, December 23, 1869, C.O. 7/138, No. 252, TNA, PRO.

48. Barbuda Commission Report, 1899, in C.O. 152/249, No. 611, TNA, PRO.

49. Garrett Hardin, "The Tragedy of the Commons," *Science* 162 (1968): 1243–1248, at 1243.

Chapter 12

The Contested Existence of a Peasantry in Martinique: Scientific Discourses, Controversies, and Evidence

Christine Chivallon

The inability of the descendants of slaves to gain control through land ownership has been seen as the recurrent element in Martinican social history, which the abolition of slavery did nothing to change. René Achéen suggested that the apparent postemancipation changes in plantation society in fact maintained structural continuity, as the abolition of slavery did not bring about any change in the structure of socioeconomic relationships. The very idea that a peasantry could be formed on the basis of land ownership following abolition was not even considered. However research on the English-speaking islands has had no difficulty in establishing such a relationship. For the French West Indies, the comment made by Hector Élisabeth echoes a widely held interpretation that was not really challenged until the 1990s: "One of the immediate consequences of abolition lay in the change in the slaves' status, and thus in their ability to produce and affirm a new identity in the future. But since the abolition of slavery was not accompanied by any fundamental change with regard to land ownership, it did not change the status of the former slaves in any real way."[1] Influential works such as those of Édouard Glissant[2] and to a lesser extent Francis Affergan[3] postulate with equal conviction the existence of this link between possession of land and the creation of an identity that would have eventually come about through economic control *but* go on immediately to affirm that in Martinique nothing, not even the abolition of slavery, allowed this link to be established.

This interpretation uses a version of history that could be termed classical as the basis for its explanation of the occupation of the inland *mornes* or hills by the newly freed slaves and their descendants. In this chapter I propose to examine this classical version of the appropriation of the *mornes* consisting of three principal arguments that will be developed successively. I will then look at the data that can be used to change this perspective and allow the recognition of a peasant agrarian group in Martinique. This chapter focuses on the argument relating to land and the method of its acquisition. It will also then attempt to demonstrate the extent to which the interpretation resulting from this data goes beyond mere factual information and leads to a complete reappraisal of the role played by the former slaves in the recomposition of postslavery society in Martinique.

The Classical Interpretation of the Development of Peasant Property in Martinique

The movement of population that followed the abolition of slavery in 1848 from the plantations in the low and medium altitude zones into the interior highlands of the island has had a lasting effect on the Martinican rural landscape. It would not be an overstatement to speak of a classical interpretation of the growth of such peasant property in Martinique.[4] It seems possible to summarize the content of what is described here as the classical version in three main propositions, referring respectively first to the method of access to the land, then to the scale of the occupation of the *mornes*, and finally to the method of land management set up by the newly freed slaves. The first proposition is that the development of "small properties" after abolition is principally the result of occupation without title, or squatting.[5] The sparsely populated inland *mornes* were available to the former slaves who appropriated the land left vacant by the local plantocracy. Jean-Baptiste Delawarde speaks of land "occupied by fraud, conscious or not" or again of settlements in "places unexploited before 1848," namely the "hilly lands of the highlands belonging to the colony or to big planters and acquired easily."[6] Guy Lasserre[7] also indicated that occupation without title was the principal mode of forming small properties: "Freedom found expression through . . . the proliferation of smallholdings resulting from the occupation without title of vacant land or land considered as such by the newly freed men."[8]

In addition to squatting there was another mode of access to land that demonstrates the way relationships based on planter domination were maintained, through the granting of gardens by the former masters as a way to keep their workforce, now crucially necessary in the context of the reorganization of the work regime. Thus Delawarde speaks of the practice by which planters gave their former slaves "personal usufruct of a plot of land situated on the outskirts of their property."[9] Guy Lasserre also mentions that "large numbers of big landowners granted free use of a kitchen garden and a cabin to those who agreed to stay on the estate."[10] Sales of land allowing the formation of smallholdings before the land reform of 1961 are regarded as only involving a few easily identifiable operations such as those undertaken at the end of the nineteenth century by the Conseil Général or the land division carried out for the benefit of the victims of the Mt. Pelée disaster in 1902.

The second proposition concerns the scale of this access to land. According to the 1935 survey, for the whole of Martinique, the number of small properties of less than 10 hectares was 5,715. In 1975, on the basis of the cadastre, Jacques Desruisseaux counted nine times as many for a land area almost three times as great. Many possible reasons for this increase have been put forward: variation in the category "farm" (used in 1975), which differs from that of "rural property" (used in 1935); the division of large estates, which was carried out between 1935 and 1975 creating smallholdings; the effects of the land reform in progress since the 1960s; and, finally, the considerable effect of the management of the small properties, which are "split up" by division due to inheritance.[11] Eugène Revert voiced reservations about the 1935 survey, going so far as to point out that in Sainte-Marie, a commune in the north of Martinique, it was surprising to have recorded only 400 properties of less than 3 hectares when a close knowledge of the land gives a total of 2,000 properties of less than half an acre alone.[12]

The third proposition concerns land management. For Guy Lasserre, inheritance is one of the principal factors in the evolution of the peasant holding. He states that the application of the civil code worked like a "machine to chop up the earth" and "too often this fragmentation only ended when the property, reduced to a patch of land, would have lost all economic value if it had been divided again."[13] This implies a certain rationality intended to protect the land as a tool of production. According to Lasserre, the small farmers do not have a "peasant mentality," they only endeavor to "escape their condition."[14] Hence the characterization of this agrarian group as comparable to a rural proletariat that has remained tied to the large estate. Delawarde took the trouble to specify in his essay that the peasants endowed with high moral qualities were "people of mixed-blood," "small farmers with light skins" and "cunning blue eyes."[15] In other words, if there were real peasants in Martinique, they had of course to resemble their counterparts from Normandy, and, therefore, they had to be whitened in the literal sense of the word.

Reevaluation of the Classical Interpretation

I now come to the second point in this chapter and to the exposé of the arguments which make a reevaluation of the classical version necessary. To do this I will use some of the research that I carried out in seven rural districts of the *mornes* and which made possible a reconstruction of the origin of the peasant hamlets and the evolution of their land and demographic structures from 1840 to 1988.[16] It is a body of data concerning both the newly freed slaves and their descendants and the land linked to this population. Available sources allowing access to the history of former slaves are reputed to be sparse. Yet the combined use of the written sources made up of the *État Civil, les registres d'individualités,*[17] *les registres paroissiaux,*[18] the cadastre and *les registres d'hypothèques,*[19] and of the oral sources provided by the testimony of the present-day inhabitants of the rural districts reveals a completely different configuration, as is borne out by the more or less complete reconstitutions of the land and demographic evolution carried out for these seven peasant hamlets. In these hamlets, the research method was the same and consisted, for each of the 70 households visited, of elaborating the genealogy of the land and people from the interviews. The results obtained allowed a link to be established between the present time and that of abolition. In the

Table 12.1 Evolution of the Union District (Morne-Vert) Land Structures from its Creation to 1988

	Property Types											
	Less than 3 hectares			From 3 to 10 hectares			Greater than 10 hectares			Total		
	AC	N	ACP	AC	N	ACP	AC	N	ACP	AC	N	ACP
Situation after the division of the Tiberge (1871–1873)	27	19	1.4	5	1	5	—	—	—	32	20	1.6
Current situation	29	39	0.7	4	1	4	—	—	—	33	40	0.8
Variations	+7%	+105%	−0.7 Ha	−20%		−1 Ha	—	—	—	+3%	+100%	−0.8 Ha

Notes: AC = Acreage in hectares (Note: 1 hectare = 2.47 acres). N = Number of properties. ACP = Average acreage per property.
Source: Author's research.

case of certain hamlets it was possible using the sources to obtain a precise description of the land situation at the transition period of abolition, as is the case for the districts of Urion, in Morne-Vert, which was formed from the division of the plantation La Tiberge (table 12.1). Above all this random prospecting within several hamlets allowed us to see from fragmentary information whether it was possible for the more exhaustive data gathered in one of these hamlets, the district of Le Caplet in Morne-Vert, to be generalized. It made possible the precise retracing of the landholdings (maps 12.1 and 12.2) and the demographic and kinship structures of the village in their entirety (figure 12.1) over the period 1840–1989. I was able to get a glimpse of the path followed by the pioneering generation of the newly freed slaves, and the manner in which their aims at abolition immediately turned toward land ownership (figure 12.2).[20]

As my sample of seven districts is not really "representative" in the statistical sense of the word, the broader view of my research depends on the work of the historian Annick François-Haugrin, which supplied parallel quantitative material.[21] While studying the process by which plantations got into debt at the time of slavery, this historian was led, on discovering the scale of the sales of

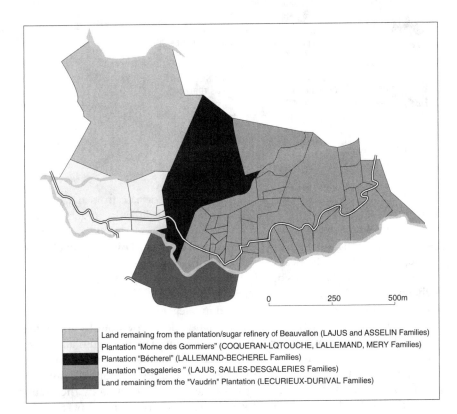

Map 12.1   Landholdings in the Caplet District around 1840

Source: Author's research.

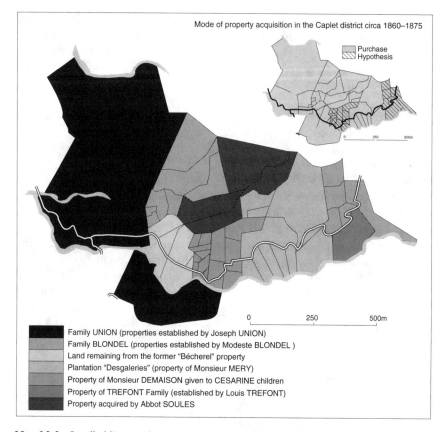

Map 12.2   Landholdings in the Caplet District around 1860–1875
Source: Author's research.

small portions of land between 1850 and 1870, to deviate from her original objective. Without this work, I would have had great difficulty in generalizing from what I found in each hamlet whose foundation was reconstituted precisely (three hamlets in Morne-Vert and one in Basse-Pointe), namely, the development of the small peasant holding from legal sales.

From François-Haugrin's quantitative study and my qualitative research, it is therefore possible to review the first argument in the classical interpretation. Peasant ownership of land occurred in a legal manner in the years after abolition through an extensive process of land sales carried out by some former masters at a time when the plantations were in danger of ruin and there was an imperative need for monetary assets. It must first be understood that the high area of the *mornes* was not available for appropriation without title as one might have thought. This is particularly well illustrated by the example of the Le Caplet district in Morne-Vert, which is a remote part of the mountainous area of Pitons du Carbet. At the beginning of the nineteenth century, this zone was completely occupied: a sugar refinery had some of its

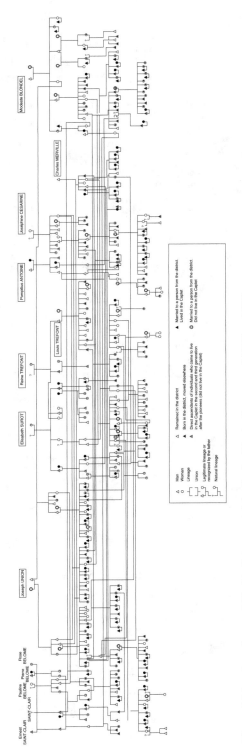

Figure 12.1 Genealogy and Kinship Structures of the Caplet District from around 1840 to 1988

Source: Author's research.

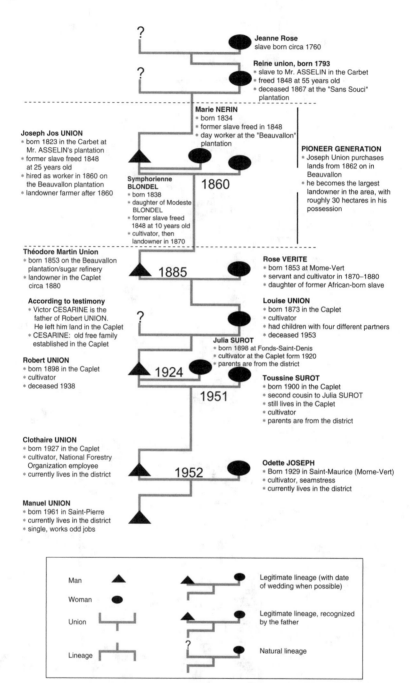

Jeanne Rose
slave born circa 1760

Reine union, born 1793
* slave to Mr. ASSELIN in the Carbet
* freed 1848 at 55 years old
* deceased 1867 at the "Sans Souci" plantation

Marie NERIN
* born 1834
* former slave freed in 1848
* day worker at the "Beauvallon" plantation

Joseph Jos UNION
* born 1823 in the Carbet at Mr. ASSELIN's plantation
* former slave freed 1848 at 25 years old
* hired as worker in 1860 on the Beauvallon plantation
* landowner farmer after 1860

Symphorienne BLONDEL
* born 1838
* daughter of Modeste BLONDEL
* former slave freed 1848 at 10 years old
* cultivator, then landowner in 1870

1860

PIONEER GENERATION
* Joseph Union purchases lands from 1862 on in Beauvallon
* he becomes the largest landowner in the area, with roughly 30 hectares in his possession

Théodore Martin Union
* born 1853 on the Beauvallon plantation/sugar refinery
* landowner in the Caplet circa 1880

1885

Rose VERITE
* born 1853 at Morne-Vert
* servant and cultivator in 1870–1880
* daughter of former African-born slave

According to testimony
* Victor CESARINE is the father of Robert UNION. He left him land in the Caplet
* CESARINE: old free family established in the Caplet

Louise UNION
* born 1873 in the Caplet
* cultivator
* had children with four different partners
* deceased 1953

Julia SUROT
* born 1898 at Fonds-Saint-Denis
* cultivator at the Caplet form 1920
* parents are from the district

Robert UNION
* born 1898 in the Caplet
* cultivator
* deceased 1938

1924

1951

Toussine SUROT
* born 1900 in the Caplet
* second cousin to Julia SUROT
* still lives in the Caplet
* cultivator
* parents are from the district

Clothaire UNION
* born 1927 in the Caplet
* cultivator, National Forestry Organization employee
* currently lives in the district

1952

Odette JOSEPH
* Born 1929 in Saint-Maurice (Morne-Vert)
* cultivator, seamstress
* currently lives in the district

Manuel UNION
* born 1961 in Saint-Pierre
* currently lives in the district
* single, works odd jobs

Man ▲	Legitimate lineage (with date of wedding when possible)
Woman ●	
Union	Legitimate lineage, recognized by the father
Lineage	Natural lineage

Figure 12.2 Caplet: Genealogy of the Union Family (Patronymic Branch)

Source: Author's research.

remaining land there; white families lived there; and other planters had reserves of "bois-debout" (forests for cutting wood). It was not a case of land left unoccupied (map 12.1). For the former slaves access to the land was not immediate but had to wait until several years after abolition. It was not until the decades of the 1860s and 1870s that change in the upland zone occurred with the settlement of the newly freed slaves and the permanent departure of the former owners. This delayed settlement of the former slaves in the highlands also reflects the constraints that the law imposed to encourage former slaves to stay on the plantations, through obliging them to prove that they had a means of subsistence (namely a recognized occupation[22]). The wishes of the purchasers and the sellers would seem to meet in the unshakeable will of the former slaves to acquire land. To my knowledge, only the historian Léo Elisabeth has paid attention to this, indicating that this demand for land had become a true popular ideology.[23] He quotes Colson, who reports a conversation held in May 1848 with some former slaves: "They all wanted the land to be shared out and it was not easy to persuade them that that could not be, and that the Republic would never commit such an injustice." And further on, "[T]hey always answered that the land belonged to God, that it was for everyone and that when they had been given their share, they would work."[24]

The former slaves showed a remarkable persistence in utilizing official procedures for land ownership as the case studies show. With such legally based procedures, the peasant group gained a patrimonial foundation that was secure. The more quantitative data given by François-Haugrin provides data for all legally owned small properties.[25] I would point out that her study included the whole northern region that represents 48 percent of Martinique. In comparison to the data gathered by Jacques Desruisseaux in the 1970s from the cadastre, the historian's data allow us to state that nearly 80 percent of small properties in existence in 1975, in the northern region, are the result of sales of plots of land carried out between 1845 and 1875.[26]

While the 1935 survey indicates 5,715 properties of less than 10 hectares, François-Haugrin identifies a stock of 7,099 sales of portions of land in the northern region alone. With such values, one comes closer to the visual assessment made by observers in the first half of the twentieth century and can better understand the gap between observations made in the field and data supplied by official statistics. From the historical data, it is possible to formulate hypotheses to explain the land structure in Martinique as it was described by Jacques Desruisseaux in 1975 on the basis of the survey. Instead of interpreting the contemporary land situation as the result of abrupt changes appearing after 1935, it can be interpreted as the almost direct heritage of the postabolition period. By applying François-Haugrin's data to the whole of Martinique, it can be seen that small properties in Martinique occupied nearly 30 percent of the island's territory and not 15 percent as the 1935 survey suggested (table 12.2). If one considers a total of 7,000 purchasers of portions of land as stated by François-Haugrin, it is possible to estimate that property ownership involved 17 percent of the rural population of the northern region.[27] But taking into account the average family size of

Table 12.2 Landholdings in Martinique in 1935

Type of property	Properties		Acreage		Average Acreage
	Number	%	Hectares	%	Hectares
Less than 3 hectares	4,696	71.8	5,876	7.3	1.25
From 3 to 10 hectares	1,019	15.6	5,924	7.4	5.81
From 10 to 40 hectares	456	7.0	8,993	11.2	20.0
From 40 to 100 hectares	157	2.4	10,669	13.3	68.0
From 100 to 200 hectares	126	2.0	17,381	21.6	138.0
From 200 to 500 hectares	71	1.04	21,099	26.2	297.1
500 hectares and more	11	0.16	10,412	13.0	946.5
Total	6,536	100	80,354	100	
			93,241[a]	**100**	
Synopsis					
Less than 10 hectares	5,715	87.4	11,800	14.7	2.0
			24,687[a]	**26%**[a]	
From 10 to 40 hectares	456	7.0	8,993	11.2	20
				10%[a]	
40 hectares and more	365	5.6	59,561	74.1	163.2
				64%[a]	

Note: [a]Hypothesis that I propose following the results of the A. François-Haugrin study.
Source: Adapted from A. Philippe Blérald, *Histoire économique de la Guadeloupe et de la Martinique du XVII ème siècle à nos jours* (Khartala, 1986), p. 140.

four persons, it is possible to propose a higher percentage, of the order of 65 percent. Even considering purchasers who became owners of several portions of land and so introduced the statistical bias of "double counting,"[28] it can be stated that at least half the rural population owned land legally during the postabolition period.

The research that I conducted in the districts provides two exhaustive sets of data: those relating to the land structure at the time of the original acquisitions by the freed slaves and those referring to the current situation as it appears in the cadastre in 1988 (table 12.1). These sets are available for two districts in Morne-Vert, Le Caplet, and Urion. A careful analysis challenges the idea that small properties have been fragmented, since the land, although small at the beginning, appears in the end not to be much divided in spite of the impression that there has been a huge increase in the portions of land. At the present time, almost everywhere it is the fourth and fifth generations since abolition who are managing the land. In 1988, at the time of my research, the sixth generation was in the process of taking over the land in certain places. Now, between the two series of data, the number of properties has multiplied by 3.7 in Urion and by 2 in Le Caplet between 1860 and 1988. This increase does not even represent one division into two parts for each generation, since even this minimal division of land would give us a multiplier equivalent to 8. And if one attempts now to apply identical methods to the results found by François-Haugrin (6,609 plots[29]) in relation to Desruisseaux' data from 1975 (19,122 properties), we find that the original number of properties has only been multiplied by 2.9 and this is without taking into account the new properties that were created between these two periods. When one knows the extreme demographic pressure in the *mornes*, this indicates how little the small properties were divided, since although the ideal would be for each child to have a share of the land, division due to inheritance concerns less than the equivalent of one subdivision for every generation.

In spite of the original smallness of the plots, and high number of claimants to the land, there has been an efficient preservation of the patrimony that guarantees its economic potential. This protection is the not the result of chance but indicates the existence of principles aimed at limiting the harmful effects of division. The methods of transmission of land discovered during the ethnographic study indicate a set of peasant rationalities. They consist of the preeminence given to males on the land and the preference for women to leave the family property, the agreements between brothers and sisters and the practices destined to compensate migrants (such as gifts in kind), and joint ownership as a way of not blocking access to land permanently, this last principle demonstrating the setting up of the family patrimony entity when the individual ownership entity proves impossible to implement. Migration also appears as a means of slowing down the division of land. This system does not suggest inconstancy; on the contrary, it shows how the peasants have managed the land to guarantee its continuity. This data seriously weakens the coherence of the classical interpretation of the small peasant property in Martinique.

A Reinterpretation of Postslavery
Society in Martinique

Now that relatively reliable data enables the recognition of a situation in which thousands of former slaves found a secure basis for land ownership, it is possible to explore several interpretative paths. If we confine ourselves only to the materials on the evolution of the land and the demography of the hamlets, these reveal regulatory principles reproduced over several generations focusing on patrimony and the family group. I outlined above the principles relating to patrimony, which enable the reproduction of a peasantry. For the family group, the stability reproduced through several generations is the outcome of collective regulation. This is shown in the choices made as far as conjugal matters are concerned. Analysis of the data indicates the existence of nuclear households organized around a conjugal couple with the presence of siblings generally from the same mother and father. The majority of women whose whole childbearing life could be reconstituted have had children with one companion. Nearly all the affiliations identified in Le Caplet refer to a status in which the paternity is recognized and is in most cases legitimate.[30]

The regulatory principles thus discovered reflect not a recurrent instability, but a social structure that reflects kinship continuity and facilitates a peasant economy as a real alternative to plantation labor. The period following abolition can therefore be defined by two trends: a tendency toward proletarianization of the ex-slave population and one that establishes itself, as Alain-Philippe Blérald states so well, as "a tendency which runs counter to the formation of the labor market," namely, the formation of an agrarian group based on domestic economy.[31]

The infamous repressive legislation of the Second Empire with its Gueydon decree embodied the wish for total proletarianization, with the imposition of an individual tax that imposed the need for money and therefore a paid occupation. However, it did not result in the expected mass return to the plantations, as is borne out by the continuous acquisition of land in the highlands and the increase in the amount of land planted in provisions. Instead, this legislation led to the peasants putting into place a *strategy of compromise* that can be identified by the two characteristics of the Martinican peasant economy: occupational pluralism in which domestic economy and salaried activity are combined and the transformation of surplus peasant produce into money. The effect of this legislation was therefore completely different from the one intended: rather than creating a rural proletariat, it resulted in the ex-slaves' partial autonomy from and partial integration into a wider economic system that constitutes the very definition of peasant societies.[32] Thus the actions of the former slaves are totally implicated in this social recomposition of postslavery society.

The situation in Martinique no longer appears so different from the one that existed in other islands in the region (see chapters 10, 13, and 17), where the process by which the peasantry was formed was similar. The difference doubtless lies in the reservations that people in the French West Indies have in recognizing the existence and also the historical role of the peasantry, while English-language works such as those by Sidney Mintz in the past[33] or more recently those of Thomas Holt[34] or again of Jean Besson[35] have described the emergence of the peasantry at the time of abolition in terms of resistance and the creation of an alternative to the plantation system.

Acknowledgment

The editors thank Daphne Besson for translating this paper from the French.

Notes

The reader may refer to the following references for a more complete approach to the chapter which is itself a synthesis of different works: Christine Chivallon, *Espace et identité à la Martinique. Paysannerie des mornes et reconquête collective (1840–1960)* (Paris: CNRS-Editions, 1998); Christine Chivallon, "Recompositions sociales à l'abolition de l'esclavage. L'importance de l'expérience des mornes dans la définition des orientations sociales à la Martinique," in Marcel Dorigny (ed.), *Esclavage, résistances et abolitions* (Paris: Les Éditions du CTHS, Comité des Travaux Historiques et Scientifiques, 1999), 417–431; Christine Chivallon, "Paysannerie et patrimoine foncier à la Martinique: de la nécessité de réévaluer quelques interprétations classiques," in *Terres d'Amériques, 3 La question de la terre dans les colonies et départements français d'Amérique, 1848–1998* (Paris: Karthala and Géode Caraïbe, 2000), 17–36. Two texts in English shed further light on peasant life in Martinique, notably from the novel *Texaco* by the Martinican writer P. Chamoiseau: see Christine Chivallon, "Space and Identity in Martinique. Towards a New Reading Focused on Space of the History of Peasantry," *Environment and Planning D: Society and Space* 13 (1995): 289–309; Christine Chivallon, "Images of Creole Diversity and Spatiality: A Reading of Patrick Chamoiseau's *Texaco*," *Ecumene* 4, no. 3 (1997): 318–336.

1. Hector Élisabeth, "Fondements réciproques de la personnalité et de la dynamique socioculturelle aux Antilles françaises," in *L'Historial Antillais* (Fort de France: Dajani, 1980), 305–319, quotation at 308.

2. Édouard Glissant, *Le discours antillais* (Paris: Seuil, 1981).

3. Francis Affergan, *Anthropologie à la Martinique* (Paris: Presses de la Fondation Nationale des Sciences Politiques, 1983).

4. See note 5.

5. The very use of the expression "peasant property" is not neutral. It is not the term favored by the classical version, which prefers to use "small property" without qualifying it further. Adding the qualifier "peasant" would amount to recognizing the existence of an agrarian group that has gained stability from some form or other of land appropriation, when in fact this interpretation specifies that the method used in the formation of the small property in Martinique does not come under legal forms recognized by the society in which it takes place and that it thus remains deeply marked by uncertain procedures that have weakened the group of small farmers by not giving it a soundly established legal base in land ownership. And, paradoxical though it may seem, in Martinique the term "small property" has now come to mean an ensemble of landed properties owing their existence to barely formalized legal procedures and constituted outside laws relating to land ownership.

6. Jean-Baptiste Delawarde, *La vie paysanne à la Martinique. Essai de géographie humaine* (Fort de France: Imprimerie Officielle, 1937), 65.

7. Guy Lasserre, "Petites propriétés et réformes foncières aux Antilles françaises," in *Les problèmes agraires des Amériques latines* (Colloques Internationaux du CNRS Paris: Éditions du CNRS, 1965), 109–124; Guy Lasserre, "La petite propriété des Antilles françaises dans la crise de l'économie de plantation," in *Etudes de géographie tropicale offertes à Pierre Gourou* (Paris: La Haye-Mouton, 1972), 539–555.

8. Lasserre, "Petites propriétés et réformes foncières," 111.

9. Delawarde, *La vie paysanne*, 64.

10. Lasserre, "Petites propriétés et réformes foncières," 111.

11. "La propriété rurale" and "Structures foncières." The argument of division due to inheritance to explain the evolution of the small property and its tendency to be split up is best in the work of Lasserre, "Petites propriétés et réformes foncières"; Lasserre, "La petite propriété des Antilles françaises."

12. Eugène Revert, *La Martinique: etude géographique*, (Paris, these d'Etat, Nouvelles Éditions Latines, 1949), 268–269.

13. Lasserre, "La petite propriété des Antilles françaises," 543.

14. Lasserre, "La petite propriété des Antilles françaises," 547.

15. Delawarde, *La vie paysanne*, 60.

16. This research was carried out in the field during 1988 and 1989 and was completed in 1992 by the submission of a doctoral thesis: Christine Guilhem-Chivallon, "Tradition et modernité dans le monde paysan martiniquais: approche

ethno-géographique" (thèse de Doctorat, Université de Bordeaux 3, Bordeaux, 1992). A more recent work (Chivallon, *Espace et identité à la Martinique*) reexamined the principle results for the period between 1840 and 1960. The hamlets studied are seven in number spread over three communes: Morne-Balai in Basse-Pointe; Urion and Le Caplet in Morne-Vert; Jossaud, la Vignette, Morne-Honoré, and Bas-Mangos in Rivière-Pilote.

17. These are registers used to record the identity of the new citizens in 1848, former slaves identified until then by a first name and a matriculation number which are recorded in these registers along with the parentage of the person (daughter or son of . . .).

18. The work on the parish registers was carried out indirectly using the database constituted by Bernard David from the same registers for his studies on the populations of Le Carbet (including le Morne-Vert up to 1949) and of Rivière-Pilote: Bernard David, "La population d'un quartier de la Martinique au début du XIXe siècle, d'après les registres paroissiaux. Rivière-Pilote 1802–1829," *Revue Française d'Histoire d'Outre-Mer* LX, no. 220 (1975): 330–363; Bernard David, "Les dernières années d'une société: le Carbet. 1810–1848," *Annales des Antilles*, Bulletin de la Société d'Histoire de la Martinique No. 20 (1977): 17–105.

19. Held in Martinique since 1806, these registers contain transcriptions of registered deeds of transfer regarding property and mention the legal nature of the act (deed under private seal or notarial deed).

20. This type of diagram is only one example among others, as is the case for table 12.1, and maps 12.1 and 12.2, as the maps corresponding to the land structures of the previous years are not included in this chapter. Other illustrations can be found in Chivallon, *Espace et identité à la Martinique*.

21. Annick François-Haugrin, "L'économie agricole de la Martinique: ses structures et ses problèmes entre 1845 et 1885" (thèse de doctorat, Université de Paris I, Paris, 1984).

22. For more details on these measures, see Chivallon, *Espace et identité à la Martinique*, 61 and 156–158.

23. Léo Elisabeth, "L'abolition de l'esclavage à la Martinique," *Annales des Antilles*, Mémoire de la Société d'Histoire de la Martinique, 1983, n 5.

24. Colson, at the time when he was President of the Society for the Reorganisation of Order and Work, quoted by Léo Elisabeth, "L'abolition de l'esclavage," 92.

25. François-Haugrin, "L'économie agricole de la Martinique."

26. The more quantitative study by François-Haugrin provides data needing to be refined to avoid confusion between a deed relating to the property, the property itself, and the purchaser of the property. Thus the cases of small proprietors who had become purchasers of several plots as well as the cases of sales concerning one and the same plot, which would have appeared as several different properties through statistical manipulation, would be taken into account. Similarly, on a comparative level, there should be clarification of the criterion used, insofar as Jacques Desruisseaux ("La propriété rurale" and "Structures foncières") fixes the upper threshold of the small property at 10 hectares while François-Haugrin ("L'économie agricole de la Martinique"), without being very precise, places the upper limit at 3 hectares. One should not, however, be too concerned about these uncertainties. The some 7,099 sales of plots of land in the historian's survey—for the northern region alone

between 1845 and 1875—reveal a large-scale phenomenon whose reliability cannot be weakened by the statistical bias introduced by the "double accounting" that I have just mentioned, and which is confirmed by the qualitative observations made in the hamlets. The constitution of the small property concerns also plots of land of more than 3 hectares, which when taken into account would compensate by a wide margin for the possible decrease that a rigorous estimate of the double counting would cause.

27. Population evaluated at 41,500 individuals in 1848–1849 according to François-Haugrin, "L'économie agricole de la Martinique," 111.

28. See note 26 above explaining "double counting."

29. Four hundred and ninety plots of land situated in the villages have been deducted from the 7,099 plots of land acquired between 1848 and 1875 in order to make a closer comparison with the data by Desruisseaux ("La propriété rurale" and "Structures foncières") based exclusively on the category "rural property." On this point, see François-Haugrin, "L'économie agricole de la Martinique," 118–122; Chivallon, *Espace et identité à la Martinique*, 89–98.

30. Legitimacy, like other colonial codes, seems to be reappropriated by the peasantry, which renews its sense. It is integrated into a set of possible designations in order to mark, via differentiations of filiations (natural, recognized, or legitimate), differential access to patrimony. In this sense legitimacy, more functional than moralistic, seems only to intervene to reinforce the existence of a basic family nucleus as well as affirming its preeminence over the familial patrimony when other filiations could compete with it for this same patrimony.

31. Alain-Philippe Blérald, *Histoire économique de la Martinique et de la Guadeloupe du XVIIe siècle à nos jours* (Paris: Karthala, 1986), 89.

32. Henri Mendras, *Sociétés paysannes* (Paris: Armand Collin, Collection U, 1976).

33. Sidney Mintz, "Petits cultivateurs et prolétaires ruraux dans la région des Caraïbes," in *Problèmes agraires des Amériques Latines* (Éditions du CNRS, 1967), 93–100; Sidney Mintz, "A Note on the Definition of Peasantries," *Journal of Peasant Studies* 1, no. 1 (1973): 91–106.

34. Thomas Holt, *The Problem of Freedom: Race, Labor, and Politics in Jamaica and Britain, 1832–1938* (Baltimore: Johns Hopkins University Press, 1992).

35. Jean Besson, "Land Tenure in the Free Villages of Trelawny, Jamaica: A Case Study in the Caribbean Peasant Response to Emancipation," *Slavery & Abolition* 5, no. 1(1984): 3–23; Jean Besson, "Religion as Resistance in Jamaican Peasant life," in Barry Chevannes (ed.), *Rastafari and Other African-Caribbean Worldviews* (New Brunswick: Rutgers University Press, 1998), 43–76.

Chapter 13

The Waxing and Waning of Land for the Peasantry in Barbados

Janet Momsen

Barbados was the only older sugar colony in the Caribbean able to increase sugar production after slavery ended, as a result of the planter's monopoly of agricultural land. Although before 1838 slaves exhibited signs of both protopeasant and protoproletarian behavior, growing much of their own food on tiny plots of plantation land and even selling surpluses on the domestic market and ginger for export, they had little opportunity to obtain their own land for farming after emancipation. Yet, gradually land did become available to the new peasantry as plantation agriculture became less profitable and the former slaves gained access to some financial capital with which to purchase land. However, as development has led to a more diversified economy, small-scale peasant farming has come under renewed threat because of increasing pressure on scarce land resources from tourism, industrialization, suburbanization, and improvements in the island's infrastructure. At the same time, agriculture is confronting a severe structural crisis because of trade liberalization with the loss of traditional protected export markets for sugar resulting in the release of land for alternative uses.

This chapter examines the adaptability of the small farm sector in the face of the changing competition between land and development in Barbados. The focus is on the period following World War II, and the detailed analysis of the changing use of farmland is based on the interpretation of aerial photographs from 1951, 1964, and 1989 and surveys of small-scale agriculture undertaken in 1963, 1987, and 2003. The chapter begins with a discussion of the value of repeat studies at a single site. This is followed by a review of the postemancipation struggles for land for small-scale farming in the face of plantation resistance. Changes in the economy of Barbados and their impact on the role of small farming in Barbados are then described. Finally the situation of small farming in Barbados over the period 1951–2003 is considered in terms of competition for land from other users.

Repeat Studies in the Caribbean

In general, there have been few long-term studies of particular field sites.[1] In the Caribbean, several people have focused their interest over a period of many years on one particular village such as Besson on Martha Brae in Jamaica[2] or on one island such as Clarke and Lowenthal on Barbuda, Skinner on Montserrat, and Mills on Carriacou as seen in their chapters in this volume.[3] However, these studies have usually emphasized in-depth understanding of a place rather than comparisons at specific points in time. Others, such as Monk and Alexander working in Margarita Island found greater economic diversity brought about by migration and the granting of duty-free status on revisiting the island after some three decades, and Brierley reported on changes noticed by a repeat study of small-scale farmers in 1982 and 1992 in Grenada.[4] None of these repeat studies, however, involved one particular economic subsector for a whole country over 40 years as do the Barbados surveys reported on here.

Survey Methodology

The farm surveys carried out in Barbados in 1987 and 2003 were designed as resurveys of the baseline survey undertaken in 1963.[5] The methodology used for the repeat surveys was a simplified version of that used in 1963. The first survey had taken as its universe a map of peasant agriculture compiled in 1960. This base map was derived from air photographs taken in 1951.[6] Land cultivated by small-scale farmers has an uneven pattern with marked clustering. The samples in every case were stratified by ecological zones and by size, with the larger farms between 1 and 10 acres being overrepresented.

In 1963, 213 surveys were completed, but in 1987 it was possible to survey only 132 farms, and in 2003, 140 largely because of the disappearance of many farms over this period. In 1987, in 24 percent of the sample areas, fewer than three farms could be surveyed, and in 2003, the target of four farms per sample area was met in only 31 percent of the areas. Undoubtedly the size of the samples and the distribution pattern of the sampled farms reflects a decline in the amount of land in small farms between the surveys as shown in maps 13.1 and 13.2 and table 13.1. However, since the same sample areas were visited in all three surveys, it is felt that sample sizes were adequate for comparison between the surveys.

The Period of the Waxing of Peasant Land

In 1838 there was virtually no unoccupied land in Barbados, and the freed slaves could obtain land only at the whim of the planters. Immediately following emancipation there was a surge of small plots of land made available to women. It is probable that this reflects planters providing land to their former slave mistresses for the support of their joint offspring.[7] Planters also provided land on the edge of estates to encourage the former slaves to continue

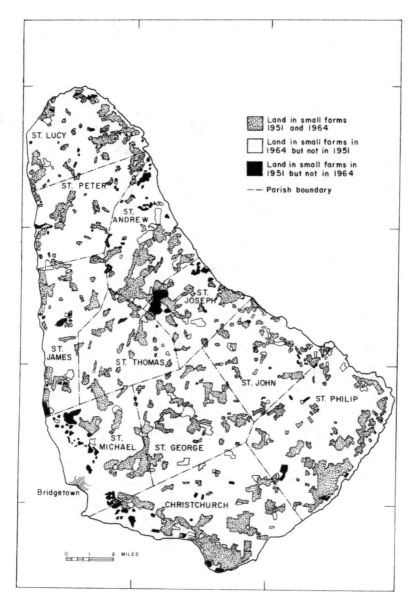

Map 13.1 The Distribution Pattern of Small Farms in Barbados, 1951 and 1964

Source: Derived from a comparison of air photographs: Air Survey Company Limited, December 1950/January 1951, at 1:10,000; and Hunting Survey Corporation Limited, November/December, 1964 at 1:10,000.

working for them. Since this land was only rented and was tied to work on the plantation it was not seen as the basis for the development of a peasantry when estates were broken up.[8] Because they were based on subdivisions of estates, the holdings are found to be associated together in "villages" of varying sizes.[9] Halcrow and Cave recognized 616 of these villages of which the

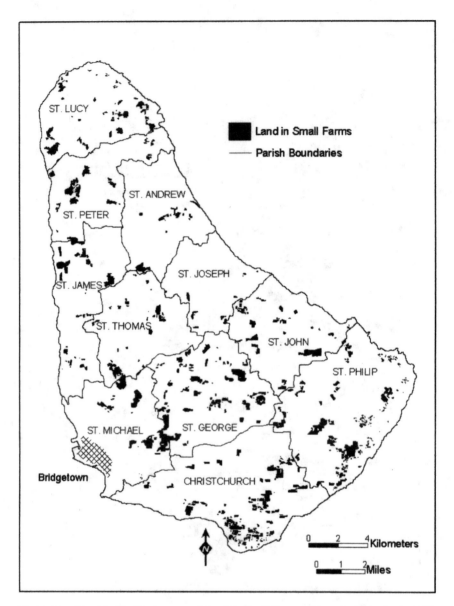

Map 13.2   The Distribution Pattern of Land in Small Peasant Farms in Barbados in 1951, 1964, and 1989

Source: Derived from a comparison of air photographs: Air Survey Company Limited, December 1950/January 1951, at 1:10,000; Hunting Survey Corporation Limited, November/December, 1964 at 1:10,000; and CIDA/Department of Energy, Mines and Resources, Canada, 1989, at 1:25,930.

1963 survey sampled 62 or just over 10 percent.[10] A corollary of the method of formation of peasant holdings lies in the quality of their land. The estates that were subdivided and sold off were generally those with poorer land. Sometimes estate land was made available to small producers in places where it

Table 13.1 The Waxing and Waning of Numbers and Acreage of Peasant Farms in Barbados, 1840–1989

Year	Number	Acreage	Notes
1840	780	—	Peasant holdings of less than 5 acres in freehold ownership
1851	3,537	—	Peasant holdings in freehold ownership
1913	13,000	—	Peasant holdings under 5 acres
1915	14,000	—	Holdings under 1 acre
1929	14,000	—	Holdings under 1 acre
	18,000	13,943	Holdings under 10 acres
	—	3,985	Holdings between 3 and 10 acres
1935	13,899	3,514	Holdings under 1 acre
	17,731	11,764	Holdings under 5 acres
	18,039	13,849	Holdings under 20 acres
1942	18,805	19,228	Holdings under 30 acres
	14,000	—	Holdings under 1 acre
	3,867	—	Holdings of 1 to 3 acres
	938	—	Holdings of 3 to 30 acres
1946	26,415	8,138	Holdings under 1 acre
	30,630	15,539	Holdings under 5 acres
	30,752	17,283	Holdings under 10 acres
1961	23,762	5,160	Holdings under 1 acre
	27,437	11,286	Holdings under 5 acres
	27,636	12,548	Holdings under 10 acres
	27,673	13,314	Holdings under 25 acres
1964–1965	27,748	15,792	Holdings under 10 acres
1965–1966	30,400	13,108	Holdings under 10 acres
1989	16,951	7,877	Holdings under 4 hectares

Sources: 1840 Sir Robert Schomburgk, *The History of Barbados* (London, 1948), 153; 1851 W. R. Sewell, *The Ordeal of Free Labour in the British West Indies* (New York, 1859), 39; 1913 W. R. Rouse, "The Moisture Balance of Barbados and Its Influence on Sugar Cane Yield," in *Two Studies in Barbadian Climatology*, Climatological Research Series No. 1, Department of Geography, McGill University, Montreal, 1966, 4; 1915 Government of Barbados, *Report of the Department of Science and Agriculture for 1915* (Bridgetown, Barbados, 1916); 1929 C. C. Skeete, *The Condition of Peasant Agriculture in Barbados* (Bridgetown, Barbados, 1930); 1935 Sir John Saint, *A Report on the Present Condition and Future Outlook of the Sugar Industry of Barbados by Delegates Appointed by the Legislature of Barbados* (1935). Draft forwarded to Mr Walcott, the Honorary Solicitor General, when Sir John was Acting Director of Agriculture in Barbados, Bridgetown, Barbados, August 21. Tables I and II; 1938 H. A. Tempany, (Compiler) *Agriculture in the West Indies*, Colonial Office No. 182 (London: HMSO, 1942), 122; 1942 *Agricultural Development in Barbados*, Despatches from the Comptroller for Development and Welfare in the West Indies (F. A. Stockdale) to H. E. the Governor of Barbados (Sir John Waddington), Bridgetown, Barbados; 1946 M. Halcrow and J. M. Cave, Department of Science and Agriculture, Bulletin No.11, Bridgetown, Barbados, 1947; 1961 British Development Division in the Caribbean, *West Indies Census of Agriculture. 1961, The Eastern Caribbean* (Bridgetown, Barbados, 1968); 1964–1965 *Current Estimates of Agriculture, April–March 1964–6* (Statistical Service, Bridgetown, Barbados, 1966), 1; 1965–1966 *Current Estimates of Agriculture, April–March 1965–66* (Statistical Service, Bridgetown, Barbados, 1968), 1; 1989 Government of Barbados, *1989 Census of Agriculture* (Ministry of Agriculture, Food and Fisheries, Bridgetown, Barbados, 1991).

had been left uncultivated by the plantation because of its poor quality or difficult nature. Shephard noted, "Much of the land now in the hands of peasant proprietors is handicapped by low fertility, steep slopes or inaccessibility."[11] Thus the postemancipation smallholders in Barbados had to struggle for land to a greater extent than their counterparts on other West Indian islands because the supply of land was very limited and the quality of land available was inferior.

Barbados is a small, tropical Anglophone island of 430 square kilometers. It is the most easterly Caribbean island, lying 435 kilometers northeast of Venezuela and is largely made up of relatively flat coral limestone with little surface water. The underlying oceanic series has been exposed in the northeastern more rugged region known as the Scotland District, encompassing the parishes of St. Andrew and St. Joseph and part of St. John, where there is marked soil erosion. English colonists established the first permanent settlement on the west coast in 1627, and Barbados remained a British colony until independence in 1966.[12] Sugarcane was introduced in 1640, and Barbados continued to be an archetypal sugar plantation economy, with sugar dominating the island's landscape and the lives of its people, until the late twentieth century.[13] Population density has been high for centuries and is currently 1,677 people per square kilometer with urban and suburban concentrations on the west and south coasts while the rest of the island remains largely agricultural. Despite a rural population density close to that of Bangladesh, in the regional context, the island has relatively high living standards and per capita incomes.

At the time of the abolition of slavery in 1834, Barbados had 36,760 hectares of agricultural land.[14] As sugar became a less profitable crop, land was slowly released by the plantations and bought by the former slaves, largely for subsistence agriculture.[15] Table 13.1 shows the pattern of this gradual transfer of land from plantation to peasant with the peak peasant acreage recorded in 1942. The West Indies Royal Commission of 1897 reported that in Barbados, unlike in the other islands, peasant farming was virtually nonexistent, so the Commissioners encouraged the plantocracy to make land available for small farmers with little success.[16]

The subdivision of plantations has been most frequent when depression in the sugar industry coincided with inflows of capital into the peasant sector. Between January 1906 and December 1910 Barbadians returning from the building of the Panama Canal brought back with them £102,456, which led to a rise in the price of small pieces of land to between £80 and £100 per acre while plantation land cost half as much.[17] Some money was sent back to wives and mothers in Barbados by the Panama migrants and was also used to buy land.[18] In 1911 subdivision of plantation land into small plots for sale was in process in the parishes of St. James, St. John, St. Michael, Christ Church, St. Thomas, and St. Philip. Subdivision in these areas was partly due to the number of returned migrants who were natives of these districts and wished to purchase land in their own home villages. On the other hand many people born in St. Lucy came back from Panama hoping to buy a farm but found there was no land available for them in that parish.[19] In St. Michael at least three estates, which had been partly subdivided in the early decades of the century, continued to be fragmented in the 1940s. These plantations and their land have given their names to districts within modern Bridgetown. Although these subdivisions may have originally been for farming they soon became part of the process of urbanization.

Between 1938 and 1940, following the economic depression of the 1930s, fragmentation in Christ Church increased, and two estates in St. James were subdivided. Those plantations that were broken up in St. Joseph, St. Andrew, and St. John were all on poor agricultural land in the Scotland District. In 1940 it was said that land for agricultural purposes was only available in a few parishes.[20] Between 1940 and 1960 subdivision was especially active in the Scotland District, and 1,270 acres of plantation land were sold out in small lots.[21]

The Waning of Land in Peasant Agriculture

A century after emancipation, in 1947, Halcrow and Cave pointed out, "The development of peasant holdings has not proceeded very far."[22] As table 13.1 and map 13.1 show land in small farming has steadily decreased since then. In the early part of this postwar period the situation may be partly explained by the coincidence of efforts on the part of peasants to obtain plots of land with increasing population pressure. After 1953 resistance to encroachment onto good plantation land increased and the subdivision of existing peasant plots began. In 1960 the Town and Country Planning Office took over responsibility for approving subdivisions of land, and of 3,166 applications granted between 1960 and 1966 only 58 were for agriculture, although some of the building lots may have included small peasant garden plots. Most of the agricultural lots were situated along the coast from St. Philip through Christ Church and St. Michael to St. Lucy, and the average size of lot was one-third to one-half acre.[23]

Innis has estimated that 21,500 acres of plantation land were released to peasants between 1860 and 1961, by small estates.[24] One-quarter of this land was in the parishes of St. Michael and Christ Church, and much of it was eventually lost to urban encroachment. In St. Andrew parish 3,464 acres, in St. George 2,364, and in St. John 1,824 acres were made available to peasants while St. Joseph also had a sizable acreage sold off to small farmers.[25] After 1960 there was an attempt to ensure that agricultural land was not divided into units too small to be viable.[26] One plantation in St. Michael was not allowed to be subdivided into lots of less than 3 acres, and in Christ Church the minimum size was 10 acres. In 1969 the Chief Agricultural Officer of Barbados said, "It is with the greatest difficulty that the minimum size into which agricultural land is permitted to be sub-divided has been held at 4 acres, and there is mounting pressure for sub-division into smaller units to enable as many persons as possible to own agricultural land."[27]

An examination of the distribution pattern of peasant holdings based on a comparison of air photographs for 1951 and 1964 shows several changes.

Much land went out of agriculture in this short period, especially around Bridgetown where it was lost to urban sprawl, and along the south and west coasts, where it has been absorbed by developments in the tourist industry. In the Scotland District government programs of soil conservation took some land out of peasant agriculture. However, this area also had some 1,147 acres of plantation land subdivided into small farm lots between 1950 and 1962.[28] Outside the Scotland District much of the spread of peasant agriculture that did occur during this period took place on sour grass pasture on the edge of gullies rather than on plantation sugar land. Overall between the two Agricultural Censuses of 1946 and 1961, the number of farms of less than 10 acres fell from 30,752 to 27,636, and their total acreage dropped even more precipitously by 27 percent (table 13.1).

Farley et al., in his report on the sugar industry in Barbados, recommended that the government of Barbados should explore ways of making land available to peasants.[29] This suggestion was not acted upon, and in 1969 the island's Chief Agricultural Officer stated, "It would therefore seem that Barbados must decide, as a matter of policy, whether the part-time farmer on his small acreage, with no implements other than the hoe and the fork, has a significant role to play in the future agricultural development of the country."[30] Almost 40 years later it seems that no clear decision has yet been made.

The most recent census of agriculture for the island, carried out in 1989, revealed that only 21,560 hectares (53,253 acres) remained in farms.[31] To make matters worse the proportion of idle land, especially on plantations, had increased to 13,000 hectares (32,110 acres). Within the plantation sector consolidation was evident with 85.3 percent of their land combined into 35 plantations under the ownership of 8 major plantation companies.[32] According to the 1989 Agricultural Census, plantations (holdings over 10 hectares or 25 acres) made up 0.8 percent of the total number of holdings, while the 16,951 small farms under 4 hectares (98.7 percent of the total) controlled only 3,189 hectares or 14.8 percent of the farmland. The average size of the almost 17,000 holdings of less than 4 hectares was 0.19 hectares or 0.46 acres. The plantations occupied 83.1 percent of the farmland, and 83 medium-sized farms (in the Barbadian context) of 4–10 hectares (25–250 acres) occupied 2.1 percent of the farmland. This heritage of plantation ownership, and the skewed control of land resources, is found throughout the region but is most acute in Barbados.[33]

Farmland has been rapidly going out of production since the mid-twentieth century. Map 13.1 shows where land in small farms was lost between 1951 and 1964. Between 1950 and 1989 the area of land in crops was reduced by more than half.[34] Some 1,900 hectares (4,700 acres) of farmland were under permanent pasture for livestock in 1989.[35] It has been estimated that between 1970 and 1985, 1.4 hectares of arable land went out of crop production each day. Between 1987 and 1989 this process accelerated to a daily rate of loss of approximately 5.3 hectares.[36] Over the period 1971–1989, about 7,700 hectares (19,000 acres) were put up for sale. Very little of this land went into the small farm sector but most of it was redesignated and redefined for residential and industrial development. Several large areas of plantation land also became golf courses.[37] These new uses reflect the changing economy of the island[38] with tourism now the primary source of foreign exchange.[39] Spatially, a coastal pattern of an urban-suburban-tourist zone with enclave manufacturing, a concentration of services, and modern retailing with many new elite residential areas, stretching from the parish of Christ Church, through St. Michael and St. James to Speightstown in St. Peter, has developed, with agriculture being largely pushed out toward the north and east of the island.[40] The areas from which peasant agriculture has disappeared are seen clearly in map 13.2.[41]

What this land-use change means to the small farmer is that agricultural land is very rarely available on the open market. When it is put up for sale it is so expensive, and the minimum size for subdivision of agricultural land at 4 acres (1.6 hectares) so large, that the capital for investment in other inputs is drained away. In 1938 the average size of smallholding was 0.3 hectares.[42] By 1989 most smallholdings (88.2 percent) were of less than 0.2 hectares (0.5 acres), and the modal size was 0.025–0.1 hectares (0.06–0.25 acres) suggesting increasing fragmentation among the smallest farms. There is no more recent source of comprehensive data, but observation and the results of the 1987 and 2003 surveys suggest that small farming has continued to decrease.

Small farms have long been concentrated on the poorest land, and this concentration is increasing. In Barbados this means on the shallow rocky soils of St. Philip and Christ Church in the south and St. Lucy in the north, where there is a very marked dry season each year. Some attempts have been made by government to supply irrigation water to these areas, but the cost of this water is prohibitive. Drought and the high cost of water were seen as major problems by 27 percent of farmers interviewed in 1987, but in 2003 they were the main problems for 53 percent of farmers interviewed. However, in Christ Church and St. Philip land has gone into residential and tourist development for which a long dry season and proximity to the airport are locational advantages as shown in map 13.2. In St. Lucy in the north of the island residential development has been slower to develop because of distance from the main city, but it was beginning in 2003. The Barbados government had set up a land settlement project in St. Lucy and provided an irrigation system, but water costs were a problem there. Small farms are also found on the red sandy soils just inland of the coast in St. Peter and St. James, but much of the coastal area of these parishes is now occupied by hotels and restaurants. Small farmland has been lost in the Scotland District, in St. Andrew and St. Joseph parishes, where farming has been restricted in an attempt to prevent further soil erosion. By the end of the 1980s small farms were surviving most successfully in the relatively favorable areas of deep black soils and weak dry seasons in St. George and St. Thomas. However, the 1987 survey found that the greatest proportion of uncultivated land on smallholdings was in the parishes of St. Michael, Christ Church, and St. George, which may indicate some speculative holding of land in these periurban areas of high land prices.[43] This was particularly the case around the city of Bridgetown where urban sprawl had overtaken former agricultural land. In the Scotland District, in St. Andrew, and St. Patrick, government soil conservation measures have led to the disappearance of several areas of smallholdings (map 13.2).

In the 2003 repeat survey, the original 58 sample areas were revisited, and, as in 1987, three farms were surveyed in each sample area. No farms were found in eight sample areas: three on the edge of Bridgetown; three in suburban areas easily accessible to Bridgetown in the parishes of Christ Church and St. Michael, where tourist and middle-class residential development has been expanding, two in St. George; one in St. Peter; and one in St. James, where land has been recently sold for residential development. In one area without farms in St. Andrew, soil erosion had made farming impossible. In a further five areas where only one farmer could be located, residential development had largely replaced farming or the land was farmed by someone who did not live in the area and so was unavailable for interview.

Conclusion

The 2003 survey revealed that there is more dynamism in small farming today than in 1987. Although crop diversity is less widely practiced, both decreases and increases in agriculture had occurred over the previous decade on more farms in 2003 than in the 1980s. However, 59 percent of farms had experienced a decrease in farming between 1993 and 2003, while 47 percent of the farms in the 1987 survey recorded no change. Most of the farmers who reported a decrease in farming activity in 2003 explained the change in terms of increasing infirmity with age or lack of time because of the demands of off-farm work. Small farmers are becoming more specialized rather than diversifying into a wider mix of crops and livestock. Production for home consumption is most important in the center and north of the island, far from market opportunities in the tourist and urban areas of the south and west.

Barbadian peasant farmers constantly reinvent themselves in the face of continuing competition for land, now from tourism and suburbanization rather than from plantations as in the past. Today small-scale agricultural producers are responding to demand from both locals and tourists for fresh, locally grown produce free from chemicals and behaving much like small organic farmers in the United States rather than traditional peasants.[44] If this latest agrarian reform is to succeed then a new generation of small-scale farmers will have to be encouraged and supported.

Acknowledgments

Thanks to Peggy Hauselt for preparing maps 13.1 and 13.2 from the air photographs and to graduate students Kelly Payson and Travis Marcotte and to 12 undergraduate students from the University of California, Davis, for work on the 2003 field survey. Thanks also to undergraduates from the University of Newcastle upon Tyne and to Dr. Richard Aspinall for help with the 1987 survey. Above all, thanks are due to Valerie Beynon for vital assistance with both the 1963 and 2003 farm surveys.

Notes

1. R. V. Kemper and A. P. Royce (eds.), *Chronicling Cultures: Long-Term Field Research in Anthropology* (Walnut Creek: Lanham, 2002; New York and Oxford: Altamira Press, 2002). Kemper and Royce discuss repeat surveys in detail but do not provide any examples from the Caribbean.

2. For example, Jean Besson, *Martha Brae's Two Histories: European Expansion and Caribbean Culture-Building in Jamaica* (Chapel Hill and London: University of North Carolina Press, 2002).

3. See, e.g., David Lowenthal and Colin Clarke, "Common Lands, Common Aims: The Distinctive Barbudan Community," in Malcolm Cross and Arnaud Marks (eds.), *Peasants, Plantations and Rural Communities in the Caribbean* (Leiden: Royal Institute of Linguistics and Anthropology, 1975; Guildford: University of Surrey Dept. of Sociology, 1975), and chapter 11 of this volume; Jonathan Skinner, *Before the Volcano: Reverberations of Identity on Montserrat* (Kingston, Jamaica: Arawak Publications, 2004), and chapter 16 of this volume; Beth Mills, "Family Land in Carriacou, Grenada and Its Meaning within the Transnational Community: Heritage, Identity, and Rooted Mobility" (Unpublished PhD dissertation, University of California, Davis, 2002), and chapter 17 of this volume.

4. Janice Monk and Charles S. Alexander, "Migration, Development and the Gender Division of Labour: Puerto Rico & Margarita Island, Venezuela," in Janet H. Momsen (ed.), *Women and Change in the Caribbean*, 167–177 (London: James Currey; Indianapolis: Indiana University Press; and Kingston, Jamaica: Ian Randle, 1993). J. S. Brierley, "The Apparent Inflexibility of Small-Scale Farmers to Changes in Grenada's Political-Economic Environment 1982–1992," in D. Barker and D. MacGregor (eds.), *Resources, Planning and Environmental Management in a Changing Caribbean* (Kingston, Jamaica: The University of the West Indies Press, 2003), 37–56.

5. Janet D. Henshall (Momsen) and Leslie J. King, "Some Structural Characteristics of Peasant Agriculture in Barbados," *Economic Geography* 42, no. 1 (1966): 74–84.

6. J. Anderson, "Land Use of Barbados" (Unpublished MA thesis, Department of Geography, McGill University, 1960).

7. Janet H. Momsen, "Gender Ideology and Land," in Christine Barrow (ed.), *Caribbean Portraits: Essays on Gender Ideologies and Identities* (Kingston, Jamaica: Ian Randle Publishers in association with the Centre for Gender and Development Studies, University of the West Indies, 1998), 115–132.

8. Woodville K. Marshall with Trevor Marshall and Bentley Gibbs, *The Establishment of a Peasantry in Barbados, 1840–1920* (Cave Hill, Barbados: Department of History, University of the West Indies. Mimeo, 1974).

9. Sidney M. Greenfield, "Land Tenure and Transmission in Barbados," *Anthropological Quarterly* 33 (1960): 165–176.

10. Magnus Halcrow and J. M. Cave, *Peasant Agriculture in Barbados*, Bulletin No. 11 (Bridgetown, Barbados: Department of Science and Agriculture, 1947).

11. C. Y. Shephard, *Peasant Agriculture in the Leeward and Windward Islands* (Trinidad: Imperial College of Tropical Agriculture, 1945), 14.

12. Hilary Beckles, *A History of Barbados from American Settlement to Nation-State* (New York: Cambridge University Press, 1990), 7.

13. I. Drummond and Terry Marsden, "A Case Study of Unsustainability: The Barbados Sugar Industry," *Geography* 80, no. 4 (1995): 342–354.

14. Christine Barrow, "The Plantation Heritage in Barbados: Implications for Food Security, Nutrition and Employment" (ISER Working Paper No. 41, Institute of Social and Economic Studies, University of the West Indies, Mona, Jamaica, 1995).

15. Marshall with Marshall and Gibbs, *The Establishment of a Peasantry in Barbados, 1840–1920.*

16. For further discussion of the importance of this Royal Commission see chapter 1.

17. Otis P. Starkey, *The Economic Geography of Barbados* (New York: Columbia University Press, 1939).

18. Momsen, "Gender Ideology and Land," 115–132.

19. C. Prescott, "The Barbadian Peasant Sector—A Problem" (Unpublished undergraduate essay, McGill University, Montreal, 1967).

20. Board of Health Minutes, Barbados Archives, Black Rock, Barbados, June 27, 1940.

21. Data compiled by author from unpublished maps and plans filed at the Scotland District Conservation Board Offices, Haggetts, St. Andrew, Barbados.

22. Halcrow and Cave, *Peasant Agriculture in Barbados,* v.

23. Janet D. Momsen, "The Geography of Land Use and Population in the Caribbean (with Special Reference to Barbados and the Windward Islands)" (Unpublished PhD dissertation, King's College, University of London, 1969).

24. Frank C. Innis, "Desarrollo planeado en un continuo de tendencias establicidas, Barbados," in *Papers of the International Geographical Union, Regional Conference in Latin America Vol. 2* (Mexico City: International Geographical Union, 1966), 80–81.

25. Innis, "Desarrollo planeado en un continuo de tendencias establicidas, Barbados," 81.

26. In 1894 the legal minimum for a subdivision was 1,220 square feet, increased to 2,400 square feet in 1928, and reduced to 1,800 square feet in 1957. Board of Health Minutes, Barbados Archives, Black Rock, St. Michael, various dates.

27. E. C. Pilgrim, "The Role and Structure of Agriculture in Barbados and the Agricultural Development Programme" (paper presented at the Fourth West Indies Agricultural Economics Conference, Barbados, mimeographed, March 1969, 20).

28. Data compiled by the author from unpublished maps and plans filed at the Scotland District Conservation Board Offices, Haggetts, St. Andrew, Barbados.

29. R. M. Farley, B. Ifill, and J. C. Brown, *Report of the Commission of Enquiry into the Barbados Sugar Industry, 1962–1963* (Bridgetown, Barbados: Government Printing Office, 1965), 82.

30. Pilgrim, "The Role and Structure of Agriculture in Barbados and the Agricultural Development Programme," 21.

31. Government of Barbados, *1989 Census of Agriculture* (Bridgetown, Barbados: Ministry of Agriculture, Food and Fisheries, 1991).

32. Barrow, *The Plantation Heritage in Barbados.*

33. Barrow, *The Plantation Heritage in Barbados.*

34. Government of Barbados, *1989 Census of Agriculture.*

35. Government of Barbados, *1989 Census of Agriculture.*

36. Barrow, *The Plantation Heritage in Barbados.*

37. One of the most recent of these new golf courses is the 18-hole course built at Sandy Lane Hotel in St. James, where Tiger Woods got married in October 2004. This course was built on a former sugar plantation to the highest international standards.

38. R. Singh, "Implications of Liberalisation for Caribbean Agriculture: Prospects for the Non-Traditional SubSector," in R. Ramsaran (ed.), *Caribbean Survival and the Global Challenge* (Kingston, Jamaica: Ian Randle, 2002), 384–415.

39. I. G. Strachan, *Paradise and Plantation: Tourism and Culture in the Anglophone Caribbean* (Charlottesville, VA, and London: University of Virginia Press, 2002).

40. Robert B. Potter, "From Plantopolis to Mini-Metropolis in the Eastern Caribbean: Reflections on Urban Sustainability," in D. F. M. McGregor, D. Barker, and S. Lloyd Evans (eds.), *Resource Sustainability and Caribbean Development* (Kingston, Jamaica: The Press, University of the West Indies, 1998), 51–68.

41. Maps of the distribution of land in peasant holdings in 1964 and 1989 can be found in Janet H. Momsen, "Caribbean Peasantry Revisited: Barbadian Farmers over Four Decades," *Southeastern Geographer* 45, no. 2 (2005): 42–57.

42. Harold A. Tempany (Compiler), *Agriculture in the West Indies*. Colonial Office (C.O.) No. 182 (London: HMSO, 1942).

43. Richard J. Aspinall and Janet D. Momsen, "Small Scale Agriculture in Barbados, 1987" (Seminar Paper No. 52, University of Newcastle upon Tyne, Department of Geography, 1987).

44. As described in Sidney W. Mintz, "The Question of a Caribbean Peasantry: A Commentary," *Caribbean Studies* 1, no. 3 (1961): 31–34.

Chapter 14

Agrobiodiversity as an Environmental Management Tool in Small-Scale Farming Landscapes: Implications for Agrochemical Use

Balfour Spence and Elizabeth Thomas-Hope

Introduction

For generations, small-scale farmers throughout the developing world have selectively nurtured a wide variety of wild and domesticated plant and animal species and in so doing, accumulated extensive knowledge about local biodiversity.[1] The process of innovation, experimentation, and knowledge sharing that has fostered the biodiversity selections of small farmers is still in vogue in spite of the global trend toward dependence on a few selected and highly experimental species of crops to increase agricultural production and enhance global food security. This selective nurturing of an array of species, especially plants, promotes enhanced levels of species diversity and related management diversity within small-scale farming systems and is commonly referred to as agrobiodiversity. Strictly speaking, agrobiodiversity (agricultural biodiversity) includes all aspects of biological diversity that have a role to play in the development of agriculture and the provision of food. In that regard, agrobiodiversity refers to the variety and variability of plants, animals, and microorganisms at genetic, species, and ecosystem levels that are critical to the sustainable functioning of the structures and processes of agroecosystems. In the Caribbean context, the diversity of species on small farms has been the mainstay of sustainability in domestic food security as, in spite of sustained reduction in output, small farms have remained the pillars of domestic food production in the Caribbean.

Agrobiodiversity is critical to environmental sustainability for a number of reasons including the fact that it facilitates the sustainable production of food and improves food security; it provides biological support to production because of the variability of nutrient demands and vulnerabilities (e.g. to pests); and it provides ecological services such as soil protection, water cycling, water quality, and air quality. Based on these benefits, high levels of agrobiodiversity are conducive to increasing environmental and economic sustainability within the agricultural system. This chapter will illustrate the characteristics of agrobiodiversity in Jamaican small farming systems, with reference to the lower Rio Grande Valley, Portland. The chapter then examines the relationship between agrobiodiversity levels and agrochemical usage, demonstrating that the conservation of higher levels of diversity of plant species reduces the need for agrochemical applications by farmers.

Characteristics of Agrobiodiversity

Agrobiodiversity is distinct from other types of species diversity in several ways:

1. There is *active management* of agrobiodiversity systems by farmers, and these systems would not survive in the absence of human interference.
2. *Indigenous knowledge and culture* are integral parts of agrobiodiversity management systems.
3. Many important biodiversity systems are based on "alien" crop species introduced from elsewhere resulting in transnational interdependence of the gene pool on which global food supply systems rely.

The agrobiodiversity of any agroecosystem is influenced by the interrelationships among human factors, environmental feedbacks, and prevailing natural environmental conditions. In that context, the level of agrobiodiversity within food production systems is informed by prevailing ecological conditions, the management capacity of farmers, farmers' access to sources of biological diversity that can influence the range of species that are part of their agromanagement systems, and farmers' access to agricultural capital such as agrochemicals that can substitute for natural capital.

Agrobiodiversity Change in Jamaica

Biodiversity loss in Jamaica, like that of the rest of the Caribbean, started early in its modern development and coincides with the plantation system of development. This system in Jamaica gained momentum in the seventeenth century with the introduction of sugarcane plantations as the economic base of the island.[2] The sugar plantation emphasized monoculture as the dominant farm management system, while mixed farming to satisfy domestic needs was left to the slave population who evolved a system of agrobiodiversity. This was characterized by a wide variety of plant species to satisfy the nutritional needs of farm households. While the plantation system engaged high levels of official support and intervention, mixed-farming systems lacked the infrastructural support that could transform them into viable commercial entities, a bias that still prevails. However, the low levels of official intervention facilitated greater retention of species and management diversity within these small-scale, mixed-farming systems.

During the early twentieth century agrodiversification was initiated within the plantation owing to the introduction of a wider variety of new crops to replace the ailing sugar industry. Thus bananas, coconuts, and citrus replaced sugar on the coastal lowlands, and coffee expanded in monoculture stands into the high altitudes. Although small farmers have access to a relatively small proportion of arable lands in Jamaica, the production of export crops was extended to those who could produce under the conditions prescribed by the export agencies to which the crops were sold for the export market. The extension of plantation-type crops to small farmers heralded dramatic changes in the species, management, and organizational diversity of small farming systems.

The notion that the promotion of these agricultural systems resulted in the serious loss of species biodiversity, agricultural management, or organizational diversity (and thus flexibility to market and other needs) has never been a matter of concern among those responsible for national development policies. This has been the case despite the significance of such losses for severe deforestation and extensive land degradation, and their implications in terms of the sustainability of farming.

Agrobiodiversity in the Rio Grande Valley, Portland, Jamaica

A study of agrobiodiversity practices among small farmers of Jamaica was conducted in the lower Rio Grande Watershed in the Parish of Portland (map 14.1), as part of an international project—People, Land Management and Environmental Change (PLEC).[3] This approach to biodiversity broadens the concept from its traditional emphasis on genetic resources to include *landscape-level* biodiversity as well as the social organization and technological inputs that support biodiversity and reduce agricultural and ecological risk. The PLEC concept of agrobiodiversity focuses on farmers' use of natural environmental diversity to satisfy livelihood objectives, including their choice of crops and animals, as well as the management strategies that apply to land, water, and the agricultural biota. Agrodiversity in this context thus includes biophysical diversity, management diversity, agrobiodiversity and organizational diversity (table 14.1). Within this context, this chapter examines the impact of agrochemical use on the agrophysical, social, and agroeconomic landscape of the Rio Grande Valley. Its relevance in the context of agrobiodiversity is in the focus on the conservation of agrobiodiversity as part of the strategy to promote the sustainability of small farming landscapes. Given this objective, it is of critical importance to understand the nature of agrochemical usage and the chemical dynamics of the area in relation to existing variations in levels of agrobiodiversity.

Agriculture is the primary economic activity in the Rio Grande Valley, and although an estimated 80.4 percent of the watershed was forested in 1998, pressure especially from banana monoculture has risen at an alarming rate. The area utilized for all land-use activities, except forest, expanded between 1986 and 1998, with an overall increase amounting to about 8 percent (1866.9 hectares). The expansion in land area utilized for human livelihood

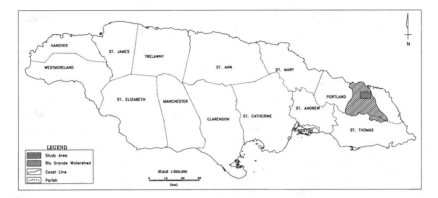

Map 14.1   Location of the PLEC Rio Grande Demonstration Site

Table 14.1   PLEC: Elements of Agrodiversity

Agrodiversity categories	Description
Biophysical diversity	The diversity of the natural environment including the intrinsic quality of the natural resource base that is used for production. It includes the natural resilience of the biophysical environment, soil characteristics, plant life and other biota. It includes physical and chemical aspects of the soil, hydrology, climate, and the variability and variation in all these elements.
Management diversity	All methods of managing the land, water, and biota for crop and livestock production, and the maintenance of soil fertility and structure. Included are biological, chemical, and physical methods of management.
Agrobiodiversity	This refers to all species and varieties used by or useful to people, with a particular emphasis on crop, plant, and animal combinations. It may include biota that are indirectly useful and emphasizes the manner in which they are used to sustain or increase production, reduce risk, and enhance conservation.
Organizational diversity	This is the diversity in the manner in which farms are operated, owned, and managed, and the use of resource endowments from different sources. Elements include labor, household size, capital assets, reliance on off-farm employment, and so on.

Source: Michael Stocking, "Diversity: A New Stocking Direction for Soil Conservation in Sustainable Utilization of Global Soil and Water Resources," *Proceedings of the 12th International Soil Conservation Conference*, Beijing, vol. 1 (2002): 53–58.

has come at the expense of the forested area that declined by about 847 hectares over the 12-year period. This pattern of land-use change has implications for flood and landslide susceptibility in the Rio Grande Valley because the removal of forest from steep slopes and disturbance of these slopes for cultivation increases rainfall runoff and reduces slope stability.

Small farming as a livelihood activity in the Rio Grande Valley of Portland, as elsewhere throughout Jamaica, is associated with poor economic returns. This situation is largely explained by the vagaries of the market and the difficulties related to transport and access to new market opportunities.[4] In addition, recurrent flooding and landslides cause repeated damage to crops and other property. Agricultural practices, especially those related to monoculture banana, further aggravate hazard impacts because the practice of removing undergrowth from banana fields allows more rapid water runoff.

Based on guidelines developed by the PLEC project, measurements of agrobiodiversity were conducted at the PLEC-Jamaica Rio Grande demonstration site.[5] This attempted to capture most aspects of the biophysical, crop, and land management diversity that characterized small farming. The measurements supported the main tenets of the PLEC project, that diversity is a feature of agricultural systems that is often overlooked in biodiversity assessments but that must be better understood in the process of biodiversity preservation and conservation.

The study identified land-use stages and field types, farm management regimes, crop and associated cropping systems, and land management practices.[6] Analysis of the farm systems at the Rio Grande site focused on the cultivated, wild, and semidomesticated plant species found on the farms in order to highlight local trends in

- the dynamics of agrobiodiversity and biodiversity, particularly impacts of land and crop management decisions and tenure arrangements on diversity;
- the environmental and socioeconomic impacts of change on diversity; and
- models of tree and field crop combinations found on small farms.

Land Management Diversity at the Rio Grande Site

Within the sampled farm units, there were five dominant land-use stages.[7] Within each land-use stage, the identified field types varied as a function of farm management and reflected a complex mix of different types of cultivated and noncultivated crops, trees, and shrubs adopted by each farmer. Within the land-use stages, field types ranged from one to eight, with Agroforest and Edge land-use stages showing the highest variations in field types. A total of 235 different species of plants were identified on the farms, including roots and tubers, vegetables, legumes, cereals, fruits, condiments, ornamental and medicinal plants, and timber trees. Approximately 70 percent of the plants were used by local residents. Use-values included food, building material, erosion and flood water control, mulch, medicine, spices, stimulants, and fencing material.

Field types on some farms changed frequently, primarily as a function of the farmer's crop and land management decisions. For example, one farm was initially characterized as having three dominant land-use stages with six field types. This farmer, occupied flatlands on the floodplains of a river where he intercropped plots of banana, coffee, and coconuts with a variety of vegetables, including pumpkin, cucumber, cabbage, pack-choi, and peppers. The farmer's decision to farm this mix of crops was based primarily on the opportunities for markets, access to technical assistance, and the availability of land. Subsequent visits with this farmer showed that changes in market availability and other socioeconomic pressures led to a change in his cropping system.

Land-Use Stages and Field Types

The results of agrobiodiversity assessments of farming systems in the Rio Grande Valley indicated that species occurrence and abundance varied according to land-use stages and field types. The Agroforest, House Garden, and Edge land-use stages were the most commonly observed within the demonstration area, constituting over 80 percent of the total sample units. These land-use stages also displayed the highest diversity of crops, fruit trees, shrubs, and other valuable plants as the *species richness index*[8] reflects (table 14.2). The Margalef Index abundance measure showed that the Agroforest, Edge, and House Garden land-use stages, respectively, contained a higher abundance than that of the orchard. Margalef Index values for the dominant land-use stages ranged from 20 to 58, while that of the banana orchards were as low as 6. From this index it may be concluded that type of land-use stage has implications for the abundance of species found on the farm. Where other plants were inter-cropped within banana fields (generating the Agroforest or House Garden land-use stage), the abundance index increased dramatically, sometimes as much as a factor of three. Another land-use stage showing high species diversity was the fallow, which was land not actively managed due to its susceptibility to flooding.

The higher diversity in the occurrence of crops and trees common to the Agroforest, House Garden, and Edge land-use stages can be attributed to the intensive management practices employed by farmers as physical and economic coping mechanisms. In many ways these strategies were consistent with the diversification of agricultural production, allowing for better market access,

Table 14.2   Species Richness by Land-Use Stages

Land-use stage	Average species richness	Incidence of the land-use stage
Agroforest	26	9
House garden	27	6
Edge	16	20
Fallow	26	1
Orchard	12	3

Source: Authors' fieldwork.

which will in turn assist in fulfilling the needs of the farmer and his household for food and cash. The management practices associated with this strategy were related to cropping types and patterns from farm to farm, further increasing agrobiodiversity at the site. These practices and approaches to crop production, land management, and livelihood security formed the basis of the "good practice" models developed by the PLEC researchers (farmers and scientists) and demonstration by expert farmers.

The field types of the sampled areas again supported the observation that variations in diversity were a function of farm management. The sampled area showed species richness that ranged from 7 to 59, with the observed variations following the trends in the land-use stages discussed above. The Agroforest land-use stage showed the highest variation in field types, with over 9 field types identified (table 14.2). Field-type species richness within this land-use stage ranged from 13 to 59. However, on farms where there was an emphasis on a mixture of banana, root crops, vegetable, fruit, and lumber trees, there was greater organizational diversity, and the species richness index was above 25.

The field type showing the highest species richness (59) was found on a farm divided into several subplots upon which a number of crops were planted for sale to the local market. This farm also showed the highest level of species abundance within the Agroforest and Edge field type. This farm and the farmer's management practices reflected the relationship between market orientation and the occurrence of diversity as this farmer sold all his produce locally. Conversely, banana farmers targeting export markets received technical support from the Banana Export Company (BECO), which promoted a loss of diversity in order to facilitate greater efficiency in cultivation and production costs. For example, the banana farmer producing for the export market will clear the banana plot to reduce "wastage" of nutrient inputs through uptake by other plants and reduce the incidence of diseases on the farm. This approach promotes a reduction in diversity and is reflected in the uniformity in field type observed in the Banana Plantation/Orchard land-use stage. The single field type within this Banana Plantation/Orchard land-use stage showed the lowest species richness values, which ranged from 7 to 19, with an average of 12. Most farms had species richness of 20 and above. It is in this environment that reliance on agrochemicals is most pronounced.

The House Garden land-use stage showed less variation within the respective field types. Other assessments of the observed field types showed that the edges also made a significant contribution to diversity, as in many instances the edge contained crops, fruit trees, and medicinal plants not commonly grown in the main farming area.

Crops and Cropping Systems at the Study Area

Diversity within the demonstration site was also examined at the level of the crops and crop management systems employed. Land-use stages and field types of the demonstration site were dominated by the banana. Within the farming systems sampled, over 75 percent of the farmers indicated that a second major crop was cultivated alongside the main income-generating crop. In addition, 61 percent of the farmers indicated that they also farmed a third income-generating crop alongside the first and second main farm crops. Commonly observed secondary and tertiary crops cultivated were plantain, yam, breadfruit, and dasheen. Some farmers also included vegetables such as tomato and legumes. Thirteen different types of vegetables were observed on the sampled farms. These included cabbage, cucumber, pumpkin, tomato, cauliflower, okra, and callaloo. Legumes are both widely cultivated and consumed in the Valley, but farmers grew limited varieties, mainly kidney beans, string beans, gungo peas, cowpeas, and broad bean.

Table 14.3 shows the combination of dominant and secondary crops selected by farmers within the Rio Grande Valley and illustrates that dasheen, plantain, and fruit trees, which when intercropped with banana, generate the Agroforest land-use stage and associated field types.

A number of trees and noncultivated species commonly thrive within each land-use stage, with the exception of the Orchard (table 14.4). Where noncultivated species were allowed to thrive, namely within the edges and the house gardens there was an associated increase in diversity. Again, it must be emphasized that this diversity was directly a function of the farmer's farm management practices for weed/wild plant control and crop and plant choice. The occurrence of medicinal and ornamental plants varied, particularly at the field-type level, and was found to be most prevalent in the Edge land-use stage.

The assessment of agrobiodiversity data at the PLEC-Jamaica demonstration site supported the premise that agricultural diversity has a significant role to play in the conservation of biological diversity. Data analysis also highlighted the following features:

- Despite socioeconomic, cultural, and political pressures, agrodiversity was flourishing within the Rio Grande Valley demonstration site, from which other farmers could learn more sustainable farm management practices.
- Coping strategies were reflected in the land-use stage variations observed.
- Substantial diversity existed in cultivated and noncultivated species, management practices/techniques, and land-use variations.

Agrodiversity and Agrochemical Use

Issues related to agrochemical use and their environmental impacts are well documented, and the desirability of farming systems to become less reliant on agrochemicals is constantly promoted. The PLEC approach of promoting agrobiodiversity within small-scale farming systems has provided a strategy for the reduction in agrochemical use through greater biological diversity and diversity in farm management practices. The conceptual relationship between agrobiodiversity and agrochemical use is demonstrated in figure 14.1.

Table 14.3 Matrix of Crop Combinations on Small Farms in the Rio Grande Valley

Dominant farm crop	Secondary crops										
	Banana	Plantain	Coconut	Dasheen	Yam	Cucumber	Coffee	Pumpkin	Melon	Pineapples	Sweet potatoes
Banana	—	5	2	2	2	—	1	—	—	—	—
Plantain	2	—	—	—	4	—	—	—	—	—	—
Coconut	—	—	—	—	—	—	—	—	1	—	—
Yam	—	—	—	—	—	1	—	—	—	2	—
Calaloo	—	—	—	—	—	—	—	1	—	—	—
Pack-Choy	—	—	—	—	—	—	—	—	—	—	—
Pineapples	—	—	1	—	—	—	—	—	—	—	1

Source: Authors' fieldwork.

Table 14.4   Land-Use Stages and Associated Cropping Systems in Rio Grande

Land-use stage	Crops commonly cultivated	Trees commonly cultivated/promoted	Medicinal/other useful plants promoted
Agroforest	Banana Plantain Dasheen Sweet potato Yam Peas/Legumes Vegetables Pineapple	Grow/Fence Stake Ackee Coconut Mango Apples Coffee Citrus	Mint (varying species Bird Pepper Aloe Vera Susumber
Housegarden	Banana Plantain Dasheen Sweet potato Yam Peas/Legumes Vegetables Pineapple	Grow/Fence stake Ackee Coconut Mango Apples Coffee Citrus Soursop Sweet sop Guinep	Ornamental Plants Mint (varying species Bird Pepper Aloe Vera Susumber
Edge	Yam Banana Plantain	Nutmeg Apple Mangoes Citrus	Grasses Mints Growstake Hogmeat Aloe vera
Orchard	Banana	Apple	Within the orchard very few aggressive wild growing plants were found: Hogmeat Marigold Guinea grass
Shrub-dominated fallow	Dasheen Coco	Coconut Yam	Bachelor button Mongoose weed Milkweed Watergrass Rat ears Cowfoot Marigold Guinea grass

Source: Authors' fieldwork.

The research on which this chapter is based was born out of the need to better understand the nature of farmers' agrochemical use and chemical dynamics within the demonstration site. The research sought to establish

1. the types of fertilizers and pesticides used by farmers;
2. the factors that influenced the farmers' use of agrochemicals;

3. the types of crops and plants present on farms, that is, patterns of agrodiversity; and
4. the relationship between agrochemical use and different levels of agrobiodiversity as reflected in different land-use stages.

The objective of this assessment was twofold: first, to understand variations in agrochemical use in relation to crop types; and second, to investigate interrelationships between agrochemical use and agrobiodiversity.

As is common in farming communities across Jamaica, the use of agrochemicals in the Rio Grande Valley was prevalent, with just over 82 percent of farmers in the study acknowledging the application of chemical fertilizers and pesticides to their crops.[9] In addition, more than 80 percent of the farmers regarded agrochemical application as a key part of crop production. The assessments demonstrated that within the Agroforest and House Garden land-use stages there were less agrochemical inputs when compared to the banana Orchard/Plantation land-use stage. Since agroforests and house gardens represented higher levels of agrodiversity than the Orchard/Plantation land-use stage, there was clear indication that increased agrodiversity coincided with lower demands for agrochemicals. For example, farms that fell within the Orchard land-use stage routinely utilized more than one and as much as five types of fertilizers. The routine use of pesticides as well as the number of pesticides employed was also higher for this land-use stage. Seven different types of fertilizers and 20 types of pesticides were used by farmers throughout the study area (see tables 14.5 and 14.6).

While the relationship between land-use stage and agropesticide use is not easily assessed, it was noticeable that pesticide use was more prevalent in some cropping systems than others. For instance, 66.6 percent of the incidence of agropesticide use was in relation to traditional export cropping systems primarily engaged in the production of banana and coffee.

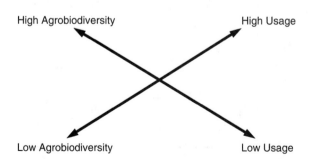

High Agrobiodiversity   High Usage

Low Agrobiodiversity   Low Usage

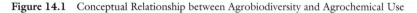

Figure 14.1   Conceptual Relationship between Agrobiodiversity and Agrochemical Use

Table 14.5 Pesticide Use at the Study Site

Categories	Pesticides	Crops	% of agrochemical users
Insecticides	Mocap	Bananas	52
	Furadan	Bananas	37
	Rugby	Bananas	19
	Decis	Vegetables	4
	Dipel	Vegetables	4
	Xentare	Vegetables	4
	Sevens	Citrus	4
	Primacide	Bananas	4
Fungicides	Anvil	Bananas	4
	Benelate	Bananas	15
	Calixin	Bananas	52
	Cocide	Vegetables	4
	Tilt	Bananas	74
	Spray Oil	Bananas	74
	Manchocide	Vegetables	4
	Ridomil	Vegetables	4
Herbicides	Roundup	Weeds	4
	Gramaxone	Weeds	93
	Diquat	Weeds	19
	Karate	Weeds	7

Source: Authors' fieldwork.

Table 14.6 Utilization of Chemical Fertilizers at the PLEC Demonstration Site

Fertilizers used	Crops	Frequency (general)	Function	% of farms using this fertilizer
Sulphate	Vegetables, Plantain, Bananas, Peppers, Coffee, (A variety of young plants)	Once	To promote growth in young plants	78
Potash	Vegetables, Plantain, Bananas, Dasheen, Coco	Once	Applied to bananas to help them to shoot	33
Miracle Gro	Vegetables	Once		7
15:5:35 (All-purpose)	Banana, Dasheen, Coco, Plantain, Vegetables, A mixture of crops	Every 10 weeks	Applied to support growth	78
Urea	Banana, Plantain	Once	To promote growth in young plants	11

Source: Authors' fieldwork.

The relationship between agrochemical use and variations in biodiversity as reflected in land-use stages was assessed by measuring the extent of association between two variables. Although five land-use stages were identified at the PLEC site, only three were employed in the analysis because agrochemicals are not normally applied to Edge and Fallow land-use stages, though these tend to have the highest levels of biodiversity. The cross-tabulations therefore focused upon House Gardens, Agroforest, and Orchard land-use stages. Both house gardens and agroforests were characterized by high levels of biodiversity, while orchard, involving mainly bananas, had significantly lower levels. Table 14.7 shows the relationship between land-use stage and total pesticide use at the study site. Given that the different land-use stages represented different levels of agrobiodiversity, the correlation coefficient of 0.610 suggests a significant relationship between agrobiodiversity and the level of pesticide usage. Pesticide usage was greatest in the Orchard land-use stage where the level of species diversity was lowest. House and Agroforest land-use stages, which are characterized by significantly higher levels of species diversity, had comparatively lower levels of pesticide usage. A similar pattern is demonstrated for fertilizer usage (table 14. 8).

In nearly 77 percent of the cases where more than 350 kilograms of fertilizer was used per season, the land-use stage coincided with Orchard.

Table 14.7 Percentage Distribution of Total Pesticide Usage (Kilograms) per Season

Land-use stage	% of pesticide usage per season			
	Lowest through 17	17.1 through 46	More than 46.0	Total
House garden	15.4		17.9	15.5
Orchard	73.1	100	75.0	75.9
Agro-forest	11.5		7.1	8.6
Total	100.0	100.0	100.0	100.0

Note: R = 0.610. R is the correlation coefficient.
Source: Authors' fieldwork.

Table 14.8 Percentage Distribution of Total Fertilizer Usage (Kilograms) per Season

Land-use stage	% of fertilizer usage per season			
	Lowest–182 kg	182.1 kg–350 kg	> 350 kg	Total (%)
House garden	6.9	41.7	11.8	15.5
Orchard	82.8	58.3	76.5	75.9
Agroforest	10.3		11.8	8.6
Total (%)	100.0	100.0	100.0	100.0

Note: R = 0.577.
Source: Authors' fieldwork.

This is in contrast to about 16 percent coinciding with house gardens and about 7 percent with agroforests.

Economic Cost of Agrochemical Use

Farmers considered fertilizers as an absolute necessity especially for the export banana crop, because of the contribution to increased yields and improved appearance of the plant. The prevalence of agrochemical use at the PLEC demonstration site has environmental as well as economic implications.[10] Environmental implications include the vulnerability to erosion and landslide of clean-weeded land under monoculture as well as the potential of heavy agrochemical usage for water pollution. In terms of the economic implications of agrochemical usage, there are no detailed measures. Record keeping on revenues and expenditure by small-scale farmers in the Caribbean is characteristically lacking, making any attempt at benefit-cost analysis of agrochemical use impossible. The cost of agrochemicals by land-use stage for the study site is indicated in table 14.9.

The total cost of agrochemicals (pesticides and fertilizers) across the land-use stages is a reflection of the number of farmers in each land-use stage as well as the mean application per farmer. The mean cost of agrochemicals by land-use stage was of particular interest here, as it allowed cost comparisons to be made between the land-use stages. For both pesticides and chemical fertilizers, orchards, which are characterized by the lowest levels of agrobiodiversity, incurred the greatest mean cost per farmer, while agroforests incurred the least mean cost. Given similarities in species richness between house gardens and agroforests, a closer agrochemical-cost relationship between these two land-use stages was anticipated. However, the relationship between the agrochemical cost on house gardens and orchards was closer than between house gardens and agroforests. The reason is not immediately clear but might be related to the fact that the agrobiodiversity of house gardens included some commercial crops such as vegetables and root crops on which agrochemicals were applied. The agroforests at the PLEC site primarily comprised food-trees for which there has been no tradition of agrochemical application or even active cultivation.

Table 14.9   Cost of Agrochemicals by Land-Use Stage at the Study Site

Land-use stage	Total pesticide cost (J$)	Mean cost (J$)	Total Fertilizer cost (J$)	Mean cost (J$)
House garden	162,938	18,104	97,400	10,822
Orchard	921,836	20,950	550,000	12,500
Agroforest	69,106	13,821	42,800	8,560

Note: US$1 = J$61.00 (approximately).
Source: Authors' fieldwork.

Conclusion

The relationship between agrochemical use and land-use stages at the study site is significant. Orchards, which are characterized by the lowest levels of agrobiodiversity among the land-use stages, are the sites of correspondingly higher levels of agrochemical use as compared with house gardens and agro-forests. As a result, farmers involved in the cultivation of orchard crops incurred significantly greater expenses for agrochemical inputs than the more biodiverse land-use stages. The relationship between biodiversity and agrochemical use and the associated cost to the farmer is shown to be considerable. Further, the relationship between fields under orchard or plantation and thus devoted to the cultivation of crops for export highlights the coincidence of reduced levels of biodiversity and increased agrochemical usage associated with the cultivation practices of crops principally intended for export. This raises concerns both about the environmental sustainability and economic viability of small farms engaged in traditional patterns of export production. The principal orchard crop in the Rio Grande Valley has been bananas cultivated for export and associated with low levels of biodiversity and high levels of agrochemical use. The recent termination of banana exports from Jamaica poses a major livelihood challenge to those farmers previously dependent on that market, but, at the same time, it provides an opportunity for the establishment of mixed-cropping systems on the banana orchard fields, thus enhancing the biodiversity on those lands.

Notes

1. See Harold Brookfield et al., "Introduction," in Harold Brookfield et al. (eds.), *Agrodiversity: Learning from Farmers across the World* (Tokyo: United Nations University Press, 2003).
2. David Watts, *The West Indies: Patterns of Development, Culture and Environmental Changes since 1492* (Cambridge: Cambridge University Press, 1987).
3. Elizabeth Thomas-Hope and Balfour Spence, "Jamaica," in Brookfield et al. (eds.), *Agrodiversity,* 270–292.
4. Amani Ishemo, Hugh Semple, and Elizabeth Thomas-Hope, "Population Mobility and the Survival of Small Farming in the Rio Grande Valley, Jamaica," *Geographical Journal* 172, no. 4 (2006): 318–330.
5. Daniel Zarin, Huijun Guo, and Luis Enu-Kwesi, "Methods for the Assessment of Plant Species Diversity in Complex Agricultural Landscapes: Guidelines for Data Collection and Analysis from the PLEC Biodiversity Advisory Group" (PLEC-BAG) (Special Issue) *PLEC News and Views* 13 (1999): 3–16.
6. Elizabeth Thomas-Hope, Balfour Spence, and Hugh Semple, "Biodiversity within the Small Farming Systems of the Rio Grande Watershed, Jamaica," in *Proceedings of the Seminario Internacional Sobre Agridiversidad Campesina* (Toluca: Mexico Autonomous University, 1999), 140–147; Elizabeth Thomas-Hope, Hugh Semple, and Balfour Spence, "Household Structure, Agrodiversity and Agro-Biodiversity on Small Farms in the Rio Grande Valley Jamaica," *PLEC News and Views* 15 (2000): 38–44; Elizabeth Thomas-Hope

and Balfour Spence, "Promoting Agro-Biodiversity under Difficulties: The Jamaica PLEC Experience," *PLEC News and Views* 19 (2002): 17–24.

7. Thomas-Hope and Spence, "Promoting Biodiversity under Difficulties."

8. A general land-use category based on vegetation structure and requiring a plant species diversity sampling strategy distinct from that of other such categories. Zarin, Guo, and Enu-Kwesi, "Methods for the Assessment of Plant Species Diversity in Complex Agricultural Landscapes."

9. Hugh Smith, "Agrochemical Use by Small Farmers in the Rio Grande Valley, Jamaica" (Unpublished MSc dissertation, Environmental Management Unit, Department of Geography and Geology, University of the West Indies, Mona, Jamaica, 2003).

10. Balfour Spence and Elizabeth Thomas-Hope, "Agro-Biodiversity and the Economic Cost of Agrochemical Use among Smallholder Farmers in the Rio Grande Valley, Jamaica," *PLEC News and Views*, n.s. 6 (2005): 3–7.

Part IV

Landscape, Migration, and Development

Chapter 15

Arboreal Landscapes of Power and Resistance

Mimi Sheller

Introduction

Land has been one of the key sites of social struggle in postslavery societies. Social relations of power, resistance, and oppositional culture building are inscribed into living landscapes of farming, dwelling, and cultivation. Claims to power (both elite and subaltern) are marked out by landscape features such as plazas, roads, pathways, vantage points, and significant trees, all of which proclaim use-rights, ownership, or the sacrality of particular places. Trees in particular have been used to identify, symbolize, demarcate, and sustain various Caribbean places, meanings, and lives. Insofar as "[n]ew meanings and uses of woods and forests have often accompanied patterns of colonial conquest," such struggles over arboreal landscapes are evident throughout the Caribbean region.[1]

Through a study of trees we can track the competing ordering, reordering, and *dis*ordering of the Caribbean landscape, and the social struggles that came to be materialized in that landscape. Drawing on literary sources and visual imagery from the Anglophone and Francophone Caribbean, this chapter traces the importance of trees in the development of plantation economies and discourses of empire—from mahogany, lignum vitae, fustic, and other dyewoods to palms, fruit trees, and botanical collections. I consider the contestation of these colonial arboreal landscapes by Afro-Caribbean agents who claimed particular trees for their own projects of survival and meaning-making—sacred ancestral trees, liberty trees, family land trees, gathering-place trees. I conclude with some suggestions for future research on trees and landscapes in the Caribbean and offer some reflections on the "cultural turn" in development studies and environmental studies.

Landscapes of Power

Trees have long been crucial to the projects of empire building, colonization, and discovery of "new worlds." Christopher Columbus dwelled on the beauty of the forests he encountered in the Antilles and of their potential economic uses. From the sixteenth century on new and useful plants were incorporated into European understanding, collected, and studied. The earliest manuscripts giving European impressions of the New World focus on unusual plants and their novel uses.[2] Early modern science was very much directed toward exploration, plant discovery, and "economic botany," including observation, collection, and appropriation.[3] Colonizing expeditions often noted the natural products to be obtained from forests of islands such as Trinidad:

> [F]rom the Abundance and Quality of its Woods and Trees, the most excellent in all the World, might bee made great advantages from some of them, issuing very rich Gumms, from others Rich Oyles, Balsoms, and Odoriferous Rossins, abundance of Woods, Proper for Dyes. The very Mountains Covered with Large Cedars, White wood and Excellent Timber for Building.[4]

Tropical hardwoods and dyewoods were highly valued, including the West Indian Cedar (*Cedrela mexicana*), used for building and furniture making; the locust (*Hymenaea courbaril*), for large beams; the extremely hard ironwood (*Bunchosia nitida*), for fencing and mill rollers; and the dyewoods fustic (*Chlorophora tinctoria*) and lignum vitae (*Guaiacum officinale*).[5] The latter was ideal for marine navigational instruments and clocks, which transformed navigational practices and enabled colonization itself to proceed.

Europeans adapted technologies of plant use from indigenous peoples besides importing plants from Africa, Asia, and the South Pacific. Botanical discovery underwrote an entirely new attitude toward the natural world, in which nature was demystified, classified, and secularized.[6] The West Indies also provided a wide range of materials that were incorporated into European material culture both in the tropics and at home, enabling innumerable new commercial and domestic products. Forests were stripped for all that was useful and cleared for agriculture, displacing indigenous rights, needs, and forms of knowledge. Deforestation was quickly evident on some Caribbean islands, and the colonists' "voracious consumption" of wood for buildings, ships, fuel, and barrels made them dependent on New England forests by the late seventeenth century. When woodland conservation became necessary, it involved conflicts between Caribs and colonists. The creation of forest reservations "became identified, especially on St. Vincent, with an exercise in political domination, population exclusion and relocation, and eventually with open conflict."[7]

Alongside economic acquisition, European colonists also made trees central in the elaboration of tropical scenery and landscape as a form of mastery. Here nature serves more as an allegorical vision of man's taming of the wilderness and an expression of his power to control and shape land. Landscapes of power already had a long provenance within Europe. In Britain, for example, from the medieval period woodland was "almost invariably the private property of the manorial lord" or the Crown. Enclosure was applied not only to arable areas but also to "common waste" and "represented the triumph of individual ownership over the rights of the rest of the community."[8] One of the reasons nonlanded entrepreneurs entered the West Indies trade was precisely so that they too could enjoy such "status landscapes," whether by building grand plantation prospects in the West Indies or by using profits to acquire or build such properties back in England.

English landscape gardening was influenced by Italian art, related "in the scope of the landscape, in the wide prospects and in the relationship between the foreground and more distant objects."[9] Richard Grove refers to the "power-conscious interest in constructing a new landscape by planting trees [and] marking out reservations" in the eighteenth-century Eastern Caribbean.[10] As Amar Wahab has shown, a power-imbued sense of "prospect" was asserted in Caribbean plantation landscapes such as those of nineteenth-century Trinidad.[11] In their efforts to open up extensive vistas to their grand homes, planters exercised some of the same autocracy of landed elites in England, but they also faced some of the same social tensions and struggles over land use and the unwelcome mobility of people and livestock across their "private" property.

Trees were enrolled into projects of spatially inscribing property, immortality, and perpetuity, which then became the stuff of landscape painting and travel writing. Palm trees especially informed initial European impressions of the region's unusual flora and became key symbolic icons representing the entire Caribbean, even nonnative imported varieties. The means of producing, representing, and viewing landscape drew on similar elements: grouping of dwellings, geometric organization, use of trees to create perspective, demarcation of property boundaries, layout of roads, and so on. This is not to say that the landscape was an entirely European imposition. The tropical environment had its own powerful effects on those who entered it, altering the European sense of scale, season, and vegetal productivity. And the agency of the enslaved, the indentured, and the emancipated also refashioned nature's uses, meanings, and contexts.

The close interpositioning of the West Indian sugar estate and the English country estate is indicative not of a linear genealogy from one to the other but of the two-way traffic of "transculturation" transforming both the colonial landscape and the home landscape.[12] The encounter with tropical trees and foliage changed the European viewer's perception of nature at home and could lead to a renewed respect for the trees and plants of the temperate regions. As Nancy Stepan argues, "To even the most enthusiastic tropicalist of the nineteenth century, it seems, tropical nature was too much—too disorderly, chaotic, large—and too different from the remembered landscape at home."[13] By midcentury, "dismay at tropical excess" was linked to notions of tropical decay, disease, and death, counterpoised against European systematic enclosure, cultivation, and scientific agricultural management.

Viewing the Barbados scenery in the early 1800s with an eye trained in viewing European landscape paintings, British traveler Daniel McKinnen sought appropriate vantage points from which he could describe the landscape like a picture:

> Along the shore to the north of Bridge Town I found the road extremely picturesque. It leads through a long avenue of shady cocoa-nut trees, over-arched by their palmated and spacious leaves, and fenced on each side by prickly pears, or the blades of aloes. In occasional openings, or through the stems of the trees, you behold the masters' dwelling-houses with the negro-huts adjoining; and over a rich vale, abounding with cotton shrubs and maize, the hills at a small distance spotted with wind-mills, sugar-works, and a few lofty cabbage-trees, or cocoa-nuts. At times the road approaches the sea and leads along the beach. . . . It then winds into the plantations, where the cultivated parterres of cotton and tropical plants are often relieved by groups of cocoa-nuts and plantains, the leaves of which, in the form of squares or quadrangular figures, have a singular effect in the landscape.[14]

McKinnen's movement through this plantation landscape gives us a sense of what Henri Lefebvre calls its "texture." Long-arched avenues such as the one described here were a proclamation of mastery, of order, and of geometrical spatial orders, marking this as a socially produced landscape. The trees dotting the hills echo the vertical drama of windmills and sugar-works. Evidence of an entrepreneurial presence, the palms were enrolled as symbols of cultivation and markers of the boundaries of plantations, scrawling property claims across the sky, while the "quadrangular figures" of the plantains also mark out tracts of cultivation enabled, of course, by slavery.

Captain J. E. Alexander also described the landscape of coffee plantations around Georgetown, Grenada, on the eve of emancipation in 1833, as if viewing the kind of map found in engravings of well-ordered slave plantations.[15] Standing on the "parterre" (suggestive of a flower bed or a theater stall), he too writes from a vantage point of mastery in which the land performs and presents itself as a map. His imagery conveys the social and economic structure by connecting the "verdant slopes" to the "coasting vessels" that carry their produce to market. Both of these viewers convey a sense of economic productivity as a well-organized and fruitful garden. Yet this "picturesque" Hesperides depended on slavery. These plantation landscapes aligned projects of cultivation, export, and profit with European visual registers of open prospect and pastoral scenery. Nevertheless, some of the trees hint at alternative appropriations of the land for other projects of cultivation, as discussed below.

Finally, a third genre of descriptive writing employs a romantic discourse of "Tropical Nature," which has come to deeply inform modern tourism in the region.[16] By the late nineteenth century the palm tree begins to evoke beauty and relaxation, rather than power and property.[17] The palm became a symbol of exotic and romantic places, corralled into Victorian "palm houses," domesticated as a garden feature. From nineteenth-century romantic prints to twentieth-century tourist brochures, the ubiquitous image of the palm sums up the Caribbean tropics so effectively that it has been turned into a brand icon and marketing logo on a wide range of products and businesses associated with the region, from Island Records to the Island Trading Company.

Released from the utilitarian purposes it may have suggested to writers in the seventeenth century, and from the landscapes of power it may have suggested to writers in the eighteenth century, the palm tree has become a symbol of leisure, relaxation, and carefree living. It beckons a hedonistic tourism, escape from the world, seductive immersion in bodily pleasures. Yet the palm also served as a major symbol of African Caribbean liberty. At the time of the French Revolution it took the place in the Caribbean of the French Liberty Tree in republican iconography. It is prominent on the National Seal of Haiti, appearing on the Haitian flag and currency, but it also occurs as a marker of emancipation in Jamaica and elsewhere.[18] These revolutionary meanings of the palm (and any earlier indigenous meaning they may have had) have been usurped by more anodyne tourist imagery. Can we, though, still recover the "underside" of the Caribbean landscape and reclaim the subaltern histories that are uprooted, appropriated, and erased by imperialism and capitalist development?

Landscapes of Resistance

Trees have long been at the center of social and political struggles in the Caribbean. In Bwa Kayman a great *mapou* tree stands, where a ceremony was reputedly held in 1791 inaugurating the slave uprising that sparked the Haitian Revolution. The *mapou*, or silk cotton, is a sacred tree, inhabited by spirits, and throughout Haiti ceremonies continue to be conducted and offerings made by *serviteurs* (devotees) of the *lwa* (spirits) under such trees. Their behemoth boughs make shaded gathering spots, mark major crossroads, allow posting of public notices, and provide shelter from floods. "Although wounded by the drought and under persistent attack from the Protestants," according to recent visitor novelist Madison Smartt Bell, "the enormous, ancient tree [at Bwa Kayman] hung on"[19] remaining a powerful symbol of the resistance of the Haitian people to foreign domination, slavery, and exploitation, marking the continuity of African traditions and ancestral spirits.[20]

But another tree was chosen to symbolize the Haitian state: the palm tree in the guise of a Liberty Tree surmounted with the Liberty Cap of the French Revolution. Both the cap and the tree of liberty have a long transatlantic symbolic role in many revolutionary upheavals. The Caribbean version picks up on the classical tradition of slave emancipation in ancient Rome interpreted via the French Revolution but perhaps also symbolizes the *potomitan* around which the dances of Voodoo ceremonies take place—linking "the heavenly and the earthly worlds."[21] The leaves of the palm are sacred to the *lwa* Aizan, who "protects markets, public places, doors and barriers,"[22] so the Liberty Tree may syncretically imply spiritual protection of Haiti's national markets, public places, and borders. When Haitian President Jean Bertrand Aristide was deposed and went into exile, he quoted Toussaint L'Ouverture: "In overthrowing me, they have uprooted the trunk of the liberty tree. It will grow back because its roots

are many and deep." He likened himself to a tree of peace that would grow
back "because its roots are L'Ouverturian."[23]

As in revolutionary Colonial America, liberty trees were planted in central
public areas and used as gathering places for public speaking in Haiti.[24] Quaker
missionary Stephen Grellet addressed huge crowds gathered at such trees during
his tour through Haiti in 1816. He described a scene near Little River:

> To accommodate such a crowd, it was considered proper to hold the meeting
> in their large market-place. About meeting time a regiment of soldiers, on their
> march to Port-au-Prince, also arrived in the town, and their officers brought
> them all to the meeting. Several thousand persons, it was supposed, were
> collected. They stood very close round me, and I was placed on the market
> cross, or rather Liberty Tree, which is planted in almost every town.[25]

Tales of uprooted liberty trees come to us from other parts of the Caribbean
as well. In their celebrations of the "First of August" Emancipation Day in
Jamaica, church congregations planted coconut palms as symbols of liberty
and held annual festivals in which the trees were watered.[26] In at least one
case, a missionary reported that his congregation "planted a cocoanut tree,
the emblem of liberty—this had been pulled up since, by some of the gentle-
men in the neighborhood, we have replanted it, and as one of the people
remarked, 'they pull up we tree, but them can't take away we August.'"[27]

More mundane trees also require attention. The fruit trees found around
kitchen gardens and on small plots of family land present more subtle forms
of cultural (and cultivational) opposition. Insofar as "protopeasantries" grew
up in the "interstices" of the plantation, as Mintz argued, those interstices
were very much botanical and temporal. Peasant culture building took place
where it did not compete with plantation commercial crops either in terms of
the spaces or the time it occupied. Hardy plants such as arrowroot and coffee
could be cultivated on marginal land, enabling small-scale production to take
hold following the abolition of slavery.[28] These small plots with their trees
offer material evidence of an alternative spatial order, or what Lefebvre calls
"superimposed spaces," which grew up in the interstices of the plantation,
interpenetrating its spaces, and eventually becoming central to postemancipation social and cultural formations.[29] The customary use of "bush," "garden,"
and "mountain" land became "part of the creative attempt to shape a new
way of life in the face of considerable hardship."[30]

Provision grounds tucked away in the hilly backlands of sugar estates and
kitchen gardens crowded around slave dwellings imply superimposed uses of
plantation spaces. Travelers noted that Jamaican plantation worker's houses
in the 1840s were usually found in "some secluded nook, approachable
through a narrow winding path" to protect their privacy and noted the "variety
and grandeur of the various trees" surrounding them.[31] Dale Tomich likewise
argues for Martinique:

> These practices both shaped and were shaped by Afro-Caribbean cultural
> forms, through which the definitions of social reality of slavery and the plantation

were at once mediated and contested. Slaves themselves created and controlled a secondary economic network which originated within the social and spatial boundaries of the plantation but which allowed for the construction of an alternative way of life that went beyond it.[32]

More than one system of cultural ordering, meaning-making, and practical usage were at work. The same cultivated tracts and majestic trees that constituted planters' claims to power and made picturesque scenery for European travel writers might have rather different resonances for those who lived and worked amongst them.

Trees are part of "material cultures" through which memories are "activated" and narrated. As Divya Tolia-Kelly has shown for the British Asian diaspora, the "prismatic qualities of material cultures ensure that these cultures become nodes of connection in a network of people, places, and narration of past stories, history, and traditions. Solid materials are charged with memories that activate common connections to pre-migratory landscapes and environments."[33] Trees can be considered one such node in a network of connections between people, places, and the stories they tell. Acts of "rememory" and "memory-history" encoded in material cultures and embedded in everyday life can challenge bounded and static nationalistic landscapes. Thus the seeding of trees into African Caribbean networks of landholding, kinship, spirituality, and historical memory activates a different "context of living" and in some cases creates "syncretized textures of remembered ecologies and landscapes" that may signify a particular "identity, history and heritage" through which other "lives, lands and homes are made part of this one."[34] In reading Caribbean landscapes in this way we can reimbue them with the more complex cultural activities and activations that actually underlay their production, cultivation, and meaningfulness.

Not only were subaltern "superimposed" landscapes culturally rich and materially productive, but they also impacted back upon the landscape of power. A thousand hands working in small ways to shape the land to their own needs, a thousand feet trudging up into the remote hills could easily outweigh the overweening gestures of the planter's prospect, the impotent laws of the colonial administrator, or the imperious gaze of the traveler. Above all, these trees also carry a spiritual meaning beyond the ken of the ruling elites. Anthropological studies from many parts of the Caribbean point to the far-ranging significance of many different trees. Alfred Métraux notes of Haiti,

> Each *lwa* has his favourite variety of tree: the *medicinier-béni* (*Tatropha cureas*) is sacred to Legba, the palm tree to Ayizan and the Twins (*marassa*), the avocado to Zaka, the mango to Ogu and the bougainvillea to Damballah etc. A tree which is a "resting place" may be recognized by the candles burning at the foot of it and the offerings left in its roots or hung in its branches.[35]

Thus trees bereft of any symbolic or spiritual significance for Europeans were in fact full of multiple meanings to various communities of African origin and were drawn into complex webs of religious significance for Voodoo in Haiti,

Candomblé in Brazil, Santeria in Cuba, and Obeah and Myalism in Jamaica. Bottles were hung in their branches, umbilical cords buried under them, and sacrifices placed at their roots.

In addition to their spiritual significance, trees planted around slave huts and on provision grounds also provided shade, building materials, medicines, and foodstuffs. Trees played a significant part in enslaved and emancipated community efforts to carve out a space for themselves, providing some degree of economic autonomy, as well as familial terrain. Fruit trees in particular were central to the creation of subaltern property and informal tenures, which were often recognized in common practice and became fundamental to systems of kinship and inheritance. Laurent Dubois observes the ways in which trees represented an alternative social cartography in the French Antilles:

> In the 1830s, the abolitionist Victor Schoelcher visited a plantation in Martinique where a huge mango tree stood in the middle of a cane field, stunting the cane that grew in its shade. The planter would have cut down the tree, but it was owned by an enslaved man, who had already promised to pass it on to his descendants. According to Schoelcher, there were similar cases involving fruit trees owned by slaves on other plantations.[36]

Such trees were part of the alternative landscape of gardens and informal markets through which the enslaved "cultivated networks that criss-crossed, and therefore undermined, the highly structured world of the plantations"; even official maps sometimes identified these "other patterns and practices that emerged within and against this order . . . a world formed by the interaction of colonial policy and daily practice."[37] In bequeathing trees to "some yet unborn" descendants, as Schoelcher put it, slaves were not only establishing competing claims to space, to land, and to productive property in trees but were also creating new systems of kinship, descent, and inheritance.[38]

In her study of Martha Brae in Jamaica, Jean Besson shows how trees planted in the period of emancipation maintained familial significance for generations. Appropriated landscapes created in the interstices of the plantation spatial order during the era of slavery carried over into the postemancipation period, marking the descent group's claim on particular plots of land. Besson further points out, "The idea that trees and land are symbols of the continuity of kin groups and communities is widely spread among Jamaican and other Caribbean peasantries, and derives from the protopeasant past."[39] Because burial practices at one time took place in familial yards, and trees often marked such gravesites, these familial plots also represented a continuation of the kin group through a physical connection with the spirits of dead ancestors. In another case, an informant remarked on the genealogy of particular trees, which had been transplanted by his ex-slave grandfather from a specific plantation.[40]

Besson's work opens our eyes to the extent to which this protopeasant past might be found in the living landscapes and "archi-textures," to use Lefebvre's term, of Jamaica's rural countryside, villages, and small towns. The very settlement patterns, plots, and provision grounds that remain in the twenty-first century—and especially their long-lived and precious trees—offer clues to the social production of space and the politics of landscape in the nineteenth century. The differing textures of landscape in different regions or even particular hamlets may have a great deal to tell us about the forms of social contestation in the slavery and postemancipation period, about the differing interpenetrations between plantation and plot in the production of space, and hence about the different textures of freedom as lived in these places. Continuities and discontinuities in spatial orders, represented in part by the planting, transplanting, and uprooting of particular species and botanical individuals, and the stories people tell about those plants, can tell us a great deal about social histories and collective memories.

Conclusion

European and North American interests in trees whether as economic resources, landscape prospect, or elements of the tourist picturesque are fundamentally at odds with Afro-Caribbean investment in trees as spiritual repositories, family land, and markers of kin relations, community, and ancestry. Without romanticizing the "indigenous" "traditional" horticulture and arboriculture, it is possible to argue that it contributed immensely to the conservation and sustainability of Caribbean lands, kin groups, culture, and communities. A better understanding of the competing landscapes of arboreal power might suggest some new solutions to the conflicts over sustainability and development in the Caribbean. Recognition of the subaltern meanings of landscapes and the spiritual and familial investment in particular trees might help in efforts at conservation.

In conclusion I want to call for a "cultural turn" in development studies, as well as a "development turn" in cultural studies, that would more fully recognize and research the contested meanings and symbolic deployments of material resources and natural entities in the social production of space. This will require greater attention to the cultural shaping of nature, a neglected area in Caribbean studies. By offering a cultural study of trees as a means of thinking about land and development in plantation societies I hope to have underlined the importance of a multimethod approach to tracing social struggles over land, landscape, place, and space.

A cultural turn in development studies requires a multimethod approach that attends not only to landscapes of power but also recognizes the landscapes of resistance that have sprung up in between, underneath, in and around the plantation, and today the tourism, landscape. These are crucial areas for a new research agenda that could begin to analyze the visual and material cultures, narratives and representations, and vernacular practices of Caribbean socioecologies.

Notes

This chapter was presented to the Society for Caribbean Studies Annual Conference, June 29–July 1, 2005, Newcastle, United Kingdom, whose participants I would like to thank for their comments. Thanks also to Divya Tolia-Kelly.

1. Phil Macnaghten and John Urry, "Bodies in the Woods," *Body and Society* 6, nos. 3–4 (2000): 167.
2. See, e.g., *The Drake Manuscript in the Pierpont Morgan Library: Histoire Naturelle des Indes* (London: Andre Deutsch Ltd., 1996).
3. On early colonial deforestation, conservation, and botanical gardens see Richard Grove, *Green Imperialism: Colonial Expansion, Tropical Island Edens and the Origins of Environmentalism, 1600–1860* (Cambridge: Cambridge University Press, 1995); Robert S. Anderson, Richard Grove, and Karis Hiebert (eds.), *Islands, Forests and Gardens of the Caribbean: Conservation and Conflict in Environmental History* (Oxford: Macmillan, 2006).
4. V. T. Harlow, *Colonizing Expeditions to the West Indies and Guiana, 1623–1667*, Works issued by the Hakluyt Society, Second Series, No. LVI (London, Hakluyt Society, 1924), cited in Amar Wahab, "Inventing 'Trinidad': Colonial Representations in the Nineteenth Century" (PhD thesis, University of Toronto, 2004), 90.
5. David Watts, *The West Indies: Patterns of Development, Culture, and Environmental Change since 1492* (Cambridge and New York: Cambridge University Press, 1990), 155.
6. Mimi Sheller, *Consuming the Caribbean* (London and New York: Routledge, 2003), 43; Grove, *Green Imperialism*.
7. On indigenous knowledge see David Arnold and Ramachandra Guha (eds.), *Nature, Culture, Imperialism: Essays on the Environmental History of South Asia* (Delhi: Oxford University Press, 1995); William Cronon, *Changes in the Land: Indians, Colonists, and the Ecology of New England* (New York: Hill and Wang, 1983), 111–112; Grove, *Green Imperialism*. Quote is from Richard Grove, "The British Empire and the Origins of Forest Conservation in the Eastern Caribbean 1700–1800," in Anderson, Grove, and Hiebert (eds.), *Islands, Forests and Gardens of the Caribbean*, 146.
8. Tom Williamson and Liz Bellamy, *Property and Landscape: A Social History of Land Ownership and the English Countryside* (London: George Philip, 1987), 79, 94.
9. Williamson and Bellamy, *Property and Landscape*, 146.
10. Grove, "Forest Conservation," 143–144.
11. Wahab, "Inventing Trinidad."
12. Mary L. Pratt, *Imperial Eyes: Travel Writing and Transculturation* (London: Routledge, 1992); Simon Gikandi, *Maps of Englishness: Writing Identity in the Culture of Colonialism* (New York: Columbia University Press, 1997); Wahab, "Inventing Trinidad."
13. Nancy Leys Stepan, *Picturing Tropical Nature* (London: Reaktion Books, 2001), 54, 48.
14. Daniel McKinnen, *A Tour Through the British West Indies in the Years 1802 and 1803, giving a particular account of the Bahama Islands* (London: J. White and R. Taylor, 1804), 18–19.

15. Captain J. E. Alexander, *Transatlantic Sketches, comprising visits to the most interesting scenes in North and South America and the West Indies, With notes on Negro Slavery and Canadian emigration.* 2 vols. (London: Richard Bentley, 1833), I: 244.

16. Sheller, *Consuming the Caribbean.*

17. E. A. Hastings Jay, *A Glimpse of the Tropics, or, Four Months Cruising in the West Indies* (London: Sampson Low, Marston & Co., 1900), 34–35.

18. See Mimi Sheller, *Democracy after Slavery: Black Publics and Peasant Radicalism in Haiti and Jamaica* (Oxford and London: Macmillan, 2000).

19. Madison Smartt Bell, "Mine of Stones: With and without the Spirits along the Cordon de l'Ouest," *Harpers Magazine,* January 2004, 56.

20. According to Protestant evangelicals such as Harvest Life Ministries, this particular tree represents a battle between Christianity and "voodoo," Jesus and Satan, good and evil. While others are working toward reforestation efforts in Haiti, they pray for the uprooting of this ancient venerated tree. See Dan Merrefield, "The Tree," *Haiti Cheri* (Publication of Harvest Life Ministries), no. 25 (September 1, 2003): 1, http://www.haiticheri.org (accessed November 22, 2004).

21. Ernst Gombrich, "The Dream of Reason: Symbolism of the French Revolution," *British Journal of Eighteenth-Century Studies* II (1979): 199; Mona Ozouf, *Festival and the French Revolution,* trans. Alan Sheridan (Cambridge, MA: Harvard University Press, 1988), 240; Laennec Hurbon, *Voodoo: Truth and Fantasy* (London: Thames and Hudson, 1995).

22. Alfred Métraux, *Voodoo in Haiti* (New York: Schocken Books, 1972 [1959]), 362.

23. Jean Bertrand Aristide, "Aristide Statement," Znet, March 6, 2004, http://www.zmag.org/content (accessed November 24, 2004).

24. J. David Harden, "Liberty Caps and Liberty Trees," *Past and Present,* February 1995, http://www.findarticles.com/p/articles/mi_m2279/is_n146/ai_17249824/print (accessed November 24, 2004).

25. Stephen Grellet [1773–1855], *Memoirs of the life and gospel labors of Stephen Grellet,* Benjamin Seebohm (ed.) (Philadelphia: H. Longstreth, 1860).

26. Woolridge to Directors, London Missionary Society, Box 2, August 2, 1839.

27. W. G. Barret to Directors, London Missionary Society, Box 2, Four Paths, August 15, 1839.

28. Jerome Handler, "The History of Arrowroot and the Origin of Peasantries in the British West Indies," *Journal of Caribbean History* 2 (May 1971): 84; see Michel-Rolph Trouillot, "Coffee Planters and Coffee Slaves in the Antilles: The Impact of a Secondary Crop," in Ira Berlin and Philip D. Morgan (eds.), *Cultivation and Culture: Labor and the Shaping of Slave Life in the Americas* (Charlottesville and London: University of Virginia, 1993), 124–137.

29. Douglas Hall, *Free Jamaica, 1838–1865: An Economic History* (New Haven: Yale University Press, 1959), 188.

30. Hymie Rubenstein, " 'Bush,' 'Garden' and 'Mountain' on the Leeward Coast of St. Vincent and the Grenadines, 1719–1995," in Anderson, Grove, and Hiebert (eds.), *Islands, Forests and Gardens of the Caribbean,* 194–213.

31. Gosse, cited in Barry Higman, *Jamaica Surveyed: Plantation Maps and Plans of the Eighteenth and Nineteenth Centuries* (Kingston, Jamaica: Institute of Jamaica Publications Ltd., 1988), 243; see Henri Lefebvre, *The Production of*

Space, trans. Donald Nicholson-Smith (Oxford and Cambridge, MA: Blackwell, 1991), 164.

32. Dale Tomich, "Une Petite Guinée: Provision Ground and Plantation in Martinique, 1830–1848," in Berlin and Morgan (eds.), *Cultivation and Culture*, 222.

33. Divya Tolia-Kelly, "Locating Processes of Identification: Studying the Precipitates of Re-Memory through Artifacts in the British Asian Home," *Transactions of the Institute of British Geographers*, n.s., 29 (2004): 314.

34. Tolia-Kelly, "Locating Processes of Identification," 315–316.

35. Métraux, *Voodoo in Haiti*, 92.

36. Laurent Dubois, *A Colony of Citizens: Revolution and Slave Emancipation in the French Caribbean, 1787–1804* (Chapel Hill and London: University of North Carolina Press, 2004), 30.

37. Dubois, *A Colony of Citizens*, 31.

38. Tomich, "Une Petite Guinée," 235.

39. Jean Besson, *Martha Brae's Two Histories: European Expansion and Caribbean Culture-Building in Jamaica* (Chapel Hill and London: University of North Carolina Press, 2002), 166.

40. Besson, *Martha Brae's Two Histories*, 176.

Chapter 16

From the Pre-Colonial to the Virtual: The Scope and Scape of Land, Landuse, and Landloss on Montserrat

Jonathan Skinner

I-Land

From a flourishing bed
To a landscape all forlorn
Nature's fury was dread
The whole of the south is gone
Lime Ghaut, Long Ground, Whites, Trials, Galways, Brodericks . . .

Greenaway (1999)[1]

This chapter is about the island Montserrat in the Eastern Caribbean, in the Leeward Islands, an island that for the past 300 years has been British and evinces its colonial history in its landuse patterns—landscapes and taskscapes so I shall argue in this chapter. The majority of islanders are direct descendants of slaves imported to the island by the British from West Africa as labor commodities under a system of plantation exploitation that lasted from the mid-seventeenth century until the mid-nineteenth century. Until 1995, those descendents numbered approximately 11,000, many tracing their names and forebears back to the plantation land estates that they had belonged to, worked and struggled and born and died on, and been buried under. Due to volcanic eruption, the present-day island population of 3,000–4,000 lives with a very different landscape and taskscape, and those who left the island or who had their lands in the south destroyed have been left to rely upon virtual notions of land.

For most of its history, Montserrat has been 39.5 square miles in size. From 1995, however, while the population of the island reduced drastically to some 3,000–4,000, the size of the island grew slightly, but most dramatically, to some 40+ square miles. Since 1995, Mount Chance has shuddered, quaked, blown ash, and broken her history of extinction. She forced inhabitants to the north of the island or to migrate overseas; she attacked and killed a number of islanders who ignored the no-go ring around her; and she grew upwards and outwards, spilling down her mountain sides to the old capital Plymouth in the west, and to Long Ground and the airport in the east. These volcano developments, 100 million tons of new rock thrown up, have been well captured in the local press, in the sale of postcards, videos, and t-shirts ("Now she puffs / But will she Blow / Trust In the Lord / And Pray it's No") and even the creative outpourings of singers, calypsonians, and poets. In local poet, academic, and Deputy Governor Howard Fergus's recent edited collection about living with the "awesome as well as awful"[2] volcano, Jacqueline Browne describes a resented tie to it:

> Living with a Mountain
> you cannot divorce
> because you have got
> children and property!
> navel string and foundation
> buried together[3]

It is common for the people of Montserrat, whether poets or not, to fix and frame identity through ancestral lines tied by blood, sociality, and geography. In this chapter I hope to show such contemporary conceptualizations of land by island Montserratians, their land, their perceptions, and relationship with land—their I-land. This chapter is thus first about the nature of land and second about landuse on Montserrat: Amerindian, colonial, partially post-colonial and now virtual.

The Scope of Land

The Negro village tends to be regarded as the physical base, the birthplace, the place where one's "navel string is buried," from which individuals venture forth to make a living knowing that they can always return to its security and the warmth of its human relationships in time of trouble.[4]

In his review of "The Caribbean Region: an Open Frontier in Anthropological Theory," the Haitian anthropologist Michel-Rolph Trouillot makes the point that the region is somewhat artificial and unnatural, one of "prefabricated enclaves" worked by a post-plantation peasantry.[5] It is not a naturally evolved region in terms of the slow diffusion of a population with some—but limited—continuity from settlement to settlement. The Caribbean region is one of sharp distinction, rupture, and displacement. In the twentieth and twenty-first centuries, West Indian people are working the land not as Mintz's "proto-peasants"[6] but as emancipated workers still suffering the consequences of globalization and "world capitalist development."[7] "Their" land is where the local and the global have always historically intersected since colonization began;[8] the region is also a place where development is similar to plantation-oriented production systems in the Asian colonies and the

Antebellum south, but it is distinctive in its colonial diversity in such a situated geographical locale, in the intersections that revolve about common experiences of European plantation development with absentee landlords and mass out-migration contributing to a "common absentee orientation" on Nevis and neighboring islands, for instance.[9] As Greenfield in Barbados and Horowitz in the French-speaking Caribbean point out, local landuse and land tenure patterns are explained as the vestiges of systems of colonial domination.[10] And yet, as Besson notes, many of these contemporary explanations of Caribbean landuse as cultural heritage—family land especially—fail to account for the complexities of local kinship relations and obligations, and the socio-economic factors leading to particular landuse patterns.[11] Such "local" factors are compounded further on Montserrat by recent shifts in the very land itself and hence the islanders' landscape.

"The landscape is a polyrhythmic composition of processes whose pulse varies from the erratic flutter of leaves to the measured drift and clash of tectonic plates." Unpacking this statement made by David Reason,[12] the anthropologist Tim Ingold[13] makes some perceptive and conceptual points about land, landuse, and the landscape that are pertinent to our consideration of land and landloss on Montserrat. First, Ingold distinguishes between land and landscape, the former as a quantity, homogeneous, "a kind of lowest common denominator of the phenomenal world"; the latter as qualitative and heterogeneous, "a contoured and textured surface" with visual qualities to it.[14] In other words, the *form* is the landscape and the *content* is the land. Ingold pushes these semantics further by—wrongly in my opinion—suggesting that the landscape is unformed, that it is unfinished and only known to those who live as part of it.[15] The landscape may be fashioned as "the homeland of our thoughts," but it is the land that is our horizon of primordial perception.[16] "The landscape is the world as it is known to those who dwell therein."[17] The landscape is apprehended as a socio-cultural perception of place.

Moreover, the work practices undertaken on the land constitute a "taskscape"—the visible acts of working and dwelling such as the well-worn tracks up and down the mountain or the ruins of estate houses and mills. Ingold explains that "the taskscape is to labour what the landscape is to land," present only so long as dwelling occurs.[18] Though introducing useful new concepts—the land as baseline and the landscape as socio-cultural view of land—Ingold takes his distinctions and analyses too far by suggesting that meaning actually resides *in* the landscape, to be "discovered," rather than held in the eye of the beholder.[19] In addition to these landscapes and taskscapes, I should like to add the "landscope" as the potential for land, the vision of what can be done to a place such as the rebuilding of a capital such as Plymouth, Montserrat, or its visionary relocation to the north of the island.

In land—or rather, *on* land—then, we have practices performed and perceived (taskscapes and landuse/scape/scope). These ties run deeper than the depth of the navel string buried in the ground after the birth of a child. If the land is the core perceptual baseline, then changes to the land force an unsettling recalibration of the self. And if that land is lost to human labor and habitation, then the reactions are intensified to the level of existential and ontological crisis; though taken for granted beneath us, the land acts as a protective and reassuring cocoon. This means that a natural disaster that reorders the land and the landscape can unsettle and lead to mental health problems on top of the death and destruction wrought. For example, the 1970 earthquake in Peru which destroyed the city of Yungay caused loss of memory, withdrawal, nervousness, insomnia, and flashback in the survivors.[20] Oliver-Smith notes that the earthquake unsettled many through its unpredictability (predictability being a cognitive need with which we are able to move forward) and by reordering or restructuring people's "mazeways"—their "mental structures of understandings about the conditions of existence which not only help us to solve the basic material problems, but also give us the means to reduce raw experience of life to some form of comprehensible order."[21]

Sketching Land and Development on Montserrat

Take it easy, stranger man
In your imperious drive
To build an ivory wall
In my black sand[22]

This verse comes from Howard Fergus's poem "This Land Is Mine," a line from Shakespeare's *The Tempest*, one of Caliban's warnings. Here, Fergus is the artful Caliban, a "barbarian" poet writing for independence at the end of the twentieth century, protecting his island from being turned into a tourist fantasy/local nightmare.[23] Originally, however, Montserrat was devoid of an indigenous population. Montserrat was first sighted and named in 1493 by Columbus who sailed nearby and named the island after the steep rocky crags overlooking the Benedictine monastery of Saint Mary of Montserrat in northern Spain. The island was not settled by colonial powers until 1632 when Irish Catholics relocated from neighboring St. Kitts. They found traces of Amerindian settlement, particularly in the east, but no indigenous population. The settlers turned planters and began to establish a "prosperous farming colony,"[24] parceling land into 19 estates and a collection of small farms, and building settlement towns such as Plymouth, many of which remained the same in name for over 300 years (see map 16.1).

By 1700, the colonial settlers had shifted from tobacco production to sugar and were producing at a level of 250 tons per year. This was to peak at 3,150 tons in 1735. Not only have the names remained around the island, but the "sugar taskscape" is still evident from several centuries ago—remains of some of the 78 stone mills, cauldrons and equipment used in making the sugar and rum are still dotted around the island (see figures 16.1 and 16.2).

It was only by the end of the eighteenth century that there was a plantation shift away from sugar to cotton: 2,000 acres in 1789 out of the total cultivation acreage on the island of 8,000 acres.[25] This form of estate taskscape

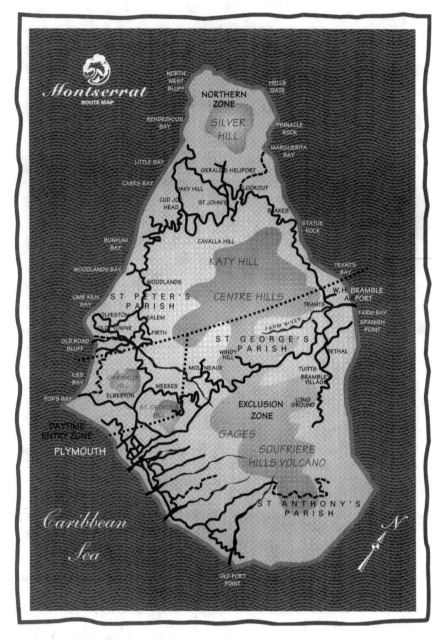

Map 16.1   Montserrat—Post-Eruption Access Zones

remained very much the same for centuries: Galways Estate in the south-west produced sugar until the 1920s when it changed over to cotton, and Fergus notes that the Waterworks Estate is one of the few estates to still remain in "white" hands—573 acres originally given to the island's Deputy Governor

Figure 16.1 Taskscape: A Ruined Stone Mill Again, Formerly the Island National Museum, 2005

Source: Photo by author.

in 1668, leased, sold, and inherited within the family until the late twentieth century when it became an exclusive recording studio and now a US$10,000 per week "unspoiled" 4,000 acre estate for tourists.[26]

In terms of land and development, the picture of the island remained largely the same following settlement and initial plantation development. The slaves working on the estates gained their freedom in 1833 only to work as apprentices and sharecroppers for the same landowners and on the same lands. In the nineteenth century, Fergus draws attention to the system of *métairie*—unpaid labor for landlords who were meant to share the crops between landowner and land laborer. Significantly, Fergus writes that "[i]n Montserrat more than in any other British colony, *métairie* was the big obstacle to peasant development."[27] It was a practice that continued into the twentieth century, and it maintained the large estate fields, the mono-crop agricultural system rather than the range of crops that small-scale farmers would develop on the land had they been allowed to. The only opportunity for small-scale land development was in small plots around the freed slaves' accommodation or as squatters on uncultivated land or some of the estates that were falling into arrears. These developments did not feed down to the freed slave. Nor did they facilitate the growth of a peasantry. Citing Berleant-Schiller, Fergus notes the rise in the number of peasants from 400 in 1862 to 1,628 in 1928, and that between those years, in 1897, there were 1,200 smallholdings recorded, many of which were less that 1 acre in size.[28]

Figure 16.2 Taskscape: Colonial Plantation Machinery in a Copse, Roche's Estate, Eastern Montserrat, 1995

Source: Photo by author.

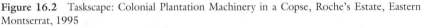

In other words, it was only toward the end of the nineteenth century that the landscape of Montserrat began to develop from that of a course roughly-hewn rug to that of a diverse patchwork quilt.

Still, through much of the twentieth century, Montserrat remained a plantocratic colony. In 1953, Fergus notes that of the total 16,300 acres of land under cultivation, nearly 6,000 acres still belonged to companies and individuals in England; the government owned 1,200 acres; and the inhabitants of the island owned 9,200.[29] It was not until the 1950s and the 1960s that the cotton industry declined and workers developed trade union recognition and the vote, effectively breaking the plantocracy. It is in this context of "land hunger," "misuse of land," and "mendicancy" as the plantation estates broke down and were broken up, that we see trade union growth and activity (plantation worker strikes) on the island which eventually led to full local government and an indigenous Chief Minister exercising rule alongside the colonial Governor.[30] W. H. Bramble, a carpenter, churchman, and cotton cultivator, was elected the first Chief Minister in 1952 (going on to rule for almost 20 years). His first activity to consolidate the erosion of "post-emancipation neo-slavery" was an attempt to shift the agricultural system away from *métairie* toward a land rental approach.[31] This proved to be unsuccessful, resulting in the—encouraged—emigration of workers and their families and the beginning of a remittance and residential tourism revenue phase in the 1960s. Bramble did manage to sell off many government lands at low prices for Montserratians to buy, and at high prices for expatriates: "[c]onsciously or not, he [Bramble] had adopted the Puerto Rican model of development by invitation, but it was for real-estate development, not industrialization."[32]

There followed a decade of house construction and land lot selling to wealthy white expatriates. More than any previous policy since the establishment of the plantation agricultural system, this strategy markedly changed the Montserrat landscape. Geographer David Weaver notes that this policy shift had a significant impact upon the landscape of the island as the GDP based on agriculture declined from 39 percent in 1962 to 4 percent by 1984. Indeed, by 1979, 3 percent of the land base was all that was being cultivated on the island.[33] Despite Montserrat's status as an "unconventional tourism product,"[34] what with poor accessibility, lack of beachfront, and susceptibility to earthquake and hurricane (plus volcano!), it is surprising that Montserrat opted for the residential tourism route for revenue, and so categorically. In 1959, tourism did not feature in the economic and "landscope" potential for the island. Yet by the 1970s, the island had fallen for tourism as de Kadt's illusory "passport to development."[35] Unfortunately, whilst Montserratians had just gained a voice and political controls, they did this at the price of selling their newly acquired land to expatriates in order to maintain the economy. By 1970, non-Montserratian tourism development companies held 2,113 hectares (nearly 25 percent of the island); this resulted in 225 "snowbird" houses constructed on these lands by 1972, predominantly for North Americans.[36] In other words, suddenly the landscape of Montserrat changed with the construction of retiree mansions along colonial tropical lines. The islanders even saw their island taskscape change from agriculture to construction/foreign settlement and their island marketed—controversially—as "The Way the Caribbean Used To Be." We might say that the tourism here was, perhaps, following a post-colonial "space-economy," as land was parceled up and used as small lots, a markedly different tourism policy and practice to the use of pre-existing plantation lands as all-inclusive destinations which was taking place on islands such as Antigua and Jamaica.[37]

Land and Landloss in the Global and the Local

In 1995, Mount Chance, a previously extinct volcano, began to erupt, a slow creeping spillage of pyroclastic ash and occasional magma (see figures 16.3 and 16.4). Evacuations were as creeping and sporadic as the flow of the

Figure 16.3   Mount Chance from Plymouth before the Volcanic Eruption, 1995
Source: Photo by author.

Figure 16.4   Mount Chance from Plymouth after the Volcanic Eruption, 2005
Source: Photo by author.

pyroclastic mudflows: sudden bursts to the north and east and west, settling, and further to the north again as the volcano changed the lie of the land and reshaped the landscape into a sublime natural wasteland, obliterating the present and historical taskscapes on the island.[38] The capital, Plymouth, was evacuated just before it came to be buried 9 feet deep by a succession of devastating waves of pyroclastic material. To the south, old estates and villages such as St. Patrick's were lost. And in the east, a delta fanned out into the Atlantic adding approximately 0.5 mile square to the size of the island. The implications of these land changes and losses were for Montserratians on the island as well as those living—or forced to live—abroad (map 16.1).

Cultural geographer Tracey Skelton reports visiting the island in June 1998 to find that two-thirds of the island's population had migrated, mostly to the United Kingdom (3,500 people, 32 percent of the population), and that three-quarters of all remaining Montserratians had had to relocate to shelters in the north.[39] From her gendered research, Skelton notes that the loss of the community, a support mechanism, and extended family for women, was the most distressing loss felt by Montserratian women.[40] Those migrants who relocated to the United Kingdom faced additional resettlement difficulties ranging from cultural and physical disorientation to schooling and social services needs, all on top of employment, accommodation, and visa difficulties to overcome. The sense of landloss was felt by both old and new migrants, perhaps even more keenly than for the asylum seeker who in many cases at least lives with the potential to return to their land.

> The first time that I heard the news of the major eruption [1997 blast], I felt a sense of immense panic. My first words to my friend was [*sic*], "Oh my God, I won't come from anywhere."[41]

This was U.K.-based Cathy Aymer's reaction to news about the major volcano eruptions. One way for evacuees to cope with the sense of dislocation was to create a version of their existing cognitive map, a simulacrum mazeway, an approximate representation that they could live by, one without the formally recognizable landscapes and taskscapes of island Montserrat. This practice was begun by the migrants to the United Kingdom in the 1950s and 1960s who are reported to have reframed the United Kingdom in terms of Montserrat's landscape: economic migrants from east Montserrat who settled in Stoke Newington referred to Birmingham as Long Ground, for example.[42] In the late 1990s, natural disaster evacuees from Montserrat congregated about Ridley Road Market in London and openly referred to it as "the Evergreen," the name for a large tree at a junction on the outskirts of Plymouth where locals "limed" and hung out.[43] Though this original place was destroyed by the volcano, sprigs of the tree were symbolically replanted and nurtured in the north of Montserrat, and "the Evergreen" was used as an expression for the internet newsgroups and discussion pages online, "the Electronic Evergreen."

In her study of the psychosocial effects of the volcano upon Montserratians resettled to the United Kingdom or relocated to the north of Montserrat, Clarice Barnes stresses the importance of the Montserrat Maroon tradition, a community support mechanism that has great use transposed as a disaster counseling intervention, one which fosters a "participative consciousness" amongst the victims.[44] From these sessions and from her interviews, Barnes is able to demonstrate the sense of loss and displacement remaining with relocatees, people with memory of a place and a life lost, many of whom felt uncomfortable and alien even in the north of the island, "trespassers" on other Montserratians' lands.[45] Montserratians from the evacuated south typically felt a loss for the physical and human environment. Skelton used the very apt expression "grief for the land" when she described personal losses after Hurricane Hugo tore across the island in 1989.[46] This sense of grief is very relevant today and has been compounded by the volcanic disaster that has removed land from the traditional land map of the island and from the islanders' cognitive landscapes and taskscapes.

As Skelton points out, there has always been a very strong "culture of land" on Montserrat, as well as on other Caribbean islands. Land is the navel string connection people have with their past, with history, and generational experience. This "mountain ground" is the "family land" described by Besson.[47] It is land reserved and retained by the family, passed on and passed down the generations. It therefore has "mystic significance," whether it is in use or not.[48] The attachment to land on Montserrat and in the Caribbean region in general is "at once physical, spiritual and emotional": land is to be used or left fallow, but to never be lost.[49] Even if the land is not used because of its associations with laboring and slavery—"a legacy which alienated people from the land"— it is still to be kept within the family.[50] The land for many West Indians thus has emotional worth more so than monetary value. This means that there is a difference between the Western notion of land in the Caribbean and the West Indian notion of land in the Caribbean. The sale of land to residential tourists—such as Skelton herself who recently bought her own villa on Montserrat—thus sets up divisions between people on the island, a "fracturing of modernity" in Skelton's own words as the local is challenged once again by the global.[51]

For many, the old Montserrat remains in their heads, a virtual Montserrat. On the internet, Chedmond Browne, an anti-colonial activist and politician on Montserrat, links the people's landlessness and landloss to their colonial status when he describes Montserrat's integration with Britain as "the path to becoming a Landless & Nationless People."[52] Proud of his people and his homeland, Browne also refers to Montserrat as a "virtual nation . . . [a] country that [now] has no physical borders . . . [a] country that can exist within others."[53] In this way, the islanders are jumping from colonial land and taskscape to the virtual, without having passed through the political post-colonial condition of independence that is felt by neighboring islanders keen also to eradicate colonial land notions and practices on their island (Jamaica, Cuba, and Haiti especially). In this virtuality, in the e-mails between Montserratians at the Electronic Evergreen, they retain their embeddedness— a rootedness to the land as well as the landscape of Montserrat. There is, thus, a physical undercurrent to even the virtual relationships, an embeddedness of relations that goes against Giddens's disembedded characterization of modernity, as the landlost villagers of St. Patrick's find a new folkloric space to shelter in.[54] From this, I would like to suggest that in this shifting, mobile landscape, Montserratians on and off the island desperately clutch at the old rhythms and patterns of living, maintaining their strong sense of dwellingness and rescuing old practices in a vain attempt to arrest the movement and change all around them.

Conclusion

And yet, as Ingold notes, "everything is suspended in movement."[55] Lands and landscapes are prone to change. There is a temporal quality about the land, one that unnerves people, particularly when "brought home" to them during a natural disaster. The eruption of Mount Chance on Montserrat is just such a case study, one of mazeway disruption. The Montserrat landscape lost is not, as Ingold would have it, "the congealed form of the taskscape," the latter an embodiment of the former.[56] As I have suggested above, the land is the core perceptual platform; the landscape a social view; the taskscape activities' remains; and landscope the potential envisioned in the land. The land then itself does not hold native readings, the remains of generations. Rather, this, for me, is the taskscape: the monuments to labor in the fences and hedges and mills across the land, the ploughs' furrows, and the footpaths' tramped.

If the post-colonial is a contestatory or oppositional consciousness, one that can even be found within the colonial regime, then we can conclude that perhaps Montserrat has been undecidedly post-colonial, particularly through the narrative of landlessness, land, and landloss that spans the centuries on the island. The present-day dramatic eradication of a familiar taskscape in the eruption of Mount Chance is only but a new threat to the ontological security of Montserrat's colonial subjects, but it is one that may well give onto a form of new "disaster imperialism" as the colonial machine returns with its ever monitoring, scrutinizing, auditing eye.[57]

Notes

1. Randy Greenaway, "South Gone," song from the album *Little Island Live Volcano: The Songs* (Baker Hill, Montserrat: Zunky Music Ltd., 1999).
2. Howard Fergus, *Volcano Verses* (Leeds: Peepal Tree Press Ltd., 2003), 9.
3. Jacqueline Browne, "Living with a Mountain," poem in Howard Fergus (ed.), *Eruption: Montserrat versus Volcano* (Montserrat: UWI School of Continuing Studies, 1996), 85–86, 85, 1.1–6.
4. Raymond Smith, "Ethnic Difference and Peasant Economy in British Guiana," in Raymond Firth and Basil Yamey (eds.), *Capital, Saving and Credit in Peasant Societies* (London: George Allen and Unwin, 1964), 303–323, at 316.
5. Michel-Rolph Trouillot, "The Caribbean Region: An Open Frontier in Anthropological Theory," *Annual Review of Anthropology* 21 (1992): 19–42, at 23.
6. Sidney Mintz, *Caribbean Transformations* (Chicago: Aldine, 1974).
7. Trouillot, "The Caribbean Region," 21.
8. Michel-Rolph Trouillot, *Peasants and Capital: Dominica in the World Economy* (London: Johns Hopkins University Press, 1988).

9. Karen Fog Olwig, *Global Culture, Island Identity: Continuity and Change in the Afro-Caribbean Community of Nevis* (Philadelphia: Harwood Academic Publishers, 1993), 2.

10. Sidney Greenfield, "Land Tenure and Transmission in Rural Barbados," *Anthropological Quarterly* 33 (1960): 165–176; Michael Horowitz, *Morne-Paysan: Peasant Village in Martinique* (New York: Holt, Rinehart and Winston, 1967).

11. Jean Besson, "A Paradox in Caribbean Attitudes to Land," in Jean Besson and Janet Momsen (eds.), *Land and Development in the Caribbean* (London: Macmillan, 1987), 13–45, 17–18.

12. David Reason, *The Unpainted Landscape* (London: Coracle Press, 1987), 40, cited in Tim Ingold, *The Perception of the Environment: Essays in Livelihood, Dwelling and Skill* (London: Routledge, 2000), 201.

13. Ingold, *The Perception of the Environment*, 189–208.

14. Ingold, *The Perception of the Environment*, 190.

15. Ingold, *The Perception of the Environment*, 193.

16. Maurice Merleau-Ponty, *Phenomenology of Perception* (London: Routledge and Kegan Paul, 1962), 24.

17. Ingold, *The Perception of the Environment*, 193.

18. Ingold, *The Perception of the Environment*, 195, 197.

19. Ingold, *The Perception of the Environment*, 208.

20. Anthony Oliver-Smith, *The Martyred City: Death and Rebirth in the Andes* (Albuquerque: University of New Mexico Press, 1986), 188.

21. Oliver-Smith, *The Martyred City*, 267.

22. Howard Fergus, *Green Innocence* (St. Augustine, Trinidad: Multimedia Production Centre, 1978), 23, ll. 1–4.

23. Jonathan Skinner, *Before the Volcano: Reverberations of Identity on Montserrat* (Kingston, Jamaica: Arawak Publications, 2004).

24. Howard Fergus, *Montserrat: History of a Caribbean Colony* (London: Macmillan Caribbean Press Ltd., 1994), 34.

25. Bryan Edwards, *The History, Civil and Commercial, of the British Colonies in the West Indies* (London: John Stockdale, 1801), 486–498.

26. Fergus, *Montserrat*, 59.

27. Fergus, *Montserrat*, 107.

28. Fergus, *Montserrat*, 111.

29. Fergus, *Montserrat*, 191.

30. Howard Fergus (ed.), *Beneath the Bananas: Poems of Montserrat* (Salem, Montserrat: UWI Montserrat, 2004), 6.

31. Fergus, *Montserrat*, 152.

32. Fergus, *Montserrat*, 163.

33. David Weaver, "Alternative Tourism in Montserrat," *Tourism Management* 16 (1995): 593–604, at 598.

34. Weaver, "Alternative Tourism," 599.

35. Emanuel De Kadt (ed.), *Tourism: Passport to Development?* (New York: Oxford University Press, 1979).

36. Weaver, "Alternative Tourism," 599.

37. David Weaver, "The Evolution of a 'Plantation' Tourism Landscape on the Caribbean Island of Antigua," *Tijdschrift voor Econ. En Soc. Geografie* 79 (1988): 319–331, at 324.

38. Jonathan Skinner, "The Eruption of Chances Peak, Montserrat, and the Narrative Containment of Risk," in Pat Caplan (ed.), *Risk Revisited* (London: Pluto Press, 2000), 156–183.

39. Tracey Skelton, "Evacuation, Relocation and Migration: Montserratian Women's Experiences of the Volcanic Disaster," in Jonathan Skinner (ed.), Island Migrations, Island Cultures (Special Edition), *Anthropology in Action* 6 (1999): 6–13, at 7–8.

40. Skelton, "Evacuation, Relocation and Migration," 11.

41. Cathy Aymer, "Migration: The Irreparable Separation of Small and Large Footprints," in Jonathan Skinner (ed.), Island Migrations, Island Cultures (Special Edition), *Anthropology in Action* 6 (1999): 29–33, at 29.

42. Stuart Philpott, *West Indian Migration: The Montserrat Case* (London: Athlone Press, 1973), 108.

43. Gertrude Shotte, "Islander in Transition: The Montserrat Case," in Jonathan Skinner (ed.), Island Migrations, Island Cultures (Special Edition), *Anthropology in Action* 6 (1999): 14–24, at 19.

44. Clarice Barnes, "The Montserrat Volcanic Disaster: A Study of Meaning, Psychosocial Effects, Coping and Intervention" (unpublished PhD thesis, University of Birmingham, 1999), 276, 30.

45. Barnes, "The Montserrat Volcanic Disaster," 200.

46. Tracey Skelton, "Globalizing Forces and Natural Disaster: What Can Be the Future for the Small Caribbean Island of Montserrat?" in Eleonore Kofman and Gillian Youngs (eds.), *Globalization: Theory and Practice* (London: Continuum, 2003), 65–78.

47. Jean Besson, "Family Land and the Caribbean Society: Toward Ethnography of Afro-Caribbean Peasantries," in Elizabeth Thomas-Hope (ed.), *Perspectives on Caribbean Regional Identity* (Liverpool: Liverpool University Press, 1984), 57–83.

48. Edith Clarke, *My Mother Who Fathered Me: A Study of Family in Three Selected Communities in Jamaica.* 2nd ed. (London: Allen and Unwin, 1966), 65.

49. Skelton, "Globalizing Forces and Natural Disaster," 325.

50. Jean Besson and Janet Momsen, "Introduction," in Besson and Momsen (eds.), *Land and Development in the Caribbean*, 1–9, at 6.

51. Tracey Skelton, ' "Cultures of Land' in the Caribbean: A Contribution to the Debate on Development and Culture," *European Journal of Development Research* 8 (1996): 71–92, at 8.

52. Chedmond Browne, "MONTSERRAT'S INTEGRATION INTO BRITAIN: The Path to Becoming a Landless & Nationless People," *Pan-Afrikan Liberator* (May 2002): 3, http://www.geocities.com/brownec/may2002.html (accessed October 21, 2005).

53. Chedmond Browne, "1st Virtual Nation," *Pan-Afrikan Liberator* (September 2000): 2, http://www.geocities.com/CapitolHill/Parliament/4751/index32.html (accessed October 21, 2005).

54. Anthony Giddens, *The Consequences of Modernity* (Cambridge: Polity Press, 1990).

55. Ingold, *The Perception of the Environment*, 200.

56. Ingold, *The Perception of the Environment*, 199.

57. James Lewis, *Development in a Disaster-Prone Place: Studies in Vulnerability* (London: Intermediate Technology Publications, 1999), 146.

Chapter 17

"Leave to Come Back": The Importance of Family Land in a Transnational Caribbean Community

Beth Mills

Anthropologists, geographers, and sociologists working in the Caribbean have recognized a form of customary, kinship-based, land tenure among Afro-Caribbean people, often referred to as family land, beginning with Edith Clarke's groundbreaking work in Jamaica in the 1950s.[1] Since this early work, important contributions to the understanding of the history, meaning, and function of this type of customary land tenure have been made by Wilson[2] in Providencia, Besson,[3] Carnegie,[4] and McKay[5] in Jamaica, Rubenstein[6] in St. Vincent, Barrow,[7] Crichlow,[8] and Dujon[9] in St. Lucia, Fog Olwig[10] in Nevis and St. John, and Maurer[11] in the British Virgin Islands.

From the many case studies and discussions a few characteristics of family land emerge as indisputable. Family land is not communal land but land where use is restricted to a particular group of people who are related by blood. Family land is only available to members of the kinship group, that is, people who share a common ancestry, and its use is defined by tradition. It is seen as a flexible resource and available for whoever's need is greatest at any given time. It is important for family members to cooperate and to feel a responsibility for each other for the arrangement to work smoothly.

It is clear from reviewing the scholarship surrounding family land tenure that it functions best when the land resource is of little or marginal market value. The arrangement tends to work smoothly in places where land sales do not command high prices due to the marginality of the environment or because of the peripheral location of the land. When economic circumstances surrounding the land shift to make it significantly more valuable, family land comes under pressure and changes in the tenure arrangement may result.

Family Land on Carriacou

Carriacou, the largest of the Grenadine islands, together with the neighboring island of Petite Martinique, and the larger island of Grenada to the south, make up the tri-island state of Grenada. The country's government is administered from St. George's, on Grenada. Residents of Carriacou and Petite Martinique have traditionally felt removed from life on the "mainland" of Grenada. Because of their proximity to each other, the two smaller islands share a history and many family ties.

The presence of family land tenure in Carriacou was first noted by Smith from his field studies in the villages of L'Esterre and Harvey Vale.[12] Smith's detailed study tracing inheritance in particular families through generations illuminated the complex way in which rights to land were transferred in these small agricultural villages. At a later date, in the mid-1980s, the relationship between family land tenure and agriculture was clarified in a restudy by the author focused on explaining agricultural land use in the village of Harvey Vale.[13] At that time, much of the land that was under cultivation in Harvey Vale was family land. A further restudy of the village by the author in 1999 indicated that an increase in tourism in the village had resulted in a decrease in the amount of land under cultivation, regardless of tenure. The same research noted an increase in tension over the division and sale of land also in response to increasing tourism.[14]

Research was conducted in five villages on Carriacou during 1999 and 2000 to uncover the extent and nature of family land on the island.[15] Results show that 80 percent of the self-identified household heads interviewed claimed a share in family land located somewhere on Carriacou. These same survey results show that essentially all people with family land had relatives living abroad who share a claim in family land.

Carriacou's geographic isolation and its history of different political juris-dictions, first as part of the French colonies, then as part of the British Colony of Grenada, and after 1974 as part of the tri-island nation of Grenada, is fundamental to understanding the evolution of family land there. Carriacou's small size, its often severe dry season, its lack of surface water and hence, the marginality of the island's agricultural production meant that the plantation economy was less successful here than on the larger Windward Islands. Consequently, by the turn of the twentieth century, essentially all the planta-tions on Carriacou were abandoned, or under absentee management, and were in the process of being subdivided and sold to residents who were descendants of slaves.

The process of land reform undertaken by the colonial government was a response to the poverty and dysfunction of the agricultural economy follow-ing the decline of plantation production on Carriacou. Land redistribution here was more of a practical and altruistic project undertaken by the govern-ment rather than a response to a resistant, organized, and antagonistic rural proletariat, as may have been the case elsewhere in the region. The historical record from the time speaks with a fairly gentle and concerned, paternalistic, voice for a change in land tenure that might work to advantage of absentee landowner and landless sharecropper or squatter. In fact, squatting on the estates of Harvey Vale and Beausejour seems to have been the precursor to, if not the inspiration for, the government idea of resettlement.[16] If the agricultural economy of Carriacou had been successful, or even functioning, at the turn of the century, it is doubtful that land reform would have unfolded as smoothly and with so little resistance from the planters, who in this instance were absentee landlords.

The evidence from Carriacou appears to contradict the idea that family land was created as an institution in response to intense land scarcity and planter opposition to peasant settlement.[17] However, given a history of plantation slavery and the hunger for land on the part of the local population on Carriacou at the time of resettlement as documented in the historical record, and the high rates of emigration for wage labor in other parts of the region at the same time, it is clear that land ownership was a symbol of personhood, freedom, and prestige as well as a pragmatic survival strategy for the residents (see chapter 18).

It may be claimed with confidence that in the view of Carriacouans, most of the island of Carriacou is family land. Two basic and sometimes overlapping definitions emerged from fieldwork done in 1999 and 2000.[18] The first understanding about family land is that it is simply undivided land. There are five locations of individual, large, undivided acreages on the island that have remained undivided from the time they were purchased from an absentee plantation owner. These areas are referred to as family land. The second understanding of family land is centered on a simple principle: the land is inherited from one's parents or other family members. Purchased land may become family land at any time if the intent of the owner is for the family to inherit equally. In this way, very small pieces of property, as little as one-quarter acre, may be regarded as family land.

Caribbean researchers have come to understand, after years of work in rural villages, that the origins and evolution of customary land tenure in the region are complex and varied. In the case of Carriacou, the origin of family land can be traced to a time period when the plantation economy had already dissolved. And family land continues to be created today on Carriacou in the total absence of plantations but in a situation of continued land scarcity.[19]

The Symbolic Nature of Family Land

Examples from throughout the region have noted the symbolic significance of family land to Caribbean communities.[20] Although members of a family (those people who share ancestors) may be dispersed and living at distances from each other, a share in family land binds them over distances. Within the family, family land may become a symbol of a common past and represent the ties of the individual to their homeland and culture.

The physical reality on the small islands of the region is that land is a very limited and scarce resource. Consequently, family land creates the impression of land as an unlimited resource by tying it to the idea of "permanence and immortality."[21] Because the land remains undivided and inalienable, it comes to symbolize the continuity of a landholding corporation, in the sense that everyone has a share. Elaborating on this point for the Jamaican village of

Martha Brae, Besson notes, "Thus when discussing family land, interrelated contrasts are reiterated by the villagers: the permanence of family land as opposed to the impermanence of man; and the immortality of the kinship corporation in opposition to the mortality of its individual members."[22] By expanding the discussion about family land beyond its economic utility and toward its symbolic significance, Besson opens the door to a understanding of Afro-Caribbean society and culture.[23]

Migration and "Rooted Mobility"

Both long-term and short-term migration have been important to Caribbean society since emancipation (compare chapter 18). Migration has been especially critical to survival on the smaller, resource-poor, and environmentally marginal islands, and there continues to be a connection between migration and family land. The evolution of family land is a process of both "rooting and uprooting" in that the limited land resources on small Caribbean islands propels migration, while a share in family land connects the migrant to home.[24] The agreement that gives symbolic value to land ownership depends on migration to prevent competing economic claims from destroying family and community ties.

Family land is important to migrant societies because it provides a base of operations for family members who are sojourners abroad. As Fog Olwig observes for St. John, "The importance of family land should be found in its value as an actual and imagined home for people who have had to make their living as 'hunters and gatherers' in the margins of the global economy, often in distant migration destinations."[25] Family land may function as an economic safety net by allowing a family member to return at any time and request use of the land, should the need arise.

Karen Fog Olwig's research on family land and community life in Nevis and St. John most closely approximates the circumstances of family land on Carriacou, Grenada. The similarities are due to the small size, drought-prone conditions, marginal agricultural economies, and consequent history of migration that Nevis, St. John, and Carriacou share. The commonalities in their geography manifest themselves in the way family land evolved in all three locations.

For the former Danish West Indies (now the U.S. Virgin Islands), family land emerged as an effective response to marginalized conditions in that part of the region. In the postemancipation period family land provided an actual residence for freed slaves as well as a symbolic home for family members whether or not it was their actual place of residence.[26] For freed slaves in the Danish West Indies the emergence of family land went hand in hand with increased migration from the islands. Its function as a symbol of home and "rootedness" was essential to the migrants.

From the case study on St. John it is clear that, like Carriacou, family land tenure worked for the negative reason that the land offered so little economic opportunity and many family members sought work off island. And similarly most St. Johnians "leave to come back," that is, they migrate with intention of earning enough money to be able to return and build a house and live.[27] But many St. Johnians, like Carriacouans, find it difficult or impossible to return once they have gone abroad and established careers and families there.

Olwig discovered that in a very important sense rooting and mobility are intimately connected in the institution of family land. It is only because some family members do stay on the island and take care of the land that makes it possible for it to remain a symbolic home for those abroad. In the case of Carriacou (and perhaps St. John) it can be argued that the integrity of family land is as important or even *more* important to those living abroad.

Like the situation on Carriacou, family land on St. John proved a viable system as long as the land had little commercial value. And, like St. John, when land prices began to rise as the island became a tourist destination, serious problems arose in regard to the land. An important difference between circumstances on St. John and Carriacou, one that should work to protect Carriacouan interest in the land, is the Grenadian law prohibiting foreign ownership of more than a few acres of land. This provision does not exist on St. John because it is administered by the American government. The dilemma that many St. Johnians now face is one that Carriacouans fear: "[W]hat was formerly a source of identity and family togetherness has become a source of contention and divisiveness."[28]

The View of Family Land from Abroad

Since emancipation, migration has kept the population of Carriacou relatively stable. Carriacouans have always responded to new opportunities abroad. During the nineteenth century men from Carriacou traveled within the Caribbean to islands where agricultural wages were higher than on Carriacou. The sphere of their migration destinations expanded in the twentieth century to include work on the Panama Canal; the oil industries of Trinidad, Aruba, and Venezuela; agricultural work in the American south; employment in the cities of England and North America.[29]

Many of the early migrants to urban centers of the North experienced prejudice and economic exploitation on their way to achieving acceptance and, in many cases, success in American, British, and Canadian societies. Opportunities for early migrants were limited, but through perseverance, and especially through diligence in pursuing higher education, many Carriacouans in New York, London, and Toronto are now professionals who contribute greatly to the country where they are resident, as well as to their families and the larger community back in Carriacou. These individuals were pioneers establishing the transnational community of today.

Remittances from family members working abroad have always been an important aspect of the Carriacou economy. Support from abroad continues to be important, but the growth of the tourist economy, especially in regard to the visitors who arrive by yacht, has helped to enhance the local economy.

Perhaps the greatest boost to the Carriacou economy in the past decade has been the growth in the construction industry. This sector has grown to accommodate the new housing demands of returning migrants, primarily those people who left for England in the 1950s and 1960s. There has also been a certain amount of new construction associated with the building of vacation homes.

The relationship between family land and migration has been important since emancipation. The newly freed slaves quickly concluded that the agricultural resource base on Carriacou was insufficient to support their advancement. The colonial administrators designed the first resettlement schemes to promote a prospering class of peasant or "yeoman" farmers. In addition to this intent, the former slaves viewed the opportunity to own land as a way to establish a foothold, an anchor, for the family. For people who had been displaced from their original homeland and whose families had been torn apart, establishing land ownership and a locus for their new families became critical. From this home ground family members were able to venture forth from the island to seek better wages and business opportunities. The small farms, though unsuccessful, that resulted from the resettlement programs on Carriacou provided the security and flexibility necessary for family members to "forage" abroad.

Family land tenure has accommodated the coming and going of people until the present time. People were welcomed back home when they chose to come, their welcome being all the warmer if they had maintained a regular flow of support through cash remittances and other gifts during their absence. In this regard, family land tenure has done more to ensure a flow of development aid than has any government program or initiative.[30]

During 1999 and 2000 interviews with Carriacouans abroad in New York City and Toronto were conducted that revealed much about the way islanders who are living abroad feel about family land back home on Carriacou.[31] With few exceptions, migrants said that land on Carriacou, and their family connections to it, were crucial to them. However, despite this sentiment, most people who have been away from Carriacou for many years have lost track of the details of the size and location of the family land parcels to which they are connected. They often have a general idea of the location of land with which they identify but cannot tell you the exact acreage or produce any legal record of their connection to the land, such as a deed. But when a person is currently maintaining a household in Carriacou while away, and coming and going at regular intervals, they have a more exact view of the status of their family land.

What all migrants who claim a share in family land expressed when interviewed is a strong conviction that the land should not be divided or sold. In many cases they have an unrealistic vision of the status of land back home. They imagine much larger allotments than exist. In some cases, it seems important to people who are abroad to imagine an undivided family land base on the island, whether or not that base actually continues to exist. There is often a gap between what the migrants imagine as their common resource back home and what is true on the ground, acre for acre. It seems that, as long as migrants do not return, their imaginations continue to feed their ties to their heritage.

One important concept that emerged through the interviews is that the land and people's heritage are synonymous. When land is divided, heritage and identity are threatened. There was a consistent plea expressed for the necessity of maintaining the heritage as "the ancestors" intended. In other words, the reason that elders initiated family land tenure was to ensure that the land remain within the family and undivided in perpetuity as a symbol of the peoples' roots. There is often the desire to remain connected to family holding and oppose the division and sale of land, particularly among family members who have been living away from the island for a generation or two.

The sentimental attachment to family land can cause conflict among family members when those who remain at home do not share the views of those abroad. At times there is a disconnection between the social and economic changes occurring at home on Carriacou and the idyllic place of the migrant's imagination. Local landowners have been under some pressure to sell their land to foreigners as the tourist economy on the island grows.

In an effort to maintain local control of the land the government does not allow foreign citizens to own more than a small portion; the limit is less than 5 acres. Despite this fact, there is a perception among many Carriacou residents that foreigners are taking over. This is a misconception given the small number of individuals who were not born on the island who own second homes and even smaller number who own businesses on Carriacou. Nonetheless, there is a fear among many that resources are shifting toward white and foreign control. The idea of keeping family land undivided and in local hands is important to some people who express anxiety regarding a loss of control over their heritage.

There has been a tremendous exodus from this tiny island over the years, and many Carriacouans have left never to return. Some, no doubt, felt little connection with the place after their departure, especially if their experiences had been particularly harsh while there. Many, however, maintained strong ties with their past and the family members back home. In fact, every Carriacouan who was interviewed abroad expressed the wish to be able to return home, at some future date. In some instances people said that they wanted to return to the exact place of their birth. This sentiment may also help to account for the many small family cemeteries associated with family land all over the island. One migrant who had been back and forth from New York for the past 30 years had recently retired to his birthplace, "right here on this spot" (where we were sitting for the interview) in order to complete the circle of his life journey.

To Carriacouans abroad family land can represent the hope of return to a simple, quiet way of life where people take care of each other. This construction of place may have little to do with the changing reality of island life today, but if the migrant does not actually return home, the idyllic, imagined place that family land represents can support and comfort in the midst of a chaotic urban lifestyle. A share in family land works as an imagined space in the minds of those abroad and through memory and nostalgia maintains the link to home.

Family land tenure on Carriacou is a complex and evolving set of relationships between people and the land. The concept of family land created by the transnational imagination is arguably the most important role of family land in contemporary Carriacouan society. It ensures cohesion among community members in urban areas abroad. It underlies the reason for support and development aid to the home economy. It is important to the identity of those who have been away for any length of time, and it is the foundation of their dream to return.

Notes

1. Edith Clarke, *My Mother Who Fathered Me: A Study of the Family in Three Selected Communities in Jamaica*. 2nd ed. (London: George Allen and Unwin, 1966).

2. Peter J. Wilson, *Crab Antics: The Social Anthropology of the English-Speaking Negro Societies of the Caribbean* (New Haven: Yale University Press, 1973).

3. Jean Besson, "Family Land and Caribbean Society: Toward an Ethnography of Afro Caribbean Peasantries," in Elizabeth Thomas-Hope (ed.), *Perspectives on Caribbean Regional Identity*, Monograph Series No. 11 (Liverpool: Liverpool University Press, Centre for Latin American Studies, 1984), 57–83; Jean Besson, "Family Land as a Model for Martha Brae's New History: Culture Building in an Afro-Caribbean Village," in Charles V. Carnegie (ed.), *Afro-Caribbean Villages in Historical Perspective* (Kingston, Jamaica: African-Caribbean Institute of Jamaica, 1987); Jean Besson, "A Paradox in Caribbean Attitudes to Land," in Jean Besson and Janet Momsen (eds.), *Land and Development in the Caribbean* (London: Macmillan, 1987), 13–45; and Jean Besson, *Martha Brae's Two Histories: European Expansion and Caribbean Culture-Building in Jamaica* (Chapel Hill and London: University of North Carolina Press, 2002).

4. Charles V. Carnegie, "Is Family Land an Institution?" in Carnegie (ed.), *Afro-Caribbean Villages in Historical Perspective*, 83–99.

5. Lesley McKay, "Tourism and Changing Attitudes to Land in Negril, Jamaica," in Besson and Momsen (eds.), *Land and Development in the Caribbean*, 132–152.

6. Hymie Rubenstein, "Folk and Mainstream Systems of Land Tenure and Use in St. Vincent," in Besson and Momsen (eds.), *Land and Development in the Caribbean*, 70–87.

7. Christine Barrow, *Family Land and Development in St. Lucia* (Cave Hill, Barbados: Institute of Social and Economic Research, University of the West Indies, 1992).

8. Michaeline A. Crichlow, "An Alternative Approach to Family Land Tenure in the Anglophone Caribbean: The Case of St. Lucia," *New West Indian Guide* 68, nos. 1 and 2: 77–99.

9. Veronica Dujon, "National Actors against World Market Pressures: Communal Land, Privatization and Agricultural Development in the Caribbean" (PhD dissertation, University of Wisconsin, Madison, 1995).

10. Karen Fog Olwig, "Cultural Complexity after Freedom: Nevis and Beyond," in Karen Fog Olwig (ed.), *Small Islands, Large Questions: Society, Culture and Resistance in the Post-Emancipation Caribbean* (London: Frank Cass, 1995), 100–120; Karen Fog Olwig, "Caribbean Family Land: A Modern Commons," *Plantation Society in the Americas* IV, nos. 2 and 3 (1997): 135–158; and Karen Fog Olwig, "Caribbean Place Identity: From Family Land to Region and Beyond," *Identities* 5, no. 4 (1999): 435–467.

11. Bill Maurer, "Fractions of Blood on Fragments of Soil: Capitalism, the Commons, and Kinship in the Caribbean," *Plantation Society in the Americas* IV, nos. 2 and 3 (1997): 159–171.

12. M. G. Smith, "The Transformation of Land Rights by Transmission in Carriacou," *Social and Economic Studies* 5, no. 2 (1956): 103–138.

13. Beth Mills, "Agriculture and Idle Land in Carriacou, Grenada with a Case Study of the Village of Harvey Vale" (unpublished MA thesis, University of New Mexico, 1987).

14. Beth Mills, "Family Land in Carriacou, Grenada and Its Meaning within the Transnational Community: Heritage, Identity, and Rooted Mobility" (unpublished PhD dissertation, University of California, Davis, 2002), 154–170.

15. Mills, "Family Land in Carriacou," 33–41.

16. British Colonial Office Papers (C.O.) 1898. Miscellaneous Paper No. 11. Grenada; C.O. 1903. Miscellaneous Paper No 24. Grenada.

17. Besson, "Family Land and Caribbean Society."

18. Mills, "Family Land in Carriacou," 131.

19. Mills, "Family Land in Carriacou," 125–131.

20. Jean Besson, "Symbolic Aspects of Land in the Caribbean: The Tenure and Transmission of Land Rights among Caribbean Peasantries," in Malcolm Cross and Arnaud Marks (eds.), *Peasants, Plantations and Rural Communities in the Caribbean* (Guildford: University of Surrey and Leiden Royal Institute of Linguistics and Anthropology, 1979), 86–116; and Olwig, "Caribbean Family Land," 136.

21. Besson, "A Paradox in Caribbean Attitudes to Land," 15.

22. Besson, "A Paradox in Caribbean Attitudes to Land," 15.

23. Besson, *Martha Brae's Two Histories*, 8–10.

24. Besson, "Family Land as a Model for Martha Brae's New History"; Jean Besson, "Land, Kinship, and Community in the Post-Emancipation Caribbean: A Regional View of the Leewards," in Olwig (ed.), *Small Islands, Large Questions*, 73–99.

25. Olwig, "Caribbean Family Land," 136.

26. Olwig, "Caribbean Family Land."

27. Olwig, "Caribbean Family Land," 149.

28. Olwig, "Caribbean Family Land," 153.

29. Donald Hill, "The Impact of Migration on the Metropolitan and Folk Society of Carriacou, Grenada," *Anthropological Papers of the American Museum of Natural History* 54, no. 2 (1977): 218–227.

30. Beth H. Mills, "The Transnational Community as an Agent for Caribbean Development," *Southeastern Geographer* 45, no. 2 (2005): 174–191.

31. Mills, "Family Land in Carriacou," 170–215.

Chapter 18

Collateral and Achievement: Land and Caribbean Migration

Margaret Byron

Introduction

The colonial legacy of unequal land distribution remains very evident in the Caribbean region. As the colonial settlers appropriated land resources after eliminating the populations they encountered there, there was virtually no preexisting peasantry, and access to land by the slave and ex-slave populations and later imported indentured laborers was largely at the discretion of the plantocracy and the colonial state.

Land was the key to production in a region dependent on agriculture and was the only alternative to their labor power for the majority of the population. Postemancipation history in the Caribbean could usefully be examined from the perspective of the struggle for land and the security that access to and control of land conveyed. It is recognized that access to land varied in each territory according to the success of sugar cultivation and to proportion of less arable, nonplantation land that existed. Throughout this complex region, however, land acquisition remained a route to greater security and a means of conveying wealth to descendants.

The laboring classes incorporated migration for work opportunities from early in the postemancipation era. While initially the remittances from such migrations assisted with subsistence of the families left behind in the home territories, over time it was also used to invest in house lots and later in land for cultivation. As the sugar industry declined, in some islands migrants found that their return coincided with the sale of estates that had ceased to be profitable sugar plantations. The wealthiest returnees, often those artisans who had the opportunity to take skilled jobs in the destination countries, used their savings to invest in relatively large landholdings upon their return. The subdivision and resale of this land created a small, relatively middle class in many territories.

The migration to Britain was the largest and most comprehensive exodus of labor from the British Caribbean colonies and ex-colonies in the postwar period. Central to this movement for many migrants was the use of land as collateral. For others, their greater income in the destination enabled them to purchase land for the first time in the home territory. This land ownership paralleled social ties in maintaining firm links between migrants and their countries of origin. It underpins the "transnational existence" for many migrants and is usually the first stage of realizing the return goal.

This chapter will examine the relationship between land ownership and migration and will discuss the role of land in the increasingly transnational condition of Caribbean communities. The first part of the chapter will consist of a brief review of some of the major elements of the region's migration history after emancipation (which first occurred in the British West Indies in 1838), noting how this related to the critical issue of ownership and access to land. The second part will consider specific migrations from the island of Nevis and will examine how migration combined with other major structural factors (such as land settlement) to grant greater agency to the workers in that island gradually leading to a change in land tenure and, indeed, in class structure. The third part will examine the continuing role of land in the transnational Caribbean communities.

Land and Migration in Historical and Geographical Context

In the years immediately following emancipation, most ex-slaves were free in name only as they still lived on the plantations, still worked for their former owners, and were now forced to spend most of the pittance they received as wages on renting huts on the plantations. However, due to the variations in size and topographical features of Caribbean territories, significantly different livelihood strategies evolved in the postemancipation years[1] Hence in the smaller, rocky sugar islands of Nevis and Montserrat, for example, where sugar cultivation declined relatively early, there is evidence of land ownership and a fledgling peasantry, long before this developed in key sugar territories such as St. Kitts and Barbados. Meanwhile in the larger island territories such as the Dominican Republic and Jamaica there was more variation in topography and peasantries developed in less cultivable areas in conjunction with plantation agriculture in the more accessible and fertile land areas. In the most mountainous islands such as most of the Windward group, sugar cultivation was far less successful with a quasi-peasantry quickly developing following slavery.

In the smaller islands of the northeastern Caribbean very few ex-slaves had the chance within their local environment to escape this status as land, the main source of a living other than their labor power, was in the control of the European planters and the colonial state.[2] At that point land ownership by ex-slaves and their descendants was restricted to those mistresses and children of white planters and estate officials who had made gifts of land to them and other freed slaves, many of whom were artisans, who had managed to save enough cash to purchase small acreages of land.[3] For the vast majority the only chance to exercise their freedom meant taking the opportunity to leave the islands to seek work in the more recently established, modern plantations of Trinidad and British Guiana in the southern Caribbean.[4] Here, while the migrants remained landless laborers, they received higher wages and had the satisfaction of exercising the freedom to leave the property and restrictions of their former slave owners. Ironically, this shortage of labor in the larger territories was largely the result of the withdrawal of the black ex-slaves from the southern Caribbean plantations to marginal land to live as peasant farmers or to live in urban areas as members of the proletariat or artisan classes. Despite the hazards of these mid-nineteenth century sea journeys from the Leeward Islands to Trinidad and British Guiana, returns and remigrations were regular occurrences for a few decades.[5]

Labor migration thus became a socioeconomic survival strategy, particularly for those small islanders with no space in which to exercise freedom. Later in the nineteenth century, as the importation of indentured laborers to Trinidad and British Guiana from the Indian subcontinent reduced the demand for workers from the region, potential migrants from the Leewards found other labor-poor destinations.[6] They were approached by labor recruitment officers from the large, sugar plantations in the Dominican Republic and, to a lesser extent, Cuba. New U.S. investments in these territories created a demand for labor which remained unfilled by local sources, and the plantations turned to the small islands of the northeastern Caribbean in search of a migrant labor force.[7] The relatively large land area and varied topography of the Dominican Republic and Cuba enabled local peasantries to develop. Empowered by their access to land these peasants could morph into semiproletarians if additional income was required but proved an unreliable and nonpliable workforce. The plantation establishment sought seasonal migrant workers as the solution to their labor needs.[8] While the extent of additional disposable income was at times negligible and some migrants returned from Santo Domingo "empty handed,"[9] this labor migration offered many the opportunity to accumulate savings[10] that contributed to early land purchases by ex-slaves and their descendants as some estates and Crown Land became available to the masses in later decades.[11] For the Leeward Islanders, these two migrations along with the movement of labor to Bermuda in the first decade of the twentieth century set the precedent for a strategy to augment meager earnings in the home territory by migration to jobs in expanding industries abroad.

Migration did not involve cutting ties with the home territories. Indeed, in many cases, the remittances enabled families and households to consolidate their socioeconomic position by purchasing property they rented or squatted on. However, this varied by island. For example, in the twin island colony of St. Kitts-Nevis very different land tenure systems evolved due to their different environmental conditions. Sugar cultivation was generally a success in St. Kitts due to favorable conditions. Investment in modernizing the sugar production system in the early twentieth century led to consolidation of the industry and a reinforcement of the control over land and the power of the plantocracy, condemning the black majority of the population to landless worker status. In Nevis, the gradual collapse of the sugar industry led first to a share-cropping arrangement, a compromise solution. For up to a century the planter class opposed the sale of land to the former slaves. After years of unprofitable sugarcane cultivation, some indebted planters resorted to sharecropping. Through this process they reduced labor costs by allowing their labor force to occupy and cultivate parts of the plantation land in return for one-third of the produce. Sharecropping was particularly common in the British islands of Nevis, St. Lucia, and Tobago and in French Martinique.[12] In Nevis estate owners gradually offered house and farm lots for sale to the existing occupants, and those who could afford it bought the property. The gulf between the societies in St. Kitts and Nevis widened significantly at this point. Richardson reports on 292 landholdings of under 10 acres in Nevis in 1929 compared to only 11 in St. Kitts.[13] So while the opportunities to migrate were grasped equally by the male populations of both islands, their earnings were only likely to be converted into landholdings in Nevis. St. Kitts was very similar to Barbados in this respect as an older, successful economy, which largely excluded the development of a peasantry in postemancipation years (see chapter 13).

In the larger territories, as exemplified earlier by the cases of Trinidad and Guyana, and including Jamaica and Hispanic Cuba and the Dominican Republic, a dual economy developed with plantation agriculture occupying the best land, while more marginal, mountainous land was the site of peasant production. The struggle for access to such land has been examined in depth by Besson in the case of Jamaica.[14]

In some cases ex-slaves squatted on Crown Land while others who had accumulated some capital attempted to purchase land. Their occupation of Crown Land was vigorously opposed by the planter class due to the associated loss of their plantation labor force. A landless proletariat was desired by the planters in their quest for a cheap and available labor force. In general, the state acted in the interests of the plantocracy taxing small producers and ensuring that land prices were above a level that the vast majority of former slaves could afford. Mainly in response to this hard-line attitude, in Jamaica, nonconformist missionaries bought land and sold small lots to people who wanted to settle in free villages around the church and village school.[15]

Finally, after 1897 (see chapter 1) land settlement schemes were introduced in some Caribbean islands.[16] This was seen by the colonial state as a solution both to those cases of unprofitable plantations and to the widespread demand for cultivable land by the ex-slave population. Selected plantations were bought by the state and subdivided and rented or sold to ex-slaves and their descendants. In French Martinique, land occupation by ex-slaves took place in the uplands (*mornes*) of the island. Groups of freed slaves organized themselves to claim land, former plantation properties that had been subdivided and eventually sold off, and gradually built hamlets and villages from groups of plots. Thus some sectors were totally occupied by freed slaves by 1880 (see chapter 12).[17]

In the Windward Islands (Dominica, St. Vincent, St. Lucia, Grenada, and Tobago), relatively late settlement by Europeans, low population density, and mountainous terrain meant that the plantation never gained the dominance over the economy and the landscape that it did in many other territories.

With the greatest opportunities for land acquisition in these islands, the postemancipation counterplantation economy developed there most rapidly. Marshall observes, "These islands, then, are more nearly communities than any of the other islands in the (British) West Indies."[18]

The opportunities to exercise their freedom were few for the ex-slave populations of the smaller, older, plantation-dominated colonies of the region and emigration, into another plantation context, was most likely. In these cases the association between lack of access to land and migration is clear and the establishment of a tradition and dependence on migration is very evident. It was lack of land and thus the material and symbolic power that land occupation and/or ownership brought that propelled the exodus. Over time, however, migration became an integral part of livelihoods in the islands, and the relationship between land and migration evolved into a much more complex entity. In the larger islands such as Jamaica, or the mountainous Windwards, migration was not simply the preserve of the landless. Migration had gradually become, for many, one means of transforming their limited lot at home, not only from a purely financial perspective but also culturally. The glamorous attire and swagger of the adventurous "Colón Man" was as attractive to would-be Jamaican migrants as was his silver (which kept him independent of the plantation bosses at home).[19] So, even in the cases of those who had access to land to farm, either on a rental or ownership basis, migration offered the chance to extend their income often with one or two family members migrating while others kept the plot going at home to spread the risk. Migration became a part of the many livelihood strategies engaged in by individuals and households in their bid to survive the difficult economic conditions in the Caribbean colonies during this era.[20]

Critically though, as early as the postemancipation decades, where land was available, migrants invested the capital they brought back home in land, livestock, and housing. The connection between land and migration was established early in this era, and over time the two became intricately related aspects of postemancipation socioeconomic status and mobility.

Migration and Land Tenure in Nevis: The Transformation of a Society

The evolution of land tenure in Nevis has been a complex interaction between social, economic, political, and environmental structures and the persistently independent agency of the ex-slave population and their descendants in the island. As discussed earlier, the migration to the southern Caribbean provided an escape for many in Nevis and surrounding small islands of the northeastern Caribbean from continuing to work for former slave masters. However, early in the postemancipation decades, many estate owners who were struggling to maintain increasingly unprofitable plantations in the island resorted to a share-cropping system in which the workers took over responsibility for allocated landholdings, usually producing a combination of the cash crops of sugarcane and cotton and food crops for subsistence and the local market. The estate owner gained two-thirds and one-half of the crop's value with the black "peasant farmer" retaining the rest. The ultimate control of the land, the vehicles, and the processing was in the hands of the planters but as Richardson and Frucht observe there was a greater degree of control by the ex-slaves over this critical land resource than in the neighboring plantation-dominated economy of St. Kitts.[21] Peasant farmers were directly responsible for feeding their families, and the cash crop income enabled them to accumulate small savings.

Although initially intended as a temporary measure to see the planters through economic depression, the share-cropping system remained intact for many decades in some parts of the island. The tension between the owners and the peasant farmers was palpable, but an accommodation existed that was gradually shifted in favor of the peasantry. Slowly, by the end of nineteenth century, unsuccessful white planters were selling their estates to speculators, some of them black returnee migrants who sold off small land plots to black peasants. Those most likely to purchase land were people who had migrated in the past or were currently engaged in labor migration, at the time to the Dominican Republic and over successive decades to Bermuda and the Dutch Antilles. Returnees from the latter destination were noted for their investment in land and small commercial enterprises.[22] The process of migration, through remittances and return, significantly increased the capital available among the local populace for land purchase and further investment. However, until the 1930s land was a very scarce commodity.

From the 1930s, access to land for would-be small farmers in Nevis was revolutionized by the introduction of land settlement schemes by the colonial state. Parallel with the increasing, albeit ad hoc, availability of land as owners of estates admitted defeat in export crop production and broke up estates into small plots for purchase or rental by the minority with the capital to do so, the colonial government purchased several estates and made the land available for rental by small farmers.[23] Momsen noted that the settlement land was less intensively cropped and more likely to be used for grazing by the tenants.[24] While there were clear differences in the utilization of settlement and private lands, peasant attachment to their land on settlements was clear and rights to occupation were passed on to later generations. The settlement land amounted to being an insurance policy for those unable to purchase any land or to expand the land area they farmed at the time, yet who recognized and desired security of legal recognition of their land occupation. The fact that this land was passed on to descendants showed that for many the right to occupy land was in itself a key element of security. It is also likely that occupants of the land foresaw that in the future tenure possibilities would change from rental to ownership at a discounted rate to tenants. Indeed over time most of the government-owned estates were made available for purchase and, unlike many of the private estates on which lots were sold to expatriates at inflated prices, nationals of the country were given priority and the prices were kept low.

Postwar Migration to Britain: Land as Catalyst and Product of the Migration Process

It has been shown above how land played a major role in the migration process. By the time that labor migration to Britain developed in the postwar years, a clear migration tradition had developed in the island of Nevis and many of its neighbors. In Nevis, returning migrants sought to invest savings in land and to establish permanent properties on it. In the 1950s when the migration gathered momentum, the first to migrate were often young persons, usually the older children in a family, whose parents raised the money for their fares by taking their title documents to the local bank as collateral for a travel loan. For the first few years in Britain, remittances were in many cases channeled into repayment of such loans. In other cases, the income from the harvest of the cash crop of sea island cotton, the family's annual cash income, was supplemented by money from the sale of a few livestock to raise the fare to England. Again remittances were relied on to replace this investment.

Access to land and its produce was essential for many to pay the cost of transport, and lack of this resource precluded travel for some. Although some stayed at "home" due to their role in the family and a dependent group of elder and/or younger relatives, many mentioned that their family had no "land papers" to take to the bank rendering impossible the journey to Britain. Once established in Britain migrants were soon to become involved in securing the land tenure of their families at home.

Ownership of their house lots transformed the lives of households in Nevis. Most owned their house. However, prior to purchasing the land, the house could not be permanently attached to the ground and thus was a very basic wooden structure set on four boulders. If the householder lost the land tenancy the house was literally lifted off the boulders onto a flat-bed truck and moved to another location after prior negotiation. There could be plumbing or electricity fittings on rented land and life was very rudimentary. Once the land was purchased, concrete foundations could be established and a kitchen and bathroom built on to the rear of the house, often with verandah at the front. A regular addition to the property was a concrete cistern adjacent to the house, which caught and stored rainwater and provided water security for the household. Both migrants who had spent a short but lucrative period in Britain and elderly relatives whose children had migrated showed me their water cisterns with pride stressing that they were built with "England money." Migrants who had spent more time in Britain, between 25 and 40 years, returning at retirement, had usually set the stage for their eventual return by purchasing house lots early in their sojourn in Britain and built substantial, modern homes to return to.[25]

Migration and in particular the postwar migrations, which coincided most closely with land becoming available on a wide scale for purchase, significantly transformed the society in Nevis from laborers with minimal control of the land resources to land-owning small farmers mixed in with a growing class of returning migrants who engaged in a range of occupations within the service sector. The remittances from migration of course also led to an increasing detachment from the land as a source of income through cultivation. The development of the service sector and in particular the tourism industry has further shifted perception of land utility to that accommodating buildings from places for cultivation for subsistence and the market.

Yet even within the Anglophone Caribbean the process of gaining access to land differed significantly from one island to another. Recent research in Barbados and St. Kitts/Nevis showed how relevant the discussions of the postemancipation access to land are to the return migration process.[26] As migrants retire and return in greater numbers they have very different land and housing options available to them. In Nevis, most returnees have owned their land for several decades, and, in general, land was purchased in or close to their community of origin. They therefore built their homes in familiar places. In Barbados and, to a lesser extent, St. Kitts, most of the island's land remained under plantation status for sugar cultivation until very recently making land for housing very scarce.[27] As the plantation sector has declined over the past 20 years, land has been released for real estate speculators and individual house lots and also purpose-built housing estates have mushroomed. Returnees have a range of options available but are often unlikely to find property in their village or town of origin and can end up living on a new housing estate with which they have no historical link. Sometimes this works out positively with communities of similarly experienced returnees forming in the parishes of St. Phillip or Christ Church in Barbados or in the hill town of Mandeville in Jamaica.[28] However, many returnees end up living relatively isolated lives in sites with which they have no symbolic connection.

The Continuing Role of Land in Transnational Caribbean Communities

The migrations from the Caribbean in the postwar era have created Caribbean communities on both sides of the North Atlantic. The transnational status of these communities and the relationship between communities in London, Manchester, New York, and Toronto with places and communities in the Caribbean has been forcefully brought to the fore in discussion of Caribbean migrations since the 1980s.[29] Land links members of generations in that migrants often left siblings or parents in charge of land while they were abroad. However, as migrant generations age and pass on, land is now a major force in continuing the transnational process started by the postwar migrant cohorts. Foreign-born descendants of migrants take advantage of dual citizenship arrangements to obtain nationality of Caribbean states in order to inherit property left to them by parents and grandparents. Through claiming this land, members of the Caribbean diaspora refresh and strengthen links with the Caribbean origin community (see chapter 17). Others investigate purchasing land in order to maintain links with the home their parents remained so connected to while simultaneously maintaining homes and lives in Britain or the United States, for example.

It is the summer holidays and I watch as three generations of a Nevisian family pack for a three-week holiday to Nevis. Grandpa is already in Nevis having left a week ago to prepare the three-bedroom house he had built on his land there 10 years ago to receive all the holiday makers. Last summer he went with his wife only but this year, their two British-born children, their spouses, and the three grandchildren are all traveling "down to Nevis" for their holidays. Lots of relatives are waiting for their arrival including Great Granddad who is 91 and will meet two of the great grandchildren for the first time. They are joined by a 17-year-old cousin from Manchester who has cajoled her mother into permitting her to travel to Nevis with the cousins from the British Midlands because she had such a wonderful time there last Christmas when she accompanied her grandmother. Such holidays will continue long after the original migrant generation pass on. The links with the land and the family are strengthened and reformed over time and generations. Maintenance of the land and buildings on it usually require that close links with family members in the Caribbean are retained and regular contact occurs. Modern communication makes this a relatively simple process. Without such material ties to land and family, the Caribbean would have a much more vague, albeit symbolic, meaning for descendant generations of the migrants.

Conclusion

Even as it expanded the horizons of the postemancipation populations, migration was also critical to cementing their place in the Caribbean territories. As occurred in several earlier migrations, migration and membership of the proletariat in urban Britain enabled acquisition of land in the Caribbean and subsequently a secure, middle-class retirement in the Caribbean. Migrants were also able to improve the socioeconomic status of their relatives in the Caribbean by assisting them with land purchase and sending remittances that often led to a decrease in agricultural productivity as people no longer needed the subsistence income they had previously earned from the farm. A large proportion of the migrants to Britain came from working class, mainly agricultural, laborer backgrounds. Most joined the proletariat in Britain in a range of jobs in the service and manufacturing sectors. Most of this migrant generation did not experience significant socioeconomic mobility in Britain. However the higher earnings meant that they could improve on and consolidate their position in the Caribbean, and hence, in the transnational context in which they existed, they experienced status improvement. Those who were in a position to do so bought property on the British housing market, and for many equity in this property and careful saving enabled them to prepare for the lifestyle in the Caribbean that none had left behind in the 1950s and 1960s. The socioeconomic mobility that they achieved extended to their relatives who, while they remained in the Caribbean, also benefited from the migration. The migrants returned permanently or intermittently to live a middle-class lifestyle. The purchase of land was the first step to attaining this social transformation.

Notes

1. See, e.g., Jean Besson, "Land, Kinship, and Community in the Post-Emancipation Caribbean: A Regional View of the Leewards," in Karen Fog Olwig (ed.), *Small Islands, Large Questions: Society, Culture and Resistance in the Post-Emancipation Caribbean* (London: Frank Cass, 1995), 73–99.
2. Douglas Hall, *Five of the Leewards, 1834–1870* (Aylesbury: Ginn & Co.).
3. Janet H. Momsen, "Gender Ideology and Land," in Christine Barrow (ed.), *Caribbean Portraits: Essays on Gender Ideologies and Identities* (Kingston, Jamaica: Ian Randle Publishers in association with the Centre for Gender and Development Studies, University of the West Indies, 1998), 115–132.
4. Bonham Richardson, "Freedom and Migration in the Leeward Caribbean, 1838–1848," *Journal of Historical Geography* 6, no. 4: 391–408; and Bonham Richardson, *Caribbean Migrants: Environment and Human Survival in St Kitts and Nevis* (Knoxville: University of Tennessee Press, 1980).
5. Richardson, "Freedom and Migration in the Leeward Caribbean."
6. Kale Madhavi, *Fragments of Empire: Capital, Anti-Slavery and Indian Indentured Labor Migration to the British Caribbean* (Philadelphia: University of Pennsylvania Press, 1998); and Walton Look Lai, *Indentured Labour, Caribbean Sugar: Chinese and Indian Migrants to the British West Indies, 1838–1918* (Baltimore: John Hopkins University Press, 1993).
7. Elizabeth Thomas Hope, "Island Systems and the Paradox of Freedom: Migration in the Post-Emancipation Leeward Islands," in Olwig (ed.), *Small Islands, Large Questions*, 161–175; and Elizabeth Thomas-Hope, "The Establishment of a Migration Tradition: British West Indian Movements to the Hispanic Caribbean in the Century after Emancipation," in Colin G. Clarke (ed.), *Caribbean Social Relations* (Liverpool: University of Liverpool Centre for Latin American Studies, 1978), 66–81.
8. Michel Baud, "The Struggle for Autonomy: Peasant Resistance to Capitalism in the Dominican Republic 1870–1924," in Malcolm Cross and Gad Heuman (eds.), *Labour in the Caribbean* (London: Macmillan, 1988), 120–140.
9. Margaret Byron, *Post War Caribbean Migration to Britain* (Aldershot: Avebury, 1994), chapter 2.
10. Richardson, *Caribbean Migrants*.
11. Richard Frucht, "A Caribbean Social Type: Neither Peasant nor Proletarian," *Social and Economic Studies* 13, no. 3 (1967): 295–300.
12. Janet H. Momsen, "Land Settlement as an Imposed Solution," in Jean Besson and Janet H. Momsen (eds.), *Land and Development in the Caribbean* (London: Macmillan, 1987), 46–69.
13. Richardson, *Caribbean Migrants*.
14. Jean Besson, "Land Tenure in the Free Villages of Trelawny, Jamaica: A Case Study in the Caribbean Peasant Response to Emancipation," *Slavery and Abolition* 5, no. 1 (1984): 3–23; Jean Besson, "A Paradox in Caribbean

Attitudes to Land," in Besson and Momsen (eds.), *Land and Development in the Caribbean*, 13–45; and Jean Besson, *Martha Brae's Two Histories: European Expansion and Caribbean Culture-Building in Jamaica* (Chapel Hill and London: University of North Carolina Press, 2002).

15. Besson, "Land Tenure in the Free Villages of Trelawny"; Besson, "A Paradox in Caribbean Attitudes to land"; and Besson, *Martha Brae's Two Histories*.

16. Momsen, "Land Settlement as an Imposed Solution."

17. See also Christine Chivallon, *Espace et identité à la Martinique. Paysannerie des mornes et reconquête collective 1840–1960* (Paris: CNRS-Editions, 2002).

18. Woodville K. Marshall, "Peasant Development in the Caribbean since 1838," in P. I. Gomes (ed.), *Rural Development in the Caribbean* (London: Hurst and St. Martin's Press, 1985), 1–14, at 10.

19. Olive Senior, "The Origins of 'Colon Man': Jamaican Emigration to Panama in the Nineteenth Century," in *West Indian Participation in the Construction of the Panama Canal, Proceedings of the Symposium Held at the University of the West Indies, Mona Jamaica* (Mona, Jamaica: LACC, 2000), 33–42.

20. Lambros Comitas, "Occupational Multiplicity in Rural Jamaica," in David Lowenthal and Lambros Comitas (eds.), *Work and Family Life: West Indian Perspectives* (New York: Anchor/Doubleday, 1973), 152–173.

21. Richardson, *Caribbean Migrants*; and Frucht, "A Caribbean Social Type."

22. Frucht, "A Caribbean Social Type."

23. Momsen, "Gender Ideology and Land."

24. Momsen, "Gender Ideology and Land," 65.

25. Margaret Byron, "Return Migration to the Eastern Caribbean: Comparative Experiences and Policy Implications," *Social and Economic Studies* 49, no. 4 (2000): 155–188.

26. Margaret Byron, "The Caribbean-Born Population in 1990s Britain: Who Will Return?" *Journal of Ethnic and Migration Studies* 25, no. 2 (1999): 285–301; and Byron; "Return Migration to the Eastern Caribbean," 155–188.

27. Mark Watson and Robert Potter, "Housing Conditions, Vernacular Architecture and State Policy in Barbados," in Robert Potter and Dennis Conway (eds.), *Self-Help Housing, the Poor and the State in the Caribbean* (Knoxville: University of Tennessee Press, 1997), 30–51.

28. Byron, "The Caribbean-Born Population in 1990s Britain"; Harry Goulbourne, "Exodus? Some Social and Policy Implications of Return Migration from the UK to the Commonwealth Caribbean in the 1990s," *Policy Studies* 20, no. 3 (1999): 157–172.

29. Linda Basch, Nina Glick Schiller, and Cristina Szanton Blanc, *Nations Unbound: Transnational Projects, Post Colonial Predicaments and Deterritorialised Nation States* (Amsterdam: Gordon and Breach, 1994); and Karen Fog Olwig, "Transnational Socio-Cultural Systems and Ethnographic Research: Views from an Extended Field Site," *International Migration Review* 37, no. 3 (2003): 787–811. See also Jean Besson, "Land, Territory and Identity in the Deterritorialized, Transnational Caribbean," in Michael Saltman (ed.), *Land and Territoriality* (Oxford: Berg, 2002), 175–208.

Notes on Contributors

David Barker is Professor and Head of the Department of Geography & Geology at the University of the West Indies, Mona campus, in Kingston, Jamaica, where he has been a Geography Lecturer since 1980. He is a coauthor of the tertiary-level textbook *Contemporary Caribbean* (2004), and a coeditor in the book series: *Environment and Development in the Caribbean: Geographical Perspectives* (1995), *Resource Sustainability and Caribbean Development* (1998), and *Resources, Planning and Environmental Management in a Changing Caribbean* (2003). Additionally, he is cofounder and editor of the regional journal *Caribbean Geography*. Dr. Barker's main research interest focuses on small-scale agriculture and indigenous knowledge, and hillside farming and environmental degradation in Jamaica.

Jean Besson, a Jamaican, is Reader in Anthropology at Goldsmiths College, University of London. Dr. Besson has also taught at the universities of Edinburgh and Aberdeen and held visiting appointments at the University of the West Indies, Mona, and the Johns Hopkins University. She has carried out research in Jamaica and the Eastern Caribbean. Her publications include *Martha Brae's Two Histories: European Expansion and Caribbean Culture-Building in Jamaica* (University of North Carolina Press, 2002), *Caribbean Narratives of Belonging: Fields of Relations, Sites of Identity* (coedited with Karen Fog Olwig, Macmillan, 2005), and *Land and Development in the Caribbean* (coedited with Janet Momsen, Macmillan, 1987).

Margaret Byron is a Lecturer in the Department of Geography, King's College, London. She has a DPhil in Geography from Oxford. Her research interests include labor migration, particularly postwar Caribbean migration to Europe and the impact of return migration to the region in recent decades. She is currently working on Caribbean communities in urban Britain and France, focusing on gender, generation, and the employment and housing histories of these multigenerational communities. Her publications include *Post War Caribbean Migration to Britain: The Unfinished Cycle* (Avebury, 1994) and, with Stephanie Condon, *Migration in Comparative Perspective: Caribbean Communities in Britain and France*, (Routledge, 2007).

Christine Chivallon is an anthropologist and geographer, employed by the CNRS (National Center of Scientific Research) in France. Dr. Chivallon's research has focused on space and identity, mainly in Caribbean societies and through Caribbean migration also in Europe, including research on the memory of slavery. Among her major recent works are *La diaspora noire des Amériques, expériences et théories à partir de la Caraïbe* (Paris, CNRS Éditions, 2004) and "Beyond Gilroy's Black Atlantic: The Experience of the African Diaspora," *Diaspora. A Journal of Transnational Studies* 11, no. 3 (2002): 359–382.

Colin Clarke is Emeritus Professor of Geography at Oxford University and an Emeritus Fellow of Jesus College. He has taught at the universities of Liverpool and Toronto and has carried out many research projects in Mexico and the Caribbean. His principal research interests are in race, ethnicity and class, urban and rural social structures and their spatial expression, and peasant transformation. Professor Clarke's most recent publications include *Class, Community and Ethnicity in Southern Mexico: Oaxaca's Peasantries* (Oxford University Press, 2000), *Kingston, Jamaica: Urban Development and Social Change, 1692–2002* (Ian Randle Publishers, 2006), and *Decolonizing the Colonial City: Urbanization and Stratification in Kingston, Jamaica* (Oxford University Press, 2006).

Lawrence S. Grossman is a Professor in the Department of Geography at Virginia Tech. He has been conducting research in the Caribbean since the late 1980s and is the author of *The Political Ecology of Bananas: Contract Farming, Peasants, and Agrarian Change in the Eastern Caribbean* (University of North Carolina Press, 1998). Dr. Grossman is currently conducting archival research on colonial environmental discourses and policies related to deforestation and soil erosion in the British Caribbean from the late 1800s to 1950.

Ellen-Rose Kambel obtained a law degree and a PhD in Social Sciences from the University of Leiden, the Netherlands. For the past 10 years, she has worked with indigenous communities in Suriname and has co-authored several books and reports on human rights, development, and gender issues. She currently works as an independent human rights trainer and researcher.

David Lowenthal is an Emeritus Professor of Geography at University College, London. He taught history at U(C) WI in Jamaica in 1956–1957 and was research associate at ISER, and then extramural consultant to the vice chancellor. The Institute of Race Relations (London) commissioned his *West Indian Societies* (Oxford University Press, 1972). With Colin Clarke he served as Barbuda advocate at the Antigua-Barbuda Independence Conference (London, 1980).

Donald Macleod is a Lecturer and Head of Tourism and Heritage at the University of Glasgow and has a doctorate in social anthropology from the University of Oxford. He has undertaken field research in the Canary Islands, the Caribbean, and Scotland, and his interests include sustainable development, globalization, cultural change, tourism, heritage, and identity. His publications include the books *Tourism, Globalization and Cultural Change* (Channel View Publications, 2004), *Niche Tourism in Question* (Glasgow University Crichton Publications, 2003), and *Tourists and Tourism* (Berg, 1997).

Learie A. Miller worked as Director for more than a decade with the Natural Resources Conservation Authority/National Environment and Planning Agency in Jamaica. He was also an adjunct faculty member of the University of the West Indies Geography Department for several years. He has a MSc degree from the University of Toronto in Environmental Management and Geomorphology and a joint Ryerson University/University of Toronto Masters in Spatial Analysis (MSA). He now works as a Resources Planner with the Kawartha Region Conservation Authority in Ontario, Canada.

Beth Mills has a Master's degree from the University of New Mexico and a PhD in Geography from the University of California, Davis. She has carried out fieldwork in the Caribbean for over 20 years, and her research focuses on questions of land use and migration in Carriacou, Grenada. Dr. Mills' broader research interests include the connection between culture and land use, transnational migration, and community development. She lives in Santa Fe, New Mexico, with her two children, where she works with local government as a land-use planner and as a part-time faculty member in the School of Architecture and Planning at the University of New Mexico.

Janet Momsen is Professor of Geography in the Department of Human and Community Development at the University of California, Davis. She has taught in Canada, the United Kingdom, Costa Rica, and Brazil. Her research interests include gender and development, rural development, agrobiodiversity, and tourism in the Caribbean, Mexico, Eastern Europe, and Bangladesh. Dr. Momsen's publications on the Caribbean include *Land and Development in the Caribbean* (coedited with Jean Besson, Macmillan, 1987), *Women and Change in the Caribbean* (James Currey and Ian Randle, 1993), and *Environmental Planning in the Caribbean* (with Jonathan Pugh, Ashgate, 2006).

Debbie A. Niemeier is a Professor of Civil and Environmental Engineering at the University of California, Davis. She is interested in issues of transportation and accessibility and is currently Director of the John Muir Institute of the Environment at UC, Davis.

Jonathan Pugh is the Academic Fellow in Territorial Governance at the University of Newcastle upon Tyne. He has a PhD in Geography from the University of London. His major interests include participatory and environmental planning in the Caribbean and the theoretical relationship between space, time, and the political. He is the coeditor, with Janet Momsen of *Environmental Planning in the Caribbean* (Ashgate, 2006) and with Robert Potter of *Participatory Planning in the Caribbean* (Ashgate, 2004).

Bonham C. Richardson is an Emeritus Professor having retired from the Geography Department at Virginia Tech in 2003. He has been doing fieldwork and archival research in the Caribbean since 1967 in Guyana, Trinidad, Carriacou, St. Kitts-Nevis, and Barbados. His most recent book is *Igniting the Caribbean's Past* (University of North Carolina Press, 2004).

Mimi Sheller is a Visiting Associate Professor in the Department of Sociology and Anthropology at Swarthmore College, USA, and Senior Research Fellow in the Centre for Mobilities Research at Lancaster University, UK. She is coeditor of the journal *Mobilities* and author of *Consuming the Caribbean* (Routledge, 2003) *Democracy after Slavery: Black Publics and Peasant Radicalism in Haiti and Jamaica* (Macmillan Caribbean, 2000), and coeditor of *Uprootings/Regroundings* (Berg, 2003), *Tourism Mobilities* (Routledge, 2004), and *Mobile Technologies of the City* (Routledge, 2006). Dr. Sheller's Caribbean research has focused on the history of Jamaica and Haiti.

Jonathan Skinner is a Lecturer in Social Anthropology at the Queen's University of Belfast. He has carried out long-term fieldwork on the island of Montserrat where he investigates colonial and postcolonial relations as expressed through calypso, poetry, development work, and political debate published as *Before the Volcano: Reverberations of Identity on Montserrat* (Arawak Publications, 2004). He also has interests in tourism and dance, edits the journal *Anthropology in Action*, and serves as EASA Publications Officer.

Balfour Spence is a Jamaican with BA and MPhil degrees from the University of the West Indies and a PhD from the University of Manitoba, Canada. He is a Lecturer in Geography at the University of the West Indies, Mona, Jamaica. His research focuses on agriculture and tourism in Jamaica.

J. David Stanfield has degrees in Mathematics (Ohio State), International Relations and Organization (American University), and Communication (Michigan State). He worked at the Land Tenure Center at the University of Wisconsin until retirement in 2004 and with the Terra Institute at Mt. Horeb, Wisconsin, from its founding in 1974 until the present day. His research has attempted to deal intellectually and practically with "land tenure" issues mainly in such places as Wisconsin, Chile, Honduras, Nicaragua, Dominican Republic, Ecuador, Syria, Egypt, the Caribbean, Albania, Georgia, Kyrgyzstan, and Afghanistan.

Glenroy Taitt is a Trinidadian and holds a PhD in History from Sussex University. He is Librarian III/Special Collections Librarian in the Main Library at the University of the West Indies, St. Augustine, Trinidad. His research interests are in French West Indian history as well as in Church history.

Elizabeth Thomas-Hope has an MA from Aberdeen University, an MSc from Pennsylvania State University, and a DPhil from Oxford. She is the James Seivright Moss-Solomon (Senior) Professor of Environmental Management at the University of the West Indies, Mona, Jamaica. Professor Thomas-Hope is a Jamaican and the author of *Explanation in Caribbean*

Migration (Macmillan Caribbean, 1992) and editor of *Solid Waste Management: Critical Issues for Developing Countries* (Canoe Press, 1998).

Rebecca Torres is an Assistant Professor in the Department of Geography at East Carolina University, Greenville, North Carolina. She has a Master's degree in International Agricultural Development and a PhD in Geography from the University of California, Davis. Dr. Torres has published widely on rural development, agricultural transformation, tourism, and migration and has carried out field research in Cuba, Mexico, Peru, and the U.S. South.

A. A. Wijetunga has wide professional and applied experience in land policy formulation, institutional and legal reform. He has worked as an independent Consultant for the World Bank, the Inter-American Development Bank, and USAID in Asia and the Caribbean. He is currently the Vice President of the Global Land Coalition. He has a Master's degree in Social Sciences from Birmingham University, UK. He did further graduate study at the University of Idaho in land-use planning for natural resources management, in land resettlement in Israel, and in institutional development in the Republic of Germany. He is currently based in Maryland.

Index

Page references in bold refer to illustrations

creation of, 235; division of, 238–39; freedmen's, 236; as imagined space, 239–40; Jamaican, 141–42; maroons', 138; migrants', 12, 236–40; on Montserrat, 229; on Nevis, 236; permanence through, 235–36; purchased, 235; role in identity, 239, 240; as survival strategy, 235; symbolism of, 235–36; in transnational communities, 11–12, 233–40, 250–51

farmers' markets, Cuban, 5, 53–62; agricultural inputs for, 5, 53, 55, 56, 57, 61; collective vendors in, 58, 59, 60; effect on black market, 62; following boat exodus of 1994, 54–55; free enterprise in, 57–58, 59, 60, 61, 62, 66n52; of Havana City, 57–61, 63n12; Havana vendors in, 57–58; land resources of, 60; numbers of, 65n51; participation in, 54–55; prices at, 59–60, 62; products offered at, 58; role in Cuban diet, 62; sales tax at, 65n41; sales volume at, 63n12; transport to, 61

farming, mixed: in British Caribbean, 32; in Jamaica, 190, 203

Fergus, Howard, 220, 223, 224; "This Land Is Mine," 222

fertilizers, 198, 199; in banana industry, 202; in Cuban agriculture, 61; use in PLEC project, 200, 201. See also agrochemicals

FINSAC (Financial Sector Adjustment Company, Jamaica), 122

fisherpeople: of Bayahibe, 112; economic opportunities for, 105n23; of Soufrière, 96, 99–100; stereotypes of, 100, 102

fishing: competition with tourism, 2, 7, 96, 107; in Dominican Republic, 112, 114, 115; environmental conservation in, 3

food production, 3, 4; agrobiodiversity in, 189; during Cuban Special Period, 53, 54–57; on Guadeloupe, 44–51, 52n23; state intervention in, 29; subsistence, 9, 13n10, 20,

25, 44, 56, 180, 250; during World War II, 4, 5, 41–51. See also agriculture

food security, global, 189

Forero, Juan, 65n51

forestation: of Antilles, 208; of Britain, 208; and colonial conquest, 207; on Guadeloupe, 46; Jamaican, 121, 128–29, 192, 202; in plantation economy, 207; of Rio Grande Valley, 192; of St. Vincent, 208; of Trinidad and Tobago, 81, 208

France, Overseas Departments of, 2

François-Haugrin, Annick, 163–64, 167, 169, 172n26

freedmen: of Barbados, 176–77; of Carriacou, 238; family land of, 236; livelihood strategies of, 244; of Montserrat, 224; on plantations, 167, 172n22, 176, 244. See also peasantry; smallholders

freedmen, of Martinique, 246; land appropriation by, 159, 160, 161, 164; land ownership of, 169; on plantations, 167, 172n22; proletarianization of, 170

free villages, 8, 136, 246; of Jamaica, 138, 144n15, 246

French Guiana, maroons of, 77

French Revolution, Liberty Cap of, 211

Froude, James Anthony, 19, 25

Frucht, Richard, 248

fruit trade, Royal Commission on, 22

Gardner, Katy, 111

Giddens, Anthony, 229

Giraldi, Alberto, 108–109

Glissant, Édouard, 159

global warming, 120

Goyave (Guadeloupe), agriculture of, 45

Grande-Terre (Guadeloupe), 41; factories of, 50

Grands-Fonds (Guadeloupe), agriculture of, 44, 49–51, 52n25

Gran Krutu (maroon gathering, Suriname), 69, 75; government reaction to, 79n23

Grant, Tom and Mary, 140–41

Great Britain: Colonial Advisory Council on Agriculture and Animal